New Challenges to Democratization

This important text explores the widespread contention that new challenges and obstacles have arisen to democratization, assessing the claim that support for democratization around the world is facing a serious challenge.

Bringing together leading international scholars of democratization, including Thomas Carothers, Michael McFaul, Laurence Whitehead, Bassma Kodmani, Nancy Bermeo, Marina Ottaway, Shaun Breslin and Renske Doorenspleet, this book examines the issues relating to developments within non-democratic states and issues related to the democratic world and its efforts to support the spread of democracy. Featuring in-depth studies on the limits of US democracy promotion, the Middle East, Russia, China and new democracies, the book sheds light on questions such as:

- Is the wave of democratization now in retreat or should we be careful not to exaggerate the importance of recent setbacks?
- Do serious, sustainable alternatives to democracy now exist?
- Is international democracy promotion finished?

New Challenges to Democratization brings together a variety of academics and writers from major think-tanks in the United States and Europe, and makes the book ideally suited to a wide international readership. This book will be of particular interest to students and scholars of democratization, comparative politics and international politics.

Peter Burnell is Professor of Politics at the University of Warwick, UK, and was also founding editor of the international journal *Democratization*.

Richard Youngs is Associate Professor at the University of Warwick, and Research Director at FRIDE in Madrid, Spain.

Democratization Studies
(Formerly Democratization Studies, Frank Cass)

Democratization Studies combines theoretical and comparative studies with detailed analyses of issues central to democratic progress and its performance, all over the world.

The books in this series aim to encourage debate on the many aspects of democratization that are of interest to policy-makers, administrators and journalists, aid and development personnel, as well as to all those involved in education.

1 **Democratization and the Media**
Edited by Vicky Randall

2 **The Resilience of Democracy**
Persistent practice, durable idea
Edited by Peter Burnell and Peter Calvert

3 **The Internet, Democracy and Democratization**
Edited by Peter Ferdinand

4 **Party Development and Democratic Change in Post-communist Europe**
Edited by Paul Lewis

5 **Democracy Assistance**
International co-operation for democratization
Edited by Peter Burnell

6 **Opposition and Democracy in South Africa**
Edited by Roger Southall

7 **The European Union and Democracy Promotion**
The case of North Africa
Edited by Richard Gillespie and Richard Youngs

8 **Democratization and the Judiciary**
Edited by Siri Gloppen, Roberto Gargarella and Elin Skaar

9 **Civil Society in Democratization**
Edited by Peter Burnell and Peter Calvert

10 **The Internet and Politics**
Citizens, voters and activists
Edited by Sarah Oates, Diana Owen and Rachel Gibson

11 **Democratization in the Muslim World**
Changing patterns of authority and power
Edited by Frederic Volpi and Francesco Cavatorta

12 **Global Democracy: For and Against**
Ethical theory, institutional design and social struggles
Raffaele Marchetti

13 **Constructing Democracy in Southern Europe**
A comparative analysis of Italy, Spain and Turkey
Lauren M. McLaren

14 **The Consolidation of Democracy**
Comparing Europe and Latin America
Carsten Q. Schneider

15 **New Challenges to Democratization**
Edited by Peter Burnell and Richard Youngs

New Challenges to Democratization

Edited by
Peter Burnell and Richard Youngs

LONDON AND NEW YORK

First published 2010 by Routledge
2 Park Square Milton Park Abingdon Oxon OX14 4RN

Simultaneously published in the USA and Canada
by Routledge
270 Madison Avenue, New York, NY 10016

Routledge is an imprint of the Taylor & Francis Group, an informa business

Transferred to Digital Printing 2010

© 2010 Peter Burnell and Richard Youngs selection and editorial matter;
individual contributors, their contributions

Typeset in Times New Roman by
Taylor & Francis Books

All rights reserved. No part of this book may be reprinted or reproduced or
utilised in any form or by any electronic, mechanical, or other means, now
known or hereafter invented, including photocopying and recording, or in
any information storage or retrieval system, without permission in writing
from the publishers.

British Library Cataloguing in Publication Data
A catalogue record for this book is available from the British Library

Library of Congress Cataloging in Publication Data
A catalog record for this book has been requested

ISBN 10: 0-415-46741-1 (hbk)
ISBN 10: 0-415-46742-X (pbk)
ISBN 10: 0-203-86997-4 (ebk)

ISBN 13: 978-0-415-46741-4 (hbk)
ISBN 13: 978-0-415-46742-1 (pbk)
ISBN 13: 978-0-203-86997-0 (ebk)

Contents

	List of figures	vii
	List of tables	viii
	List of contributors	ix
	Acknowledgements	x
	List of abbreviations	xi
1	New challenges to democratization PETER BURNELL	1
2	State sovereignty and democracy: an awkward coupling LAURENCE WHITEHEAD	23
3	Ideological challenges to democracy: do they exist? MARINA OTTAWAY	42
4	The continuing backlash against democracy promotion THOMAS CAROTHERS	59
5	Democracy assistance and the search for security NANCY BERMEO	73
6	Public support versus dissatisfaction in new democracies: an 'inside challenge'? RENSKE DOORENSPLEET	93
7	External sources and consequences of Russia's "sovereign democracy" MICHAEL MCFAUL AND REGINE A SPECTOR	116
8	Democratizing one-party rule in China SHAUN BRESLIN	134

vi *Contents*

9 Democratization by whom? Resistance to democracy promotion
in the Middle East   153
BASSMA KODMANI

10 Energy: a reinforced obstacle to democratization?   171
RICHARD YOUNGS

11 Addressing democracy's challenges   188
PETER BURNELL AND RICHARD YOUNGS

Bibliography   201
Index   216

List of figures

5.1	Ratio of US military aid to democracy aid	76
5.2	US military aid by regime type	79
5.3	US arms sales by regime type	80
5.4	Proportion of French, German, and British arms sales going to dictatorships	80
5.5	US foreign military sales, 1990–2008	87

List of tables

5.1	Ratio of US military aid to democracy aid	81
5.2	Average democracy, military and economic aid: countries that remained dictatorships vs countries that became democracies	82
5.3	Average annual increase in democracies during six US presidencies	85
5.4	US security priorities receiving democracy aid, 2003–4	86
5.5	Additions to the standard list of US weapons aid recipients 2002–7	88
6.1	The global trend of freedom: number of free, partly free and not free countries in the world	96
6.2	Support for democracy in new democracies	103
6.3	Cross-tabulation of support for democracy and satisfaction with democracy in Panama	106
6.4	Cross-tabulation of support for democracy and satisfaction with democracy in Benin	107
6.5	Cross-tabulation of support for democracy and satisfaction with democracy in Hungary	109
7.1	Major events/trends in Russian media, non-governmental organizations and elections (2001–7)	122
10.1	Freedom House scores of key oil producers, 2001–2 to 2007	173

Contributors

Nancy Bermeo, Nuffield Professor of Comparative Politics, Nuffield College, University of Oxford and Director of the Centre for the Study of Inequality and Democracy.

Shaun Breslin, Professor of Politics, University of Warwick.

Peter Burnell, Professor of Politics and International Studies, University of Warwick.

Thomas Carothers, Vice President for Studies, International Politics and Governance, Carnegie Endowment for International Peace, Washington, DC.

Renske Doorenspleet, Associate Professor, Director of the Centre for Studies in Democratization, Department of Politics and International Studies, University of Warwick.

Bassma Kodmani, Executive Director, Arab Reform Initiative, Paris.

Michael McFaul, Special Assistant to the President of the United States and Director for Russian and Eurasian Affairs at the National Security Council.

Marina Ottaway, Director, Middle East Program, Carnegie Endowment for International Peace, Washington, DC.

Regine Spector, Visiting Research and Lecturer, University of Massachusetts, Amherst.

Laurence Whitehead, Official Fellow in Politics, Nuffield College, Oxford.

Richard Youngs, Associate Professor, Department of Politics and International Studies, University of Warwick and Research Director, Fundación para las Relaciones Internacionales y el Diálogo Exterior (FRIDE), Madrid.

Acknowledgements

The editors wish to thank the Centre for European Policy Studies in Brussels, FRIDE, and the Department of Politics and International Studies at Warwick University for supporting the conference at which the initial versions of the book's chapters were debated. We would also like to thank the commentators who participated and offered helpful comments.

List of abbreviations

ACP	Africa-Caribbean-Pacific group of countries
AEI	Advanced Energy Initiative
ANOVA	analysis of variance
CCP	Chinese Communist Party
CIS	Commonwealth of Independent States
CSCE	Conference on Security and Cooperation in Europe
CSTO	Collective Security Treaty Organization
DG	Democracy and Governance office (USAID)
EITI	Extractive Industries Transparency Initiative
ENP	European Neighbourhood Policy
EU	European Union
FH	Freedom House
FIS	Front Islamique du Salut (Algeria)
FMF	foreign military finance (USA)
FMS	foreign military sales (USA)
FRIDE	Fundación para las Relaciones Internacionales y el Diálogo Exterior (Madrid)
FSB	Federal Security Service (Russia)
HIV/AIDS	human immunodeficiency virus/acquired immune deficiency syndrome
KGB	Committee for State Security (USSR)
LNG	liquified natural gas
MGIMO	Moscow State Institute for International Relations
NATO	North Atlantic Treaty Organization
NGO	non-governmental organization
OAS	Organization of American States
ODIHR	Office for Democratic Institutions and Human Rights (OSCE)
OECD	Organisation for Economic Cooperation and Development
OPEC	Organization of Petroleum Exporting Countries
OSCE	Organization for Security and Cooperation in Europe
PJD	Justice and Development Party of Morocco
PRC	People's Republic of China
SADC	Southern African Development Community

xii *List of abbreviations*

SARS	severe acute respiratory syndrome
SCO	Shanghai Cooperation Organization
SIPRI	Stockholm International Peace Research Institute
TIV	trend indicator value
TRC	Truth and Reconciliation Commission (South Africa)
UAE	United Arab Emirates
UN	United Nations
USA	United States of America
USAID	United States Agency for International Development
WTO	World Trade Organization

1 New challenges to democratization

Peter Burnell

Introduction

Readers familiar with the general discourse on contemporary democratization and on international promotion of democracy today could be forgiven for thinking that both of these are currently in crisis – or if they are not there yet, then they are heading remorselessly in that direction. For example, Larry Diamond, over the past 20 years or so one of the most prominent scholars in the US writing about democratization, has surmised that a new 'reverse wave' of democracy might be underway, with resistance to democratization or, even, democratic regression being particularly marked in a number of 'swing states' that possess significant demographic and economic size.[1] In 2008, democratic progress in small countries with little importance on the world stage such as the Maldives, Bhutan and Nepal have to be balanced against the negative political trends inside a resurgent power like Russia and the forceful clampdown on protestors in China that surrounded the run-up to the Olympic Games in Beijing.

The reasons range widely, over the effects of singular decisions such as the waging of war on Iraq to developments of a more deep-seated and structural kind. They include both recent political developments inside countries and some disturbing economic as well as political trends at the level of the international system. At the country level, the increasing concentration of power in Russia under former President Putin is a prominent example. Internationally, the consequences for democracy in the developing world of large hikes in the price of major internationally traded commodities, most notably oil, are no less troubling, notwithstanding the sharp price corrections late in 2008. The same is true of the apparent appeal for some developing country leaders of a national model that generates development without democracy, as found in China, whose dramatic economic growth helped fuel the commodity price hikes in the first place. The evidence is that neither economic liberalization nor genuine economic progress offer a guarantee of significant democratic reform.

In the Middle East, the dreams of US President George Bush that freedom and democracy would spread in the wake of the fall of Saddam Hussein's

2   Peter Burnell

regime in Iraq have turned out to lack substance. Instead there is talk of the exceptionalism of the Arab world, or of the world of Islam. In Latin America and elsewhere the disappointment that has been expressed by ordinary people with democracy's seeming inability to address their economic and social ills is palpable. And the European Union's project of enlargement, which has been a major force for consolidating democratic transitions in Central and Eastern Europe, appears to have run out of steam.

Meanwhile the industry that has built up around the international promotion of democracy seems to be facing a 'backlash', substantially but not wholly due to the use of external military force to remove governments in Afghanistan and Iraq. The mood among democracy practitioners now appears to be that their activity badly needs a new image. More hard evidence that it really can achieve favourable results, at a time when the commitment to democracy support of both government and society in the US seems to be waning, would be most welcome not just in the US but in Europe too. The enhancement of national security takes priority. At the minimum, and as a US Congressional Research Service Report for Congress (2007) put it, 'The democracy promotion ideal is now under close scrutiny.' Various security issues all looked at through a short to medium perspective appear to be uppermost in the foreign policy deliberations of the established democracies. Of course, this miasma does not constitute a judgement on the contemporary state of democratization any more than that process of change equates to the condition of democracy itself. Nevertheless the presence of what seem to be parallel worrying trends concerning both democratization and democracy promotion does raise the possibility that there could be mutual reinforcement.

Democracy is of course a much-contested concept. But in most of the discourse on democratization and in the understandings held by democracy promoters also there are certain widely accepted notions of electoral democracy and liberal democracy, the latter characterized in particular by a fuller set of civil liberties and freedoms for individuals and minority groups. None of the datasets claiming to describe trends in democracy around the world are without their critics. But one of the most prominent examples, the Freedom House annual survey of political rights and civil liberties in the world, appears to offer compelling evidence. The survey for 2007 indicated not just that the total number of democracies had reached a plateau (it stood at 121 in 2007) but that levels of freedom were starting to erode.[2] The trend is broadly based, with examples in South Asia, the former Soviet Union, the Middle East and North Africa, and Sub-Saharan Africa. Four times as many countries experienced a decline in freedom during 2007 as registered improvement. The signs are that, in very general terms, 2008 will tell a similar story of modest declines in freedom affecting some countries in most regions.

More particularly, the task of stabilizing new democracies and preventing democracies in transition from falling back now appears more difficult than we used to think. Meanwhile the resistance mounted by the opponents of

New challenges to democratization 3

reform in many of the non-democracies looks as firm as ever: highly authoritarian regimes are among the most durable regimes, and semi-democratic regimes are vulnerable by comparison (Hadenius and Teorell 2007). In addition, we are all now more aware of the existence of many fragile and failing states, the Democratic Republic of the Congo, for example. These provide particularly hostile terrain for establishing democracy. The staging of elections has proven to be premature. The challenges in these different categories of country are all different. The fact of difference compounds the challenge facing democracy promoters, who cannot hope to alight on a single model or just one approach to promoting democracy that would suit all circumstances. Their ability to transfer lessons of experience from one country or set of countries to another is severely circumscribed, which makes their task more difficult.

The aim of this book is to explore the widespread contention that new challenges and obstacles have arisen to democratization and to the spread of democracy around the world. This means exploring what lies behind the claims that a crisis exists or is now looming, and assessing their accuracy. And it means doing it in a format that brings together the several different strands of the debate. The book makes no assumption that all the more pessimistic claims are correct. After all, while Hadenius and Teorell (2007) calculate that more than three-quarters of transitions from authoritarian rule in the years 1972–2003 produced not democracy but yet another authoritarian regime, they also claim that because multiparty regimes are now common among authoritarian regimes, this offers a hopeful sign for democracy's future. Similarly, far from international democracy support having now been discredited and disowned in all quarters, in 2008, Britain's Foreign Minister David Miliband said unequivocally in a speech entitled 'The Democratic Imperative', 'I am unapologetic about a mission to help democracy spread throughout the world.'[3] While less vocal on the issue than his predecessor in the White House, US President Obama in his inaugural speech on 20 January 2009 hinted more at a new approach to freedom and democracy support, not a policy of abandonment.

Rather than take sides, then, this book seeks to interrogate the arguments, to try to establish where the balance of evidence and reasoning lies. Based on the evidence and reasoning provided in the intervening chapters, the final chapter will sum up the forces and conditions where detailed knowledge can help us not to predict with certainty the future of democratization or even the future of democracy promotion but, rather, to establish the most important influences that may well have a significant bearing on the outlook for both of these.

The central questions to be borne in mind throughout can be summarized very simply: is democratization in trouble and, if so, what is the nature of the problem and how serious is it? Are viable alternatives to democracy now coming forward? Is old-style democracy promotion past its sell-by date, and, if so, are actors who are central to it developing an effective response? And

4 *Peter Burnell*

what can the new challenges facing democratization and democracy promotion tell us about the future for democratization and the global political order?[4]

Crisis or challenge?

Crisis is a much-overworked word in social science generally and in politics in particular. In this book, the word challenge is preferred. Certainly, challenges singly or in combination can turn into a crisis. And almost by definition a crisis itself poses a challenge, notably where the sentiment is that if the crisis is not overcome then the consequences will be intolerable. And yet too often the use of the term crisis rests on a weak conceptualization or no precise definition at all, and goes beyond what an objective study of all the evidence would support. With hindsight, many 'crises' have turned out to be a false or one-sided diagnosis: the patient recovered, and the 'crisis' did not then seem so critical after all. One aim of this book is to establish whether the challenges currently facing democratization and democracy promotion warrant us saying that there is now a decisive moment, a time of especially great difficulty or danger.

Certainly a challenge can be a trial. But there are no a priori grounds for thinking it must be insuperable. Moreover it can be a catalyst for action that overcomes obstacles, solves problems. Some challenges persist, some are defeated; others just fade away. New challenges come along to add to or replace old ones. Failure throws up challenges but then so does success. The democratic transitions that occurred in such impressive numbers in the early 1990s brought about the challenge of consolidating democracy. This has proven to be very demanding, unrealistic, in many cases.

In Africa, for instance, there is the challenge of converting the increasing trend to institutionalize elections as the means whereby government is determined – a development that Lindberg (2006) for one considers very positive for democratization – into making the entire electoral process consistently and uniformly free and fair.[5] For the European Union (EU), its successful strategy of using politically conditioned accession to the EU as an incentive to the consolidation of new democracies in post-communist Europe has brought the challenge of repeating this record of democratic achievement, now that EU enlargement is almost finished and nearby states have no prospect of being offered membership. A record of success can mean that it is the really hard cases or the most difficult extra moves that are left. And while democratization today faces not one challenge but several, the many new or emerging or prospective democracies are themselves all different: they may be facing challenges that are peculiar to them as individuals as well as others that are common to a larger group.

The mainstream understanding of democratization that is centred on movement towards western-style liberal democracy is accompanied by a complex, contested and still evolving discourse on how to explain democratization – the 'causes', the conditions or prerequisites – and on reasons for the absence of democratic reform initiatives in certain places and the failure to democratize successfully in some others. The forces accounting for trends in democratization are both domestic – internal to the countries – and international. They extend to the growing number of influences in world politics that are transnational or transterritorial and supranational. While a consensus exists that domestic forces are uppermost in explaining the long-term prospects of democratization at the country level, compared to short-term fluctuations, analyses of democratization have come to pay increasing attention to international and transnational influences as well. Among these, the international promotion of democracy by the deliberate actions of democracies and certain inter-governmental organizations and their agents is a leading example. While not necessarily the most significant influence when compared with, say, shifts in the global political economy, the international promotion of democracy is controversial. The challenges it now faces – challenges that include the diffusion if not quite the deliberate export of alternative political models exhibiting illiberal and authoritarian values – are a notable feature of the contemporary international landscape of democracy. There may be links running in both directions between the challenges to democratization and challenges to the promotion of democracy.

Important analytical distinctions should be made between the practical challenges to democratization which reformers on the ground may be most acutely aware of, the challenges that face the international promotion of democracy, and the intellectual challenge of making sense of what is going on – explaining developments and trying to hazard well-grounded predictions about the future. The past 20 or more years have seen an enormous expansion in our knowledge and in the amount of theorizing about democratic change. This has helped overcome some of the myths that previously stood in the way of support for democratization. One such myth was the view that developing countries face a cruel choice whereby they cannot realistically expect to pursue both economic development and democratic reform simultaneously, without running a major risk of jeopardizing one or both of these goals. Another was that only authoritarian rule can deliver the economic liberalization which is needed if economic growth and development are to be sustained. But while not necessarily arguing that the more we know, the less we understand, there is a sense in which the failures of democratization must push scholars to think harder about the relevance of western-derived analytical frameworks and models of democracy and democratic change to societies whose political traditions, social structure and culture may be fundamentally different. Renewed attention to making more sense of democratic regression now begins to look somewhat overdue. And as we have come to explore democratization more thoroughly, so the challenge of integrating the methods of inquiry used in single country studies and comparative politics has gained in importance. The rationale for combining comparative politics with the study of international affairs has become more obvious too. A holistic

6 *Peter Burnell*

approach to the study of democratization, one that tries to integrate the best of all relevant disciplines, makes heavy demands. But its potential to add insights is increasingly apparent now that approaches as diverse as political economy, gender and development studies, international relations and area studies have all had an opportunity to offer their distinctive insights.[6]

A selection of puzzles

Although it is hard to justify selecting just a few from the many puzzles that continue to baffle students of democratization, three will be mentioned for the purpose of illustration. Typical of the state of the discourse is that scholars do not all agree on which puzzles deserve priority of attention. But on the larger canvas there is the never-ending struggle to find a plausible balance between structure and agency in couching explanations of democratization-related phenomena. Focusing in more closely, the way that informal institutions not only influence political outcomes but might actually be of service to democratic objectives also offers a highly intriguing and, perhaps, underrated subject – one that demands further study.[7]

More pressing even than the above could be the need to curb what has been called the increasing 'babel' in democratization studies (Armony and Schamis 2005), more specifically the proliferation of different categories and sub-categories depicting specific types and sub-types of democratic, semi-democratic and non-democratic regime (each with their qualifying adjective), to the point where the great array of alternative labels now on offer risks contributing more confusion than clarity. Of course, one possibility is that the babel is an accurate depiction of the reality on the ground. But if it really does make a good job of capturing the rich diversity of the political *actualité*, then that may be an uncomfortable truth for some analysts.

So at one level we see played out in the study of democratization the conflicting perspectives of social scientists unable to agree on how amenable the study of politics is to truly social scientific aspirations. These aspirations look for high-level generalizations or law-like propositions; the more universal, the better. And yet the attraction of instilling some overall coherence within the ever-increasing volume of democratization studies and the great variety of country and thematic specializations it contains is understandable: this must be regarded as a major on-going challenge. Knowing where to stop – that is to say, to sense where democratization does not offer an appropriate lens or reference point for capturing the political realities, and when to accept that different concepts or analytical frameworks would work best – is of course another challenge. This may be no easy judgement call to make, at any time. Remember that Samuel Huntington (1984), whose idea of the 'third wave' of democratization made such a great impact on the study of democratization in the early 1990s, felt confident enough before the momentous events that destroyed the Soviet Union and communist regimes in Europe to say that the likelihood of democratic development in Eastern Europe is virtually nil.

New challenges to democratization   7

Similarly, inflated talk of the 'end of history', meaning the end of ideological evolution and a convergence on western ideas of liberal democracy that subsequently sprung up now looks rather misplaced, a recent historical curiosity even. Later suggestions that international democracy promotion has become a world value, which places the onus of justification on critics who would reject this claim, too might now look as though they are being overtaken by events (McFaul 2004–5). 'Knowing where to stop' could apply with particular force when trying to comprehend political developments in states where externally driven attempts to substitute liberal democracy for autocracy have clearly failed or continue to face a stiff uphill struggle, as in Afghanistan and Iraq.[8]

While the challenges for democratization at the country level, those which beset the spread of democracy and those that face international democracy promotion, and the challenge of increasing our comprehension, are all analytically distinct, there are further distinctions to be made in terms of origins. That refers to where, what, or who is the source of the challenge, as well as what exactly is being challenged. Here it is worth noting that democratization has been challenged by: first, competing ideas or value systems. These include some versions of nationalism, developmentalism and fundamentalist religious beliefs. The distinctive combinations of capitalism and authoritarian rule that China and Russia now display currently receive a good deal of attention in speculations about a coming global struggle over ideology. Second, there is the challenge from political interests or interested groups who oppose democratic change. This includes organized forces resisting democratic reform inside their own country (challenges from within), and states or political regimes whose foreign posture regrets the international spread of democracy and objects to being on the receiving end of democracy promotion. And, third, there is the challenge set by developments at the international systemic level (challenges from without), which includes some of the trends closely associated with globalization. In the light of debates over who must carry the greatest responsibility for making a success of (or alternatively undermining) democratization, a further potentially useful distinction is between challenges from above, namely ruling elites including anti-reform elements and the international democracy practitioners, and challenges from below, that is to say popular currents in society, the grass-roots.[9] And although it is logical to think that reactionaries with their feet in the past can be a threat to democratic progress (think of North Korea, for example), there are also examples where sustained democratic momentum has been held back, reversed even, by groups who at first resembled democracy's friends. These are the people whose support subsequently proved to be only as strong as their calculation that political reform would advance their own particular interests. Democratization creates both winners and losers; it may not be possible to identify in advance the crucial members of every group and on what time line. But expectations regarding the advantages and disadvantages of reform that turn out to be false can sway opinion and sentiment just as can the disappointment

8   *Peter Burnell*

of aspirations: the subject of dissatisfied democrats is returned to at length later (see Chapter 6 by Renske Doorenspleet).

New challenges for old?

The challenge facing democratization now is quite simply to regain the momentum at a time when the reservations and doubts appear to be much more serious than before, in regard to the following: gaining new recruits to the existing number of democracies, especially liberal democracies; consolidating and improving the quality of the new democracies; preventing or slowing down the erosion of democracy where that is occurring; equipping the international democracy promotion industry with positive yet realistic ideas about what it might achieve in the future and the tools or approach; and, finally, refreshing our willingness to venture bold, credible and testable statements in answer to the big questions about the what, how, why and when of democratization.

The number of democracies and the number of people who live in democracies have probably never been greater. Furthermore the number of organizations, governmental and inter-governmental, official as well as autonomous or semi-autonomous but publicly funded, and the financial resources committed to promoting democracy around the world (probably now in excess of US$5 billion per annum) are also all at an all-time high. A degree of institutionalization has taken place in the democracy support industry. However, not only do the majority of new democracies qualify only as electoral democracies and some of them are (in Freedom House parlance) no better than partly free, but the 'third wave' has halted and may even be in retreat. Some of the most recent advances, including the 'colour' revolutions in Ukraine, Georgia and Kyrgyzstan, look increasingly insecure. Of course none of democracy's achievements necessarily mean that all the old challenges have been conclusively overcome. On the contrary, it is easy find new democracies where problems like the debilitating conflicts to which heterogeneous societies are sometimes prone show few signs of disappearing. The aftermath of the disputed Kenyan presidential election in January 2008 is an example of the increase in inter-communal violence. And in Pakistan, the challenge of persuading the military and its backers at home and abroad that the army's exercise of political power impedes political stability rather than provides an essential condition for security probably remains undiminished. Notwithstanding the relative success of the March 2008 elections (all the more impressive given the assassination of leading opposition figure Benazir Bhutto in the previous December), the future of Pakistan's politics still looks uncertain, and remains vulnerable to crises involving relations with India, Kashmir, and Afghanistan.

But what is new about the challenges now facing democratization; what are the challenges that are new? The answer here is grouped under the following seven sub-headings – ideological competition; declining morale; the strength of the opposition; ambivalent interest from the West; the changing international context; the limits to international democracy promotion; and evaluating democracy assistance – before a final section places the challenges in perspective. The intention is to introduce the broad picture, not pre-empt the more in-depth accounts that pick up on each of these themes in the chapters to follow.

Competing ideologies

Communism no longer poses a threat, and neither does the Brezhnev doctrine by which Soviet leaders presumed the right to invade states where they judged intervention necessary to prop up a communist regime. However, the ideational appeal of democracy certainly now appears more ambivalent than the universal value that was attributed by Sen (1999). The political alternatives posed by certain versions of Islamic thought, which are gaining ground in some countries and particular social strata in Africa and South Asia as well as the Middle East, and by models of national development that emphasize a concentration of political power and restrictions on individual rights, and by forms of populism that contest the traditional accountability mechanisms of representative democracy (as in Venezuela under President Chávez) all seem to be on the rise. Recent evidence from public attitude surveys in many parts of the world tell us that support for the idea of democracy may not be as strong or widespread now as it was even just a few years ago. In Chapter 3, Marina Ottaway spells out the relevant ideologies in more detail and assesses the extent to which they really do challenge democracy – or more significantly, the nature of the threat – with much greater discrimination.

Furthermore, in the twenty-first century, the predisposition of leaders like Chávez and the well-resourced efforts of Saudi Arabia to export their own brand of politics or religious thinking to other countries bring to the competition for global allegiance a dimension that was not so evident in the 1990s. In a similar vein, there is a concern that organized resistance to liberal democracy's spread by governments with opposing ideologies could be moving to a collective and regional basis, for example, through the Shanghai Cooperation Organization – an intergovernmental mutual security pact founded in 2001. The Organization's member states, which include Russia, China and Central Asian states, together make up a quarter of the world's people. We should not assume that the emerging political and diplomatic challenge that the growing power of China and Russia is now seen to pose to the leading democracies translates automatically into a threat to the prospects and processes of democratization elsewhere. But although significant political differences and some long-standing disputes do exist among the regimes that have been associated with an 'authoritarian axis', their exchanges directed at resisting the spread of democracy could evolve into more systematic cooperation on proactive strategies to bolster and promote authoritarian rule abroad. In a regional example, the attempts of the Organization for Security

10   *Peter Burnell*

and Cooperation in Europe (OSCE) to mount credible election observations in countries of the Commonwealth of Independent States have been increasingly thwarted by Russia and its allies (Boonstra 2007); and the potentially anti-democratic consequences of the interest that Russia shows in influencing the politics of neighbouring states like Georgia and Ukraine is now widely recognized.[10]

Declining morale

For some societies there is now the challenge of overcoming the disappointments that experiments in democratic reform in the 1990s have brought in their wake. We now understand more than ever that the transition to consolidated democracy and, after that, progress in improving the quality of democracy are far from assured: success has many influencing conditions, and the chances that positive conditions will come together at the same time in one place are comparatively rare. While a failed attempt to democratize offers the chance of learning from experience and of being better prepared next time, democracy's sceptics and opponents can gain in this way too. Societies that have endured violent conflict may be especially prone to a kind of vicious circle. Attempts to build democracy in the circumstances of a fragile peace can all too easily founder, especially if the international community does not provide enough of the right kind of support for state capacity and economic and social reconstruction as well. A democratic setback can then be the catalyst for reigniting conflict, thus reproducing once again what is by now a familiar historical sequence of events (Collier et al. 2003). Afghanistan is an important test case, and the omens do not look good. In Iraq too, the future remains uncertain as the number of foreign troops in the country runs down.

Even in the more peaceful situation of many of Latin America's democracies, growing popular disenchantment with the polity's inability to meet the welfare aspirations of the great majority is beginning to show signs of prejudicing attitudes towards democracy. Lack of confidence in the political institutions and in the performance (and integrity, even) of the politicians is a major contributory factor. The political consequences can include increasing receptiveness towards populist leaders or, worse from a democratic perspective, the return of military coups. Public attitude surveys conducted recently in other parts of the world, East Asia in particular, seem to provide even more striking evidence of an erosion of commitment to democracy following discontent with economic performance.[11] An intellectual challenge lies in interpreting the significance of such discontents in new democracies; the more practical challenge is to make democracy more meaningful to people in ways that accord with their felt needs and wants. This can mean more aspects of human security than just material welfare alone.

In Russia, the picture is even more graphic: the political liberalization of the first half of the 1990s is associated by many Russians with all-round chaos and national decline, leading to loss of influence in the world. At the same time Russia was viewed by the West as a new democracy. In contrast, the 'managed democracy' and 'sovereign democracy' which emerged under President Putin in effect meant a renewed concentration of executive power and an erosion of liberties such as press freedom. This seems to have won widespread support in the country, by offering not just the return of political stability but a renewal of great power status for Russia in regional and wider world affairs. The way this has come about and more particularly the provocation provided by the so-called coloured revolutions are examined further, by Michael McFaul and Regine A. Spector in Chapter 7.

The strength of the opposition

As Thomas Carothers has pointed out in regard to the 'grey zone' of semi-authoritarian states that fall somewhere between liberal democracy and thoroughgoing autocracy, political elites whose desire to hold onto power exceeds their commitment to genuinely responsive, representative and accountable rule have shown great resilience, perhaps more so than truly ruthless tyrants. They have learned how to manipulate the limited processes of political liberalization in ways that avoid – and perhaps postpone indefinitely – irresistible pressures for more far-reaching political reform. Egypt and Jordan are two often-quoted examples. While a readiness to resort to overt repression still persists in some places, such as Myanmar where in 2007 the military squashed widespread political protest by Buddhist monks, semi-authoritarians in other countries have employed more subtle techniques. These include various ruses put in place even before a general election is held, or when the count is tabulated or, as in Zimbabwe's case in 2008 even after a result has been announced – to ensure that they hold onto power. The electoral process considered in its entirety then falls far short of being free and completely fair – creating a form of 'electoral authoritarianism' (Schedler 2006). We now have a keener appreciation of these possibilities than in the early days of the 'third wave', when the so-called electoral fallacy clouded the issue. But the electoral weaknesses are not the only problem: Puddington (2007) distinguishes other contributing factors to a 'pushback against democracy', such as repression of civil society actors and legalistic devices such as economic pressure to disadvantage political opponents.

Ambivalent interest from the West

In the post-post-Cold War period, the international context has thrown up new challenges to international stability and security that, together with the foreign policy responses these have elicited from the major powers, create problems for democratization. Chief among these of course has been the train of events set in motion by 9/11 and the 'war on terror'. Notwithstanding the democratic peace thesis, which says democracies do not go to war with democracies, and undercutting the view expressed by President Bush among

12   *Peter Burnell*

others that political repression is conducive to the emergence of terrorists, the pursuit of security objectives has taken priority over consistent and wholehearted support for democratic breakthroughs in countries judged strategically important by the West. The willingness of the US government to conclude massive arms deals with Egypt and Saudi Arabia in 2007 is illustrative. In fact, the connection between US military aid and sales, on the one hand, and the objectives of democracy assistance, on the other, has received far too little attention up until now. In the first in-depth attempt to investigate this subject, Nancy Bermeo in Chapter 5 makes some striking observations, with profound implications for the international promotion of democracy.

The possibility that Iran might become a nuclear power is also concentrating minds in the West in a way that pushes that country's democratic shortfalls more into the background, even though Iran's nuclear ambitions and the domestic political vulnerability of President Ahmadinejad are not unconnected. (Indeed, the prospect of a nuclear Iran emerging without liberal democratic credentials and seeking to play a bigger role in regional politics causes considerable anxiety.) Meanwhile the grounds on which European governments are prepared to relegate their commitment to support democracy's advance around the world not just to European regional security interests and concerns for stability in the neighbourhood but to individual national interests as well has been receiving close attention, for example, by Richard Youngs (2006, 2008) and Annette Jünemann and Michèle Knodt (2007) among others.[12] The complicity of both European and US policy in explaining the weak record of democratization and the future prospects for democracy in the Middle East specifically is spelled out by Bassma Kodmani, in Chapter 9.

The changing international context

On the surface, the new architecture of global governance looks potentially more encouraging to the spread of democracy than at any time since 1945. For in addition to the way an assortment of intergovernmental agencies have taken on mandates to support democratic trends and lend some political and diplomatic support, by the early 1990s, the era when East–West rivalry in the Security Council and a North–South divide in the General Assembly inhibited a role for the United Nations (UN) seemed well past. Today more than 100 member states at the UN belong to the so-called Community of Democracies, a loose arrangement of members professing a commitment to support democratization worldwide. And even the Bretton Woods institutions, the World Bank in particular, have made adjustments in their lending to governments so as to accommodate the perceived developmental benefits of improvements in governance, human rights and democratic arrangements.

In contrast to these favourable trends, however, some major developments in the global economy have only added to the challenges. The relatively successful economic performance of some countries in recent years including a

New challenges to democratization   13

number of Europe's newer democracies, and India and China too, should be reckoned a very positive achievement for their people. But many developing countries continue to be absolutely very poor (before late 2008 made even poorer if they relied on imported energy and even now susceptible to tightening world food markets): their average living standards fall further behind those of the West. And yet at the same time their (in some cases very limited) contact with the economic forces of globalization serves to increase the inequality inside these countries. Such developments are not positive for democratization. For oil-importing, least developed countries, the dramatic increase in the price of oil added a major burden, while for the oil-exporters the political significance of international trends in energy prices works in a different and, at times surprisingly conflicting, set of ways, as Richard Youngs explains in Chapter 10.

Back in the 1970s, Arab oil-exporting countries attempted to use the cartel power of the Organization of Petroleum Exporting Countries (OPEC) and the Organization of Arab Petroleum Exporting Countries to put pressure on the West to moderate support for Israel, during Israel's open conflict with nearby Arab states. Around that time also there were indications that the OPEC bloc might use its oil power to support developing world countries in their collective endeavour to negotiate a New International Economic Order, alongside moves in the United Nations Conference on Trade and Development and the Non-aligned Movement to achieve similar ends. At the time these developments were seen in the West as a threat to international financial stability and prosperity. In the event, neither of these two examples of the political uses of oil achieved their ends. Furthermore, the international banking system proceeded to recycle the oil surpluses although in ways that led later to intolerable levels of Third World debt. The consequences of oil for democratization were not to the forefront of anyone's thinking during all that time.

In contrast, what we see now is the spectre of a different and possibly more potent side to the politics of oil supply. Developing world producers, and more especially Saudi Arabia and countries in the Gulf, have been given an opportunity to continue as illiberal and fairly stable rentier states. Their rulers feel no compelling need to be accountable to society through the ballot box. The more general boom in commodity markets and the drive of Asian companies to do business with developing countries where they have economic interests produces similar consequences. For example, in several African countries, China is now a major market (with oil and gas accounting for around 60 per cent of Africa's exports), source of finance and, even, supplier of construction expertise. China's private sector has been in the forefront of this process. A similar story can be found in parts of Latin America. So in at least some developing countries the pressure to concede demands from the West to become more democratic is being diluted. The logic of a development model that does not posit liberal democracy as a necessary condition is made more persuasive. And as Shaun Breslin shows in some detail, in Chapter 8, China itself offers no comfort to the social scientists who might wish to argue

14 *Peter Burnell*

that sooner or later liberal democratic reform must follow on from the county's rapid industrialization, social and economic development: on the contrary, different possible scenarios look at least as if not more convincing.

China aside, and notwithstanding evidence of steady improvement in some human development indicators and growth in the numbers of non-poor in the developing world, the developmental conditions for stable democracy that Lipset (1959) famously brought to prominence many years ago (and broadly confirmed in much subsequent literature) still do not exist in a large group of countries. Indeed, average life expectancy has actually fallen quite dramatically in several African countries, partly because of the impact of HIV/AIDS. The view that strongly authoritarian rule is essential if policy measures designed to bring structural adjustment to the economy are to be politically feasible has also long been buried. In the 1990s, Latin America and Central and Eastern Europe showed that democratic rule has the ability to oversee policies associated with the so-called Washington consensus and to withstand the associated traumas, even if democratically elected governments pay a price for this at the ballot box. But even where economic growth has occurred and led to increased inequality – a pattern that seems inescapable under the impact of marketization and neo-liberal economic reform – the potential for social conflict becomes sharper. In turn, this can render the stabilization of democratic rule more difficult, even while making democracy's claim to be able to mange conflict peacefully that much more important.

At the same time, the concern to reduce poverty that institutions such as the World Bank rediscovered in the past two decades or so, while potentially beneficial to democracy's social underpinnings still risks introducing yet further distortions into the patterns of accountability. External accountability to donors vies with domestic political accountability; solutions for rebalancing such arrangements do not necessarily serve the cause of full democratic accountability. For example, even the poverty reduction strategy programmes that are now considered mandatory in return for access to concessionary international finance, while bringing civil society leaders into the consultation process, have been seen to marginalize legislatures and political parties from this policy domain. Question marks are placed against how representative, how accountable, and how influential on public policy the leaders of civil society really are. In theory, the movement by international donors to go beyond their former insistence on attaching economic conditions to financial support and now to show intense interest in improving governance does give greater scope to influence political change in ways that align with democracy. For instance, support for measures to improve transparency in government for the purpose of fighting corruption can be a service to democracy. At the same time, however, the trend that is now fashionable among donors to switch from offering tied project aid to general budgetary support gives rulers more discretion over the allocation of patronage. Patronage provides power-holders with a valuable instrument for retaining power; democracy's quality can suffer all too easily as a result.

The limits to international democracy promotion

The usual tendency to view international democracy promotion as a dependent variable is, perhaps, unsurprising. The notable increase in democracy aid in the 1990s came after the 'third wave' of democratization had already begun (Carothers 1999: 44–5). New democratic transitions creating the opportunity for such aid to take place, in particular, the political events in Central and Eastern Europe that followed the end of Soviet power were especially helpful. In a rather different vein it has been argued that our knowledge of the impact of democracy assistance and whether it really works has been held back by the confusion among scholars about what democracy means and their inability to agree on indicators of democratic progress or devise convincing methods for its measurement.[13]

Yet democracy promotion must also be conceived as an independent variable, one that is intended to have effect. Which means that a deteriorating environment for democracy promotion must be considered as potentially bad for democratization – assuming of course that democratic initiatives derive some benefit from appropriate international support and that international involvement may further the chances of such initiatives being launched in the first place (assumptions that must not be taken for granted, as Kodmani shows in respect of experience in the Arab world, in Chapter 9). The mood in the democracy promotion industry especially in the United States has become less confident over recent years. This stems not simply from recognition that the challenge of democratization itself now looks to be harder than previously thought and that some of the emerging democracies have stalled or begun to travel in the wrong direction. As a striking example the largely unexpected military coup against Prime Minister Thaksin Shinawatra's government in Thailand in September 2006, and then renewed political turmoil in Bangkok in late 2008, came as a shock. But the mood among democracy practitioners is also in part a consequence of the way democracy support has come to be associated with 'regime change' – the forcible removal of governments in Afghanistan and Iraq by US and allied military invasion – and how this has been used by democracy's opponents to discredit the peaceful methods and different objectives of most democracy assistance. No less troubling, perhaps, has been the realization that strong international support for holding – possibly for the first time ever – reasonably free and fair elections does not necessarily produce an outcome deemed favourable to the interests of the West or, even, to democracy in the long run. In this regard the victory of an internationally proscribed terrorist organization, Hamas, in the Palestinian Authority elections in January 2006 can be viewed as a major wake-up call. Not only has it forced government-inspired democracy promoters in the West to reveal their true intentions but the harm done to reputations, self-questioning and recriminations seem to have exceeded anything produced by the West's acquiescence in Algeria's 1991 military coup. Although that coup prevented the Front Islamique du Salut from winning Algeria's National Assembly

16   *Peter Burnell*

elections and taking power then, it occurred before all the idealistic-sounding rhetoric and mythology of international support for democratic elections had the chance to build up. The bigger the bubble, the sharper the deflation, later.

Until the invasions of Afghanistan (2001) and Iraq (2003), the idea that state sovereignty ruled out international intervention in the internal politics of a country except in very special circumstances (most notably where the politics harmed the security of other countries) seemed to be eroding. However, the limits posed by sovereignty now draw renewed support, thanks to the reactions provoked by the examples set by regime change. Formerly, the idea of a different kind of 'regime change' did not seem so fantastic, namely one that refers to the gradual evolution of an international regime of law, custom and convention that would allow collectively endorsed intervention in the internal affairs of countries for the defence and promotion of the rights of its citizens even against their own government. The idea of a people's right to democratic governance and then of a corresponding responsibility of enforcement attaching to the international community in general, and the established democracies specifically, became a topic of debate.[14] The implications of such ideas would go well beyond the status quo ante and interventions aimed at halting genocide or comparable gross abuse of fundamental human rights. Now, however, and partly as a result of reactions against efforts to secure 'regime change' and the Bush administration's unilateral espousal of a doctrine of 'preventive intervention' (giving licence to the use of force by the US where the government deems it necessary to pre-empt the possibility of a longer-term threat to the US national interest), approaches to democracy promotion other than wholly consensual ones look as unlikely as ever to gain universal legitimation. As Laurence Whitehead argues in Chapter 2, state sovereignty and international democratization represent 'an awkward coupling' but they do need to be rendered mutually supportive. China has been a forceful advocate of non-intervention, which presents a model of global order that seems firmly rooted in the past. Naturally, illiberal regime of all stripes can draw comfort; it resonates strongly with governments such as those in Sudan and Myanmar that have been shielded from western pressure.

It seems unlikely then that the United Nations will be granted more interventionist powers to promote democracy, or a major increase in its resources, any time soon. And while regional inter-governmental organizations in Africa, Latin America and Asia might be looked to instead, the evidence that they can be relied on to take the lead in enforcing respect for democratic norms inside the member states remains patchy and unconvincing.[15] The record of the Organization of American States is somewhat better than most but nevertheless has major limitations (Legler et al. 2007). However, a challenge for all of these organizations and for analysts too is how and where to strike a balance between traditional ideas of sovereignty and the more recently developed interest in empowering human beings everywhere with certain political rights and civil liberties irrespective of the political preferences of their government – a government that may or may not be the

New challenges to democratization 17

product of a free and fair election. These questions have been made more pressing by trends in cultural globalization and, in the 1990s, the undoubted spread of norms associated with freedom and democracy.

The larger grounds for declining optimism about the prospects for democracy promotion, especially in the US, have been elaborated elsewhere, most authoritatively by Thomas Carothers (2006, 2007b), who extends, updates and reflects on the reasons in Chapter 4.[16] For the EU, in contrast, the distinctive challenge is to repeat its successful strategy of supporting democratic consolidation of post-communist European states by making offers of conditional membership of the EU. As the process of EU enlargement comes to an end and states in the neighbourhood as well as others much farther away have no prospect of membership, and as many of them lack liberal democracy's most generally accepted conditions or credentials, the EU's ability to exert influence is much reduced. The issue of Turkey's ambition to join the EU has become more contentious. To impose further delay could risk undermining the forces for liberal democracy that have been gaining ground there. However, the wisdom of allowing Turkey to join divides opinion among existing EU states more sharply now than ever. The accession of Ukraine, whose leaders have also said that EU membership is a goal but who have been rebuffed by the EU, would be no less taxing for the EU. For although even just a firm promise of eventual accession would offer support to democratic consolidation in Ukraine, the damage it might cause to Europe's already tense relationship with Russia would require very skilful political and diplomatic management. The same is no less true in regard to Georgia.

Evaluating democracy assistance

The challenge of proving that democracy assistance is effective and of demonstrating which aspects perform best (addressed in Burnell 2007) is now compounded by the new challenge of innovating ways of addressing democratic shortcomings that previously were judged too sensitive politically or too difficult to warrant much support, but are now increasingly thought to be too important to neglect. Examples include help with building viable political parties with strong roots in society and competitive party systems,[17] and legislative strengthening, where experience shows that in order to be effective, innocuous programmes like funding a parliamentary library or extra computer facilities must be supplemented by efforts to bring parliaments closer to society. That means trying to change the political incentive structure that influences the behaviour of elected politicians, and increasing citizen involvement, which are objectives that prompt resistance not only from government circles but also among parliamentarians.

In any case, there is a growing impression that evaluating democracy assistance in close detail may offer very limited value anyway, if the exercise is divorced not just from all the other approaches to promoting democracy but from the different ways in which international factors tout court impinge on

18   *Peter Burnell*

the prospects for democracy. Some such factors are unintended and unforeseen, like the international financial disruption and global economic downturn that are following hard on the heels of the 2007 collapse in the US subprime mortgage industry and accompanying bank failures. But many such factors are the product of deliberate action, where the consequences should have been fairly easy to predict.[18]

The challenges in perspective

The new challenges to democratization should be kept in perspective in three ways: (1) other challenges; (2) challenges can be beneficial; and (3) the constraints on treatment owing to standard book length.

First, the challenges to democratization are not the only challenges, political or non-political, and they may not be the most important. Indeed, the presence of quite basic material threats to the human condition and to individual security in the widest sense in many parts of the world make it a challenge to keep the issue of democratization at the forefront, especially for statesmen and policy-makers in the global arena. For some of the poorest countries, Bangladesh, for instance, just coping with the humanitarian consequences of the environmental impact of global warming will tax the collective will, not just the state's limited finances and organizational capabilities. For the international community, identifying and addressing the causes of state failure and remedying some of its symptoms in parts of Africa, for instance should remain high on the agenda, where moral and other considerations combine with mutual self-interest to demand that solutions be found. Even in the academic arena the lack of consensus shows there is still much analytical and other work to do. For example, competing arguments pit the importance of establishing the rule of law before tackling other conditions requisite to democratic progress against the idea that democracy and the rule of law are so intimately linked that efforts to advance both must always be made together (see Journal of Democracy 2007a). Perhaps dwarfing all of this is the global economic recession that seems bound to occupy 2009 and possibly 2010 as well, and whose consequences are likely to touch everything, with increase in uncertainty almost guaranteed.

Second, however, the challenges are not all bad. What may appear to be a challenge from one perspective or at a given time may turn out to be an opportunity. It may elicit a response that proves to be a powerful constructive force. The fall of the Berlin Wall and the collapse of the Soviet Union were both seen at the time as potentially disruptive for regional and world stability. They swept away a settled order that had prevented nuclear war and, like the more recent financial events, put a very uncertain future in its place. But these developments bear some responsibility for the fact that there are now many more democracies in the world today than existed before 1989. In a more specific example of how daunting challenges may take on a new aspect, the task of building a harmonious multi-racial democracy in South Africa after

New challenges to democratization   19

apartheid looked monumental to some, not least because of the emotional and psychological legacy of apartheid. The Truth and Reconciliation Commission (TRC) was invented to address this problem. And while not without its critics among the country's black population, the TRC has since been credited with making a remarkable contribution to building the new democratic South Africa – so much so that several other countries with a recent history of violence have now borrowed the idea. Without difficulties, there would be no struggle, and there is a view that struggle helps to bring about and consolidate many of the most exacting political goods such as freedom – whether freedom from foreign oppression or domestic tyranny.[19] Here the words of John Stuart Mill come to mind:

> When a people has had the misfortune to be ruled by a government under which the feelings and the virtues needful for maintaining freedom could not develop themselves, it is during an arduous struggle to become free by their own efforts that these feelings and virtues have the best chance of springing up. Men become attached to what they have long fought for and made sacrifices for; they learn to appreciate that on which their thoughts have been much engaged.
>
> (1867: 175)

Third, in this volume, as in any other book, there are pragmatic reasons for drawing the boundaries. The book is not about challenges facing democracy in its heartland, even though a growing literature on the democratic shortcomings of established democracies reveals evidence of increasing weaknesses and new assaults on the people's freedoms. And there is the democratic deficit of the European Union too. This is especially striking given its pertinence to the EU's most recent recruits, who gained or regained liberal democratic governance for themselves only very recently, following the end of communism. The omission of chapters on the established democracies is not meant to deny the wisdom of saying that one of the biggest challenges facing the international diffusion of support for democratic ideals now is the refurbishment of democracy and its reputation in the very countries that have stood in the forefront in the past, the United States especially.

Indeed, a challenge faced by democrats in prospective, new or emerging democracies is how to avoid being discouraged by the negative developments they see in the older democracies, and how to prevent these developments spreading. This means more than just being allowed to pioneer their own path to greater democracy and not being required to follow trajectories of democratic progress that the older democracies might claim to exemplify from their own past. It means appraising the significance of potential new threats to democracy and its quality in the established democracies too: the low or declining levels of political participation (the 75 per cent voter turnout in Spain, and in the US, the increase in turnout to 61 per cent, that mobilized young people especially, being noteworthy exceptions in 2008); the growing

20 *Peter Burnell*

power of concentrated private ownership of the mass media and its 'dumbing down' (as in Britain and Italy, for example); the erosion of civil liberties that accompanied measures to combat (the fear of) terrorism; the increasing presidentialization (executive-centredness) and the difficulty that legislatures and political parties encounter when trying to hold political leaders to account (typical of many democracies); the reduced levels of trust in politicians (everywhere); the proneness to extremist tendencies among small minorities, which degrades the larger social capital and damage inter-communal relations more generally (some of Europe's multi-cultural societies being especially vulnerable); and the challenge of maintaining political self-determination in a world of growing transnationalization, that transfers political decision-making to technocratic and bureaucratic sites of regional and global governance. Finally, and raised in Chapter 3 by Ottaway, there is a question mark against whether the ideological fragmentation that is witnessed in established democracies poses a kind of threat in the long run – if not there, then in newer democracies that take after them. But perhaps in this weighty but far from comprehensive list of challenges it is the issue of how to democratize polycentric and multi-level governance that perhaps merits most a truly global response. And a global response demands the full engagement not just of the established and the new democracies but of all countries, whether democratically organized or not, which is why it looks so extraordinarily difficult.

In conclusion, then, this book seeks to identify new challenges to democratization. It does this against a background that does not view the prospects for democratization and the fortunes of international democracy promotion as one and the same thing but instead recognizes there are connections between the two. Democracy promotion is not the single most important influence on the future for democracy. And the state of democracy in the world by itself does not determine everything that happens in democracy promotion. That democracy is currently under threat in certain places is clear; a failure to consolidate democratic progress and to deepen democracy in some countries, and the resilience shown by some authoritarian regimes, are also evident. The challenge of putting precise figures on the trends will be revisited in the final chapter. But the substantive chapters that lie in between will help us move towards a balanced assessment of how far the claim that democratization is now facing new challenges is warranted by the evidence provided, and the seriousness of the threat(s). Merely speculative judgements must be avoided. But it should be possible to get the measure of conditions that will have an important bearing on the future of democratization, even if general statements must be qualified where appropriate and tailored to reflect individual cases. In very broad terms, the sequencing of the chapters reflects this point, corresponding loosely to a movement from the general to the particular, from the international to the more specific, and in no way represents an order of importance or makes a statement comparing the respective insights.

The progress of democracy always has faced and doubtless always will face challenges. The future of democratization remains highly contingent. And although establishing what is new about the challenges may not be too onerous, evaluating their import ultimately will be a matter of judgement.

Notes

1 Diamond contributing to a transatlantic seminar on 'Countering anti-democratic strategies', cited in Democracy Digest: The Bulletin of the Transatlantic Democracy Network (February 2008). Diamond (2008a) contains a fuller account of his views on the outlook for democratization.
2 Freedom House data can be accessed at www.freedomhouse.org. A more positive assessment can be found in the Bertelsmann Transformation Index 2008, which reported that, on average, scores for what it calls 'defective democracies' actually improved somewhat, reflecting increased levels of political participation – albeit in elections of doubtful value (Bertelsmann Stiftung 2008).
3 David Miliband's Aung Suu Kyi Lecture at the University of Oxford took place on 12 February 2008.
4 The further ahead the projection, the greater the uncertainties. For example, the US National Intelligence Council in its report, *Global Trends 2025: A Transformed World*, while expressing optimism about the long-term prospects for greater democratization listed many 'key' and 'relative' uncertainties that suggest conditions might be much less favourable over the next decade or so.
5 In a complementary development emphasizing the greater influence that formal rules could exercise over the political conduct of elites, Posner and Young (2007) note how Africa's presidents now usually resort to constitutional means to try to get term limits on their office relaxed, instead of using fiat or force. Presumably further progress would take the form of even fewer designs on achieving such extensions.
6 For elaboration, see Burnell (2003).
7 A recent advance is Helmke and Levitsky (2006). Defining informal institutions as socially shared rules, usually unwritten, that are created, communicated, and enforced outside officially sanctioned channels, they argue that such institutions can at times reinforce formal institutions by making them more effective, enhancing their stability, or substitute for their poor performance.
8 As Whitehead (2009) argues, theoretical models derived from existing academic literature on democratization are unlikely to offer much insight into the political future in countries such as these.
9 Bermeo (2003) found evidence for the argument that elites bear primary responsibility for aborted transitions to democracy.
10 See Chapter 7 by McFaul and Spector in this book, and also Ambrosio (2009) for a pioneering account of the use of outward-oriented as well as domestic strategies for the restoration of strong authoritarian rule in Russia.
11 See evidence assembled in Journal of Democracy (2007b).
12 Mathieson and Youngs (2006) show that even the constituency of European politicians who might be expected to be most supportive of democracy promotion are in fact ambiguous or confused.
13 See, for example, Sarles (2007: 49). Burnell (2008b: 10–13) argues that the supply of and the demand for democracy assistance may be mutually constitutive.
14 Franck (1992) and subsequent writings recommending an easing of the restrictions imposed by the UN Charter on justifiable military intervention made a prominent contribution to the debate. See Fox and Roth (2000).

22 *Peter Burnell*

15 For example, a statistical inquiry by Ulfelder (2008) that concluded that for the most part, participation in the major intergovernmental organizations and the UN human rights regime has made little difference to the chances that countries would attempt or sustain democracy.
16 See also Burnell (2008b).
17 For as Ottaway explains in Chapter 3, comparatively speaking, too much emphasis may have been placed by democracy assistance on capacity-building in civil society.
18 Elaborated in Burnell (2006, 2008a). Nardulli (2008) and Magen and Morlino (2008) offer further evidence of growing interest in the wider international context for democratization.
19 Democracy arises 'not from the ashes of war but from a history of struggle, civic work, and economic development'. Barber (2003: 165).

2 State sovereignty and democracy
An awkward coupling

Laurence Whitehead

Over the centuries, democratic government has taken many forms and has had a variety of partners. Consider democracy and the town hall, or city state; democracy of the landowners; democracy and the property qualification; universal male suffrage and democracy; democracy and ethnic purity; even we have seen the celebration – most improbably of all – of a slave-owning democracy. At different times and in different historical settings, it has been accepted that democracy is inextricably linked to Protestantism, to Christianity, to secularization, to social equality, to socialism, and then – most insistently since 1990 – to capitalism. Yet all of these couplings have proved transient. There is a broad set of political institutions, traditions, and values that we can call democratic, which have persisted (or mutated) as property-owners, empires, religious commitments, and models of economic organization have succeeded one another on the historical stage.

In the post-Cold War period, democracy seemed to flourish (and mutate) as the claims of state sovereignty were said to subside. Under conditions of unipolar US supremacy, with global democracy on the advance, with state socialism discredited and eclipsed, and with liberalized markets extending into every recess of human society, the 'decline of the state' was celebrated by liberal internationalists who regarded state sovereignty as yet another impediment to individual freedom and the promotion of universal standards of human and political rights. Like slavery, like empire, like the command economy, it should be rolled back and eventually eliminated in order to maximize the liberty of all.

From this perspective, the curbing of sovereigntist illusions would clear the way for the establishment of a more secure and encompassing democratic order, one derived from permanent features of human nature undistorted by nationalist division and manipulation. Evidently, the variant of democracy promotion by the liberal internationalists was a modification of what earlier theorists had taken to be the essential characteristics of the creed. But this was not new. Each time the democratic tradition has moved from one partner to the next it has been adjusted to the new social context in which it must operate, without ever yielding its claim to moral and institutional continuity.

24 *Laurence Whitehead*

So by the late 1990s, globalized democracy, no longer closely associated with national sovereignty, had become the most fashionable and rapidly expanding variant of resurgent liberal doctrine. In the name of democracy, international organizations adopted new mandates, such as the 'responsibility to protect', and regional charters of democratic standard-setting and conditionality. These declaratory statements of willingness to encroach upon the sovereignty of nations in order to serve the higher good of democratic universalism were not purely rhetorical. At the theoretical level, they were bolstered by 'research' purportedly showing that democracies never fight each other, so that the extension of democracy into recalcitrant jurisdictions could be recast as the establishment of a universal peace. At the more practical level, this produced coordinated military operations claiming to introduce democracy into Haiti, Timor, Kosovo, Afghanistan and Iraq (the list is neither exhaustive nor closed). In all these cases (and others that may still be to come), the national sovereignty of internationally recognized member states of the United Nations was suspended without the consent of the governments involved, in operations that involved what I shall generically refer to henceforth as 'coercive democratizations'. The coercion in question could be mainly economic sanctions, although it always also involved the injection of an armed force controlled from outside the target state. Here 'democratization' refers to the stated intentions and internationally approved authorizations of these operations without prejudice to the actual results they may eventually produce.

One crucial feature of coercive democratization is that it requires an at least temporary and conditional forced suspension of sovereignty in the target state. This raises fundamental issues of procedure: who decides?; who verifies the legitimacy of a given decision?; to whom are the results accountable?; what redress is available in the event of disproportionate force or unnecessary collateral damage? It also poses major difficulties for democratic theory – especially as regards the normally assumed interdependence between sovereignty and democracy. The suspension of sovereignty requires a decision on the part of external powers to act in the interests of a political community that is unable to formulate its own preferences, owing to the suppression of democracy there. But what if those preferences excluded such a drastic remedy? What if, even after the intervention has occurred, the newly enfranchised beneficiaries of this external gift of democracy are not grateful, but hostile? In any case, coercive intervention is rarely a purely surgical operation, and nor are self-healing and the restoration of popular sovereignty the sole outcomes. Intervention nearly always creates 'facts on the ground'. New vested interests arise and need protection; old authorities are damaged or displaced and must not be allowed to return; economic and strategic balances are altered according to the necessities of the occupying powers. The more controversial and resisted the occupation, the more far-reaching will be this redistribution of costs and opportunities. Finally, once sovereignty has been suspended for the first time, local expectations and patterns of behaviour are

State sovereignty and democracy 25

likely to change. The comparative record suggests that after the first foreign intervention both domestic actors and external patrons may become habituated to cycles of repetition that preclude a durable and cumulative democratic progression. (Haiti provides one vivid example of this possibility.)

So, in this chapter, I provide a critical assessment of the lessons arising from these hubristic experiments in coercive democratization. In contrast to the liberal internationalist utopia just outlined, I consider that state sovereignty provides an underpinning to democracy that can hardly be dispensed with. This is not an unconditional defence of state sovereignty in all circumstances (there was a time before the modern state when democratic practices were already worth promoting, and there may well be a time in future centuries when they can be more richly developed even after the nation state as we currently know it has disappeared). It is a more limited and contextual correction to the analytical failings of the West's most recent generation of democracy crusaders. If we are to overcome the severe challenges to the advance of democracy around the world that have arisen over the past decade we need to undertake a theoretical as well as practical critique of this anti-sovereignty discourse.

The coupling of democracy and state sovereignty may be awkward and contingent, but it is also a necessary partnership, at least for the present generation. It is not enough to respect the sovereignty of those states that can be unambiguously assigned to the 'democratic' side of the global community. There are still far too many states (with supporting populations) whose democratic credentials are insecure, contested, or outright lacking. They will continue to exist, and to play an active part in the international community. They will often even provide services such as security and identity to their subject populations, who may therefore feel threatened when their sovereignty is contested from without. And, in most cases, these states will be the most plausible, if not the sole bearers of national hopes for eventual progress with democratization as well. So the suspension of their sovereignty is neither a practical nor a prudent method of advancing the course of democracy in the world, except under the most extremely restricted circumstances.

Many liberal internationalists lost their sense of reality in their hubristic desire to remake the entire world in accordance with their utopia. Their overreach has produced a backlash which will last for a substantial period. That backlash is sufficiently severe to present a major challenge to prior hopes of a rapidly more democratized international community. It is not the only impediment. Other contributors to this volume are addressing other challenges. In this chapter, I therefore limit myself to the sovereignist backlash and, in particular, to the resistance provoked by recent and ongoing ventures in coercive democratization.

The chapter is organized as follows: first, I recapitulate some rather traditional arguments concerning the indispensability of state sovereignty as a foundation for modern democracy. I recognize the awkwardness of this linkage, and acknowledge the limit cases where it becomes untenable. But I argue

26   *Laurence Whitehead*

that, at least for the present generation, these two items cannot be decoupled without putting democratic stability at risk. I then summarize two rival positions currently in contention: the claim that a community of democracies could best secure its sovereignty and freedom by banding together and demanding that all other states conform to their standards; versus the rival contention that democracy promotion and protection should begin at home, and be founded on the principle that one should 'do as one would be done by'. In the next section, I focus more specifically on the issues that arise in the course of democratization (when new democratic rules of the game need to be stabilized and internalized in societies with recent experience of authoritarian rule). I outline the 'counter-hegemonic' potential of democratization (the potential conflict between international order and the extension of democracy), with illustrations provided by the specific domain of 'grass roots politics'. The final section is prospective and policy-oriented. I consider the implications of the preceding theoretical and comparative arguments when applied to the specific geopolitical realities and dilemmas that will face the western democracies once the hubris of liberal internationalism has subsided and the backlash in favour of state authority has run its course.

Democracy and sovereignty: still joined at the hip

In accordance with the United Nations system established after the Second World War, the entire globe is divided into territorially demarcated and sovereign nation states, each formally equal, and all bound by some common ethical and legal considerations. These states are immensely varied in scale and power, of course. China has more than 100,000 times the population of Tuvalu, yet both have an equal vote in the General Assembly (although China also has a permanent seat in the Security Council). Some residual jurisdictions remain outside this institutional framework (most notably Taiwan, but also Puerto Rico, among others) and there are also various conflict-ridden exceptions (the Basque country, Cyprus, Kashmir, South Ossetia, Tibet, Transdinistria, and so forth). But the grid of territorial states enjoying formal mutual recognition within this system is remarkably comprehensive and has been long-lasting. The procedures for creating new units and merging old ones are broadly understood and widely accepted as necessary underpinnings of international order. Hence, Iraq could not be allowed to forcibly conquer and incorporate Kuwait in 1990. For the same reason, the international order is challenged when Kosovo is separated from Serbia without the consent of the Serbian authorities; or when the unresolved situation of the enclaves in Georgia is unilaterally altered by force, whichever side bears the responsibility.

Democracy existed as both an ideal and a political practice long before the UN system was brought into existence by the victorious Allies after 1945, and in some form or other it would no doubt continue to attract adherents and demonstrate its merits, even if this international system of nation states were

State sovereignty and democracy 27

somehow to disappear. For example, it is in principle perfectly possible to envisage a global democratic regime, with uniform civil and political rights for the entire human race, and with institutional procedures designed to ensure the competitive election of the world's governing authorities, and their accountability to the people. Both the ideal and the practice can readily be elaborated from our existing stock of democratic theory and experience, even if the means to get from here to there remain obscure; and even though the consequences for existing variants of distribution of power and authority – including existing forms of democratic power and authority – would be extremely disruptive.

One could invoke the European Union to demonstrate how a regional community of states, each preserving its current identity and boundaries, might nevertheless 'pool sovereignty' to the point at which the key question became the quality of democratic institutions and practices at the aggregate regional level, rather than solely within each separate member state (The failed Lisbon Treaty of December 2007 was an attempt to nudge Europe slightly in that direction.) It is also quite feasible to redirect attention to the sub-national level, and to envisage a system in which municipalities, or local regions enjoyed a great degree of autonomy and provided the core constituent ingredients of the democratic order (the Swiss cantons provide us with a practical illustration of how this might be developed).

Nevertheless, at least for the present generation, there is no escaping the centrality of the existing nation state as prime and indispensable bearer of whatever aspirations there may be, either for political democracy as an end-state, or for democratization as a route towards greater popular participation in the exercise of public authority.

The reasons why democracy and the sovereign state are currently 'joined at the hip' are well known, and need only be very briefly rehearsed here. First, every democracy requires a precisely defined demos. The only way to establish the views of the majority of the citizenry (the body of individuals each entitled to one equal vote) is by creating a precise and clearly acceptable inventory of who is included, or excluded, and why. The same applies to monitoring the rights and duties that accompany citizenship. So, either a nation state, or a large region, or a canton, or, indeed, a world government is needed to compile the electoral register, to ensure fair play and equality of access, and to settle electoral disputes. In the world as it is currently constituted, the legal and administrative structures capable of delivering these outcomes are almost invariably located in the nation state. Indeed, it is widely regarded as a key attribute of national sovereignty for the state to organize and supervise its own elections (often, but not invariably, in concordance with international standards and assisted by external observers, who must nevertheless operate in accordance with the local laws).

Second, given the general absence of trustworthy or authoritative institutions outside the state, most people throughout the world turn to their national authorities as a prime source of orientation and identity-formation.

28 *Laurence Whitehead*

This is true of many of those living under authoritarian rule, as well as for most citizens of secure democracies. It is not always quite so true in newly-established and fragile democracies (Russians in Baltic Republics or Kurds in Turkey, for example, may look primarily to a neighbouring state). Even in stronger democracies, there may be a temptation to look to a Great Power or regional hegemon as a source of reassurance when domestic political insecurities arise (thus, some Latin American states look to Washington, and some Francophone countries to Paris). There are certainly alternative non-state sources of orientation and identity formation (the Vatican, the European Commission, the Dalai Lama, and even the UN, for example). But none of these are capable of sustaining political cohesion on their own. To the extent that they provide political leadership or inspiration, this will express itself primarily through national political structures (for instance, through Christian Democratic parties, pro-integration movements, or Buddhist parties).

Third, despite the huge inequalities between states, they all share some basic morphological features that favour coexistence and encourage them to collude in maintaining the state system and in marginalizing non-state challengers. Even those citizens with the misfortune to be trapped on the wrong side of a national boundary, saddled with the burdens of allegiance to a poor, weak, or oppressive state, are often likely to consider themselves better placed than the refugees, stateless persons, or undocumented migrants who can neither invoke the rights pertaining to their place of birth, or to the citizenship entitlements provided to the natives in their current place of abode.

The current global financial crisis is likely to reinforce these pro-state reflexes, as is the sense of insecurity generated by terrorism, drug trafficking, and the heavy-handed security responses that these elicit. Even citizens of the most venerable and high-quality democracies are liable to feel defensive in such conditions, and it is to their own national authorities that they will turn for protection, rather than to any higher level of cosmopolitan inspiration, or broader community of like-minded democrats. Those seeking a hearing from recent and more fragile democratic regions are likely to feel still more exposed. Perhaps they will sometimes prefer the protection of a strong external power, but even in this case, the safest course will typically be to urge the national authorities in question to reinforce their ties with a protector state. Citizens fearful of the fragility of their democratic institutions are unlikely to advocate a generalized weakening of state sovereignty even if they do accept the inevitability of unequal alliances. As for those still living under some variant of authoritarian rule, the present climate of crisis and insecurity is likely to increase the premium on collective discipline, and to discourage any behaviour that can be stigmatized as disloyalty. More generally, the discredit in which liberal internationalism is currently held, and the associated crumbling of unipolarity and free market fundamentalism, seem likely to boost the centrality of state authority across regime types. (Admittedly, there are also some 'rogue regimes' and failing states where the destabilizing effects of crisis are less predictable, but these are mostly marginal cases.)

In the case of most democracies, this defensive pro-state climate probably encourages already existing tendencies towards what Guillermo O'Donnell called *democradura* (in other words, relatively tough security regulations; limited tolerance of deviance; a willingness to narrow the range of 'rights' that are reliably guaranteed; and scaling back on the incorporation of excluded groups). In the case of most authoritarian regimes, it probably produces symmetrical effects, such as a heightened suspicion of democratic idealists, a renewed determination to maintain social discipline, if necessary by repressive means. In neither case do these pro-state reactions necessarily involve the permanent or definitive suppression of democratic aspirations. The change in climate may favour temporary 'emergency' measures that can then be relaxed later, when the crisis has passed. Even the most authoritarian regimes will need to carry public opinion with them in times of hardship, so they may be more likely to conduct 'controlled' elections, rather than to repudiate popular sovereignty on principle. The current Russian discourse on 'sovereign democracy' is often dismissed in the West as no more than a fig leaf for complete regression into autocracy, but this is too Manichean a view. Not only in Putin's Moscow, but also in more liberal London, and Washington, the authorities are trying to balance the need to respond to mainstream public opinion with a strong desire (on security and national interest grounds) to restrict public debate within 'safe' limits.

An awkward coupling

Thus far, we have highlighted a 'backlash' against democratic cosmopolitanism and the emergence of 'pro-state reflexes'. It is equally important both to recognize the ambiguity of these currents, and at the same time to keep them in perspective. The globalizing and state-eroding tendencies of the 1990s may have gone into abeyance, but they have by no means disappeared and could perfectly well resurface in a few more years. In any case, they leave behind them legacies of interdependence and mutual commitment that will continue to limit state autonomy (especially in Europe). The uneven but widespread advance of democratic aspirations and democratization in the 1990s cannot be easily forgotten. It created a set of expectations about democratic performance against which the quality of democracy established in different states will continue to be monitored and critically evaluated.

However, at least for the current generation, it seems clear that state sovereignty will continue to underpin the international system, and that the state will remain the indispensable vehicle for those who wish to advance towards a more democratic world order. It will continue to be seen as the best hope, even for the large proportion of the world's population currently living under authoritarian rule. (In China, for example, a successful and effective sovereign state may not guarantee personal freedom and political pluralism, but it almost certainly provides the best hope of moving in that direction, and those seen as advocating a curbing of the authority of the Chinese state are

30 *Laurence Whitehead*

unlikely to win popular support for their less successful and legitimate recommendation.) As noted above, there are a few peripheral cases where it may be unavoidable to resort to the temporary suspension of state sovereignty, in order to avert genocide or humanitarian disaster. But such operations need to be kept to an absolute minimum, both because of the adverse consequences that we now know can attend them, and because the rhetoric of humanitarian intervention is so easily hijacked and manipulated.

The image of defenceless victims being sheltered by an altruistic international community presents a rare and improbable limit case. Genuine democrats should always think twice before embracing such schemes. Are the imagined beneficiaries truly keen to see their sovereign institutions supplanted? Are those who take it upon themselves to speak for the voiceless really as disinterested as they claim? Once evangelical liberators find an excuse to meddle in the affairs of other states in the name of the common good, they can prove themselves insensitive and disposed to over-reach. We can expect such experiences to provoke a widespread, powerful and well-grounded anti-interventionist backlash. (If the North Atlantic Treaty Organization (NATO) can do this in Kosovo, for instance, how will they like it now that Moscow has done the same in Ossetia?) Of course, not all such operations are identical. (Grenada was a success, and East Timor was also a belated and necessary corrective to earlier failings.) Controls over who makes decisions of this kind, and how the latter are legitimated and monitored, are crucial. Unfortunately, the international community has not proved sufficiently rigorous and discriminating, at least not over the past decade. As a result, indiscriminate and abusive misuse of this discourse, especially by self-serving and self-deceiving neo-conservative governments, has discredited the whole idea of humanitarian intervention, even where it may be needed, and that discredit is likely to hang over the international community for a considerable period to come.

In consequence, at least for the present and perhaps for future decades, those who are sincere about championing the cause of democratic advance around the world will need to fall back on a well-tried 'awkward coupling' between democracy and the preservation of state sovereignty. This must still be defended as an un-eliminable praxis if not an ethically impeccable principle, for regulating political relationships within and between nations. But what does that mean, in practical terms, for the cooperation between communities of democratic states, and for their relations with those they classify as non-democratic?

Democracy-militant and sovereignty-militant positions

At the risk of over-simplification, it seems worth contrasting two stylized responses. The first (which can be labelled 'democracy-militant') holds that all true democracies should work together to induce or even compel non-democracies to change their regimes. This does not necessarily commit the

State sovereignty and democracy   31

democracies to infringing the sovereignty of the non-democracies, but it clearly places the latter 'on probation' (in contrast to the security of sovereignty that is attributed to all true democracies). This is liable to be seen by the non-democracies as threatening and intrusive. Indeed, the recent practices of NATO and the behaviour of different ad hoc coalitions of Washington allies lend considerable plausibility to that perception.

The second response starts from the opposite premise and can be called 'sovereignty-militant'. It holds that except in truly extreme conditions that would have to be certified by the UN Security Council, all states – self-styled democracies and non-democracies alike – are entitled to conduct their internal affairs without the sovereignty-breaching intervention of others. In return, they are also expected to refrain from interfering with the sovereignty of their neighbours, however much they disagree over questions of regime type. This is the classic Westphalian[1] or post-1945 state system, an underlying rationale for which is that it serves the cause of minimizing warfare. It does not prevent communities of democratic states from seeking to promote their political values and practices among the non-democracies. It only precludes them from using sovereignty-destroying methods to do so. Thus, the European Union did not violate the Westphalian system when it set up the Copenhagen Criteria (1993), specifying the political reforms that it would require for the accession of any new member to its club; nor when it called for a 'democracy clause' to be attached to its cooperation agreements with members of the Africa-Caribbean-Pacific (ACP) grouping of states. But the Helms–Burton Law in the US does encroach upon Cuban sovereignty when it enforces extra-territorial economic sanctions that are only to be lifted when Washington-prescribed and approved elections are held, with the current national leaders disqualified from standing.

It would be wrong to dichotomize these two possibilities. In fact, a good deal of recent US–EU negotiations over Cuba and the 'Colour' Revolutions has consisted of attempts to shade the differences between them. NATO is also being drawn into such issues (e.g. in Georgia) as is the Organization of American States (OAS) and the Southern African Development Community (SADC) (with regard to Zimbabwe). Once it is acknowledged that there may be exceptional circumstances where sovereignty has to be temporarily suspended under UN auspices (as in East Timor, for example), then the contrast between the two options becomes a matter of degree, a question of interpretation in each specific context, rather than an unbridgeable divide. However, for the purposes of this discussion it is more important to probe the underlying principles at stake in the two cases, rather than become enmeshed in the complexities of specific applications.

The most fundamental question concerning both approaches is which states are held to qualify as democracies, immune from the rightful suspension of their own sovereignty, and (according to the democracy-militant school) also entitled to encroach on the sovereignty of the rest. The US is exceptionally confident that whatever criteria may be used, it must qualify on both counts

32 *Laurence Whitehead*

(elsewhere I have discussed the exceptional nature of this belief as an example of what I have labelled 'democratic immanence'). A few other old democracies share the same assumption, although probably with less assertiveness. But the original architects of the 'Community of Democracies' established in 2000 during the Clinton administration soon found that not all of Washington shared their confidence. India, the Philippines and South Africa, for example, all joined the community but remained alert to the risks of democratic evangelism, and were inclined to empathize with the governments it might threaten. They have therefore shown

> no desire to break ranks with their domestic constituencies and allies aboard who value protection of national sovereignty and economic relations over respect for democratic norms. More importantly even our closest allies block any serious progress towards strengthening the Community of Democracies. They view it, incorrectly, as a U.S. plot to undermine and ultimately eliminate, the UN.
>
> (Halperin and Piccone 2008: 6)

Perhaps these US authors are right, and the original community as well as the more recently mooted and more ambitious League of Democracies proposed by Senator McCain, are not in fact intended to undermine the existing international state system. But the question of which states are to be admitted soon raises the issue of who is to decide, and who will control the behaviour of the community (or League) towards those states that are not included. Is Iraq now a democracy, and eligible to join? Is Georgia? Presumably, Russia would have been a prime candidate for inclusion under President Yeltsin. Is it now to be expelled under President Putin? And what are the consequences for the established democracies of taking sides between, say, Georgia and Russia, or between Iraq and Iran, when the issues in contention in these disputes are not solely – perhaps not even primarily – about regime-type? Equally contentious would be the consequences for such a community of not intervening when democratic principles were seen as being at risk.

Democracy and peace: two questionable syllogisms

These queries direct attention to two quite fundamental issues that underpin the practicalities of coordinating the policies of democratic states. The first concerns a questionable syllogism about the relationship between democracy and peace. The second concerns whether the promotion of democracy can be effectively pursued by militant and sovereignty-threatening means abroad, without undermining the quality of democratic example that needs to be observed domestically.

From these two premises, we would have to conclude that any state engaging in armed resistance to the extra-territorial deployment of US military power thereby reveals itself as not a real democracy.

State sovereignty and democracy   33

Stated in this form the inadequacies of the reasoning are fairly apparent, but a militant assemblage of US-led democracies would be pressed to go along with the general thrust of the argument. As can be seen in various conflict settings, the first reflex for determining which contender merits the support of the democratic world is not a careful assessment of the relative quality of democratic governance in, say, Colombia as opposed to Venezuela, or Iran as opposed to Pakistan, or even the Ukraine as opposed to Russia. The short cut is to ask which is the most reliable ally of the West in whatever war (or crusade) it happens to become entangled. So there are strong grounds to doubt whether the 'democracy militant' approach is well calibrated either to promote international peace or to encourage the spread of democracy. More emphasis on sovereignty-respecting incentives to democratize would seem long overdue.

This conclusion can be reinforced from a second angle. The EU Copenhagen Criteria set quite exacting democratic standards for the states seeking to join the Union. Much of the incentive to meet these standards arose from the economic prosperity and legal protections that are associated with EU membership. But these were also strongly reinforced by the perception that the enlarged EU would be a custodian of democratic values and practices. Although it is still clearly necessary to improve and upgrade the democratic components of the European integration project, from the standpoint of candidate states and their citizens these standards were already correctly perceived as a substantial improvement on what was otherwise available. In other words, good standards of human rights protection, media freedom, political pluralism, and institutions of accountability, among others, all reinforced the desire of aspiring members to reform their domestic political arrangements so as to qualify for accession. Maintaining high standards of democratic performance at home can be seen as a crucial component of efforts to encourage democracy abroad. This applies not just to democracies in Europe but also to those in North America and, indeed, everywhere else.

Recent US-led efforts to export democracy by coercive means have not served to enhance the quality of democracy at home. To the contrary, it has seemed to many outside observers that previous standards of human rights observance and rule of law guarantees may have been compromised by the tensions associated with external belligerence and counter-terrorism. The western leaders most vocal about the need to export regime change to other countries have not been the most conscientious about displaying their accountability to their home electorates. Media pluralism and the tolerance of dissent have been shown in a poor light. Practices of domestic surveillance and heightened powers for security forces may have been necessary, but they have not added to the international appeal of the western democratic model. Respect for international law, the sovereignty of other nations, and pluralism of political alternatives could all be regarded as integral components of what makes western democracy so widely attractive. If so, strategies of democracy promotion that jeopardize these assets are clearly counter-productive.

34 *Laurence Whitehead*

Democratization-with-sovereignty can be counter-hegemonic

Under Cold War conditions, popular sovereignty was liable to be qualified by the over-riding requirement to limit domestic political innovations to changes not deemed threatening to the vital security interests of the Great Powers. This was obviously true with the Soviet bloc (as illustrated in Czechoslovakia in 1968) but also applied to the western alliance (the Dominican Republic in 1964, or Chile in 1970, for example). Yet newly enfranchised electorates in such countries as Portugal and Greece could not always be counted upon to acquiesce to this logic. They might feel that their freedoms could not be secure so long as the old repressive security forces remained in place, and the old external protectors continued to rely on these authoritarian enclaves to protect their interests. Opposition parties emerging from clandestine activity might wish to close military bases occupied by foreign allies' forces or break commitments to those who had turned a blind eye to their sufferings under undemocratic rule. Or voters might simply consider that the time had come when their chosen leaders should put the best interests of their nation ahead of the externally derived preferences of historical allies. For one or other of these reasons democratization under Cold War conditions was frequently constrained by anxieties concerning its possible 'counter-hegemonic' potential.

During the 1990s, this type of anxiety receded into the background and a 'liberal internationalist' set of assumptions came to the fore (resurfacing in a different guise since 2001). Following the dismantling of the Berlin Wall and the disintegration of the Soviet bloc, US and much of world opinion gravitated towards a series of ambitious propositions that provided the underpinnings to the democracy promotion activism of the 1990s. These liberal internationalist ideas included:

1 Unipolarity: Political, economist, military, and cultural leadership of the world were all lodged in one nation. The US would no doubt listen to its allies and attempt to work in partnership with them, but Washington alone was 'bound to lead', exercising a unique privilege and responsibility.
2 Democratization enhances security: Democracies did not go to war with each other. They respected international law and so would not engage in military adventurism. The spread of democracy would be conducive to disarmament negotiations and the spread of a 'peace dividend'. Strengthening the international rule of law would isolate and incapacitate residual 'rogue' states and violent non-state actors.
3 Globalization promotes uniform market standards: As democracies spread and increased cooperation, then international market coordination would be extended and generalized. Businesses and citizens would be increasingly free to enter into commitments outside their countries of origin, with the assurance that foreign international courts and

State sovereignty and democracy   35

regulatory agencies would uphold similar protections to those available in domestic jurisdictions. Global markets would spread prosperity and inclusiveness.

4 Liberal individualism displaces collectivist ideologies: Admittedly, there was a debate here between 'end of history' and 'clash of civilization' interpretations. It was generally accepted that western liberalism had defeated its secular rivals (communism, fascism, imperialism, state-centric nationalism), but there was room for differences about broader cultural, and in particular religious loyalties. For some, liberalism expressed universal features of human nature that would generate the same demands for democracy and rights in all parts of the world, regardless of historical traditions and identities; for others, there were still dragons to slay – illiberal religious and cultural traditions that would have to be confronted and defeated in the same way that the West had faced down Soviet commissions. Obviously, this unresolved debate acquired a new salience after September 11.

5 Fortunately, in any case, the unipolar power is inherently benevolent: Washington would promote democracy and the rule of law not just because that would best serve US interests (which, given (2) and (4), it clearly would), but also and more profoundly because it was in the nature of the US system to propagate for others the benefits that American democracy confers on its own people. Not all politically and economically dominant powers would have acted with equal benevolence. America's democratic allies might not necessarily embody the 'last best hope' for humanity in the same way as the US had done. Ungrateful partners might sour that benevolence if they took it too much for granted (since the American people would have limited patience for allied freeloaders and anti-American critics). But during the 1990s, these potential frictions between the US and her democratic allies were muted. After all, new democracies were coming into being at an unprecedented pace. As they emerged, they generally joined the community of grateful partners of the unipolar power.

Even those emerging democratic groupings that had been most suspicious of western collusion with authoritarian rulers during the Cold War were often attracted to such liberal internationalist positions. This could have been partly due to the belief that after the disappearance of bipolarity there was no alternative, but more positively than that, many centre-left politicians and opinion formers in the new democracies became more confident that if they rallied to this new international consensus, there would be space within it for a plurality of viewpoints. They may also have turned to external sources of reinforcement for their democratization efforts because of a lingering concern over the persistence of authoritarian memories and reflexes within their own countries. If they still harboured some anxieties about risks of some kind of liberal imperialism, they could plausibly argue that under unipolar conditions

36   *Laurence Whitehead*

the best defence against that might be to enhance liberal internationalist ideas and practices with the maximum of enthusiasm. One way or another, many of those most actively engaged in campaigns for democratization became progressively more disposed to put more faith in international collaborative efforts to promote freedom and rights, even at the price of some dilution of traditional commitments to national sovereignty. As a result, during the 1990s, the 'counter-hegemonic' potential of democratization was increasingly downplayed and marginalized in many democracies, both old and new.

However, over the past decade or so, evidence has once again accumulated to demonstrate the recurrent presence of such potential. In East-Central Europe, for example, the 'triple transitions' – which included a shift from state to market, and from eastern to western security structures, as well as from communism to multi-party democracy – obviously constituted a massive repudiation of pre-existing Soviet hegemony. This was especially marked in the Baltic Republics, where the restoration of national sovereignty involved the break-up of the Soviet Union, and a shift of political power from the Russian-speaking minorities to the national majorities. So long as democratization only involved the repudiation of former ties to Moscow, liberal internationalists had few concerns about this form of counter-hegemonic realignment. Moreover, since these new democratic regimes also sought admission into the European Union and NATO, they had strong incentives to curb their nationalist and sovereigntist inclinations. They proved willing to accept a huge volume of externally written legislation (the 'acquis communautaire') and to restructure their military and security arrangements to suit the desires of their western partners. However, once they were securely inside the EU and NATO, the traditional logic of national democratic politics resumed its operation. Poland under the Kaczynski twins[2] provided a particularly eloquent illustration of the unexpected channels through which sovereigntist, and even counter-hegemonic political reflexes can reassert themselves as democratization proceeds. But so long as the Russian Federation remains a potentially threatening presence, these traditions are likely to remain in check.

Latin America provides a second source of evidence. There is, of course, ample scope for debate about how well such recently elected or re-elected political leaders as President Chávez of Venezuela, President Morales of Bolivia, or President Correa of Ecuador, serve the democratic aspirations of their respective nations. Regardless of the position taken on that debate, it is clear that all of these leaders owe their public offices to their success in genuinely competitive electoral processes. It is also clear that one strong strand in their electoral campaigns has been their insistence (in contrast to their predecessors and their campaign antagonists), on a form defence of national sovereignty, and their willingness to clash with dominant external powers if necessary to defend what they saw as the interests of their people. In addition to these three particularly conspicuous examples, there are a growing number of other seriously competitive electoral processes in neighbouring Latin

State sovereignty and democracy 37

American countries where strong campaigns have been launched emphasizing similar themes of national dignity and counter-hegemonic affirmation. Whether or not particular candidates running on such platforms actually make it into office, the evidence is now unmistakable that these western hemispheric democratizations also carry counter-hegemonic potential.

There are other examples beyond Eastern Europe and Latin America. Elections in Turkey and Iran could be cited; and a striking variant of this issue is at the heart of recent electoral contests in Taiwan. The counter-hegemonic potential of democratization is not only apparent in many contemporary new democracies. It is also a looming presence in a large range of other countries where the risks of open democratic contestation are currently being blocked by domestic and/or international forces. For example, if there were to be free elections in Egypt, or indeed elsewhere in the Maghreb, it seems likely that the electorate might be seriously attracted to candidates and parties who would be seen by most western power holders as dangerously destabilizing (see Chapter 9 in this volume). To curtail that counter-hegemonic potential, the western democracies have recently seemed willing to rein back their democracy-promoting rhetoric and their liberal internationalist enthusiasms. When they made an exception (for Palestine), the result was a victory for Hamas which proved unacceptable to them, and they therefore reversed course.

This is not the place to delve more deeply into the complexities of the various cases just cited. The list is long enough to indicate that the 'all good things go together' liberal internationalism of the 1990s has proved untenable as a general rule, and to demonstrate that in contemporary conditions, just as was the case during the Cold War, democratization-with-sovereignty can prove highly unsettling to dominant powers and regional hierarchies. The most uncomfortable illustrations of this phenomenon arise where the liberal internationalists have pursued the logic of their reasoning to its extreme, and have over-ridden the sovereignty of well-established states (Serbia with regard to Kosovo; Iraq and the Kurds) claiming to act on behalf of oppressed citizens who, once their oppression has ended, may use their sovereignty in ways unacceptable to their self-appointed liberators.

In a recent volume, Alexander Cooley has probed more deeply into one quite specific aspect of these broader issues. In 2006, the US officially maintained 766 military institutions overseas (Cooley 2008: 5). These raise delicate issues of sovereignty in most of the countries where they are located. In Cooley's words, 'The presence of a foreign military force on the territory of another sovereign country goes against the most fundamental analytic principles of Westphalian sovereignty and non-intrusion in the domestic affairs of a host country.'[3]

Cooley probes the complexities of the shifting and varied legal provisions designed to cope with this situation including the question of criminal liability for actions taken by these non-national forces, the question of whether some uses of these bases can be vetoed by host governments, and so forth. For the

38 *Laurence Whitehead*

purposes of this chapter, his most important conclusion concerns the frequent instabilities and conflicts that arise when such bases are located in democratizing, as opposed to either authoritarian or fully consolidated democratic regimes.

> Maintaining permanent bases in democratizing hosts such as Afghanistan and Iraq may become politically impossible for the United States when these regimes no longer depend on the United States for their political support. Further, pressing for democratization within base-host countries that lack consolidated institutions and in which anti-Americanism is already high may actually trigger a populist anti-base backlash, and jeopardize the future legal status of the U.S. military presence.
>
> (ibid.: 28)

Whereas Cooley's interpretation stresses an institutional variable (lack of credible mechanisms for stabilizing the terms on which the host country accepts the US base), it would also be possible read his case studies, and his conclusion, in a more substantive way. At least some of his case material – from Okinawa in Japan, the Philippines, South Korea, Spain and Turkey – can be invoked as evidence that sovereign democracies are liable to reject the extra-territorial pretensions of foreign military establishments on grounds of principle, and not just because of procedural problems. This should not be so difficult for American political scientists to grasp, given the way their own democracy would react to the prospect of housing foreign military bases on US soil.

The strength of weak ties: sovereign democracies in an interdependent and multipolar world system

Liberal internationalism and US hegemony have both suffered major setbacks since the beginning of the new millennium. In the US, despite the many hopes invested in the Obama administration, and the many Clinton administration appointees flocking back to Washington, DC, at the beginning of 2009, it is not realistic to suppose that unipolarity is about to be restored, or that the severe damage done to global democratic idealism during the Bush administration can readily be undone. At the same time, however, it is equally unrealistic to visualize a return to the national sovereignty paradigm of the pre-globalization era, or to suppose that the multiple and overlapping legal and normative shifts in favour of the international reinforcement of democratic practices will simply fade away. Transnational and 'inter-mestic' issues (such as energy security, illegal migration, and international crime) are accumulating all the time, and raising the tension between the sovereign ideal and the enhanced international cooperation required to tackle such problems. Indeed, as these transnational issues become more salient, they reveal the extent of the single sovereign state's impotence in the face of joint problems.

State sovereignty and democracy 39

In the near term, a sense of mounting threat is more likely to provoke fear and nationalist backlash than constructive international cooperation, so we face the prospect of a messy and perhaps unstable intermediate position, with continuing political interdependence between democratic regimes that continue to value national sovereignty highly and will have to tolerate a pluralism of ideological models in a multi-polar world, and in which the US-led version of democracy promotion is just one among a variety of competing projects for regional and global order.

From what has been sketched earlier in this chapter, it will be apparent that this prospect carries with it much potential for friction and conflict. However, the emerging pluralist distribution of power and legitimacy more or less precludes the return to a unified liberal internationalist consensus. All but the weakest states in the system will try to preserve or restore their sovereignty, and many will be expected by their citizens to hold out for versions of national independence that their dominant neighbours are liable to view as irresponsible or counter-hegemonic.

New democratic regimes are likely to flirt with relatively provocative assertions of nationalism that appeal to sectors of their electorate. In addition, regimes that most liberals would be unwilling to classify as democracies (such as Putin's Russia, communist-ruled China or the Iran of the Ayatollahs) can also be expected to promote sovereigntist doctrines to justify non-compliance with western expectations and conditionalities. However, in the three major instances just listed, whether they are viewed as semi-democratic or neo-authoritarian, it needs to be recognized that public opinion still constrains the scope for political leaders to buckle to external demands. The 2009 global economic retrenchment triggered by the excesses of the western liberalized financial system reinforces popular nationalist reflexes, and further reduces the appeal of liberal internationalism.

In his recent volume, *On Global Order*, Andrew Hurrell (2007) undertakes a far-reaching re-examination of how the current global political order might be restructured to address the collective challenges arising from globalization and interdependence, given the starting point of an inherited 'anarchical society' of highly unequal but formally sovereign states. He explores the pros and cons of a variety of approaches, including procedural formulae and regional groupings, as well as what he terms 'liberal solidarism', and more traditional power-based, hierarchical (and ultimately imperialistic) solutions. In the end, he concludes that:

> even in the twenty-first century it is very difficult to avoid the state ... Even if we share a cosmopolitan concern for individuals we need to recognize that state strength is an important determinant of the capacity of individuals or groups to manage the costs and benefits of globalization; that states play a crucial role in securing and protecting cultural identity; and that the political agency of states acting internationally is necessary to achieve the mutuality and reciprocity that has surely to be

40 *Laurence Whitehead*

central to a shared scheme of global social cooperation and a meaningful social justice community.

(ibid.: 317)

Recent western experiments in coercive democratization have conveyed the impression that the powerful can lightly suspend state sovereignty in the name of a collective duty to protect individual rights. But far from inaugurating an irresistible forward surge in the dissemination of a western-favoured variant of democracy, this disregard for sovereignty has been widely perceived as a threat to be resisted. Given this scenario, many realists would predict a return to international disorder and the disintegration of any global democratic project. But traditional realism has long ceased to provide effective tools for predicting the course of world politics, let alone for prescribing how power should be deployed since it cannot account for complex interdependence.

An alternative insight can be derived from what some sociologists have chosen to label 'the strength of weak ties'. This is an idea derived from social network theory, and is normally applied to various types of interaction between individuals in a community. It is not common currency in international studies, but it could serve as a corrective to overly ambitious attempts either to describe or to prescribe a viable international order. The original argument was that individuals in society (here we can substitute individual sovereign democracies and potential democracies which must interact in an increasingly interdependent and multi-polar world system) may form 'strong ties' with a small cluster of close associates but may also form 'weak ties' with a much larger community of more loosely connected partners.

Let us visualize the world's roughly 200 territorially bounded and formally sovereign states as participating in a fairly low-density network (one in which many of the possible relational lines are weak or even absent), and some closely connected clusters that are related to one another in part through dense direct interactions, but also in considerable part through looser ties that may flow mainly through third parties. For example, the democracies of the European Union are strongly linked, and there is a parallel, if weaker, cluster of democracies in South America. But these two clusters of states are much more weakly linked to each other through bi-regional and sub-regional connections, and some of the most significant links are mediated by a third party – the US.

This is where Mark Granovetter's idea about 'weak ties' becomes relevant. The key insight is that it is these weak ties that provide much of the connectivity to the system as a whole. According to his perspective, 'Social systems lacking in weak ties will be fragmented and incoherent. New ideas will spread slowly, scientific endeavours will be handicapped, and subgroups separated by race, ethnicity, geography and other characteristics will have difficulty reaching a modus vivendi' (Granovetter 1983: 202). By contrast, overdependence on strong ties ('coalitions of the willing' or hierarchical alliance structures such as NATO) reduces the cognitive flexibility needed to maintain and adapt a community to new challenges.

State sovereignty and democracy   41

My conclusion is that under contemporary conditions, if democracy is to flourish in the international system as a whole, it will still have to be grounded on a basic respect for state sovereignty – especially for the sovereignty of the weaker states in the system, and even in those states where electoral opinion is out of line with the views prevailing in the currently dominant western democracies. Given the counter-hegemonic potential of democratization, we should not expect all democracies to want to sign up to a US-led 'community of democracies', and still less to a 'coalition of the willing'. Any genuinely pluralist and multi-polar international order will need to recognize, and to build on, the 'strength of weak ties'.

Notes

1 After the Peace of Westphalia, 1648.
2 In July 2006, President Lech Kaczynski appointed his brother Jaroslav as Prime Minister.
3 The use of unmanned drones to spy on, and bomb, citizens of foreign states is an even more striking anomaly here.

3 Ideological challenges to democracy
Do they exist?

Marina Ottaway

The collapse of socialist regimes in Eastern Europe and the end of the Cold War led to hasty predictions about the triumph of democracy. Reality has proven more complicated: in most countries, the initial wave of transformations has led to the emergence of regimes that are less than democratic, and the pace of transformation has significantly slowed down recently. While no full-fledged ideological challenge to democracy exists in the world today—not even political Islam, as I will argue below—the idea of democracy itself has failed to electrify the populations of most countries to demand change and sweep authoritarian regimes out of office.

The major obstacles to democracy in today's world are political. These include the authoritarian or semi-authoritarian regimes that have no intention of surrendering power; the opposition parties and movements that are too weak, divided or incompetent to force regimes to change; and weak external pressure from democratic states that falls far short of what might be needed to overcome the resilience of incumbent governments. There have been successful democratic transformations since the end of the Cold War of course, but also many transitions from authoritarianism to semi-authoritarianism but no further, as governments learn to hide their grip on power behind a façade of elections and formally democratic institutions and processes.[1] These political obstacles have slowed down the transformation toward democratization to a trickle and caused a reversal in the process in some countries, including Russia. Democracy, Larry Diamond (2008b) has argued, has entered a period of recession with 38 countries worldwide backsliding during 2007 on the Freedom House index. Indeed, there is insufficient evidence at this point to conclude that democracy is the inevitable destiny of all countries because, although ideological challenges are weak, political challenges are strong.

Among the political obstacles to democratization are also the well-intentioned but at times misguided efforts by the "international community"—read Western democracies but primarily the United States—to promote democracy. Western democracies have undertaken a broad array of programs in order to promote democracy. They have helped organize and monitor elections, supported civil society organization, tried to strengthen institutions and particularly the judiciary, and encouraged the development of

Ideological challenges to democracy   43

independent media, all with varying degrees of success. But at times they have also intervened more decisively, for example by promoting the overthrow of President Slobodan Milošević in Serbia under the thin cover of a "getting out the vote" effort. They have also supported—though less decisively than sometimes claimed—the so-called "colored" revolutions in Georgia and Ukraine (see Chapter 7 by McFaul and Spector). Such interventions made incumbent governments more hostile to democracy promotion programs than they had been initially. The greatest political damage, though, was done in the Arab world where the democracy agenda—neglected throughout the 1990s—was re-launched at the same time as the 2003 war in Iraq. This created strong suspicions, not only on the part of governments but also among democracy advocates, that the real goal of democracy promotion was the replacement of incumbent regimes with new ones friendly to the United States.[2] The suspicions and resentment generated by some so-called democracy promotion efforts thus added a layer of international complications to the already difficult political process entailed in the replacing of authoritarian systems with democratic ones.

Although ideological challenges are not the main reason for the failure of democratic transformations, they do exist, at least in a partial or fragmented form. Full-fledged ideologies, conceived as a body of integrated ideas that proclaim a value system that supports a socio-economic and political program (the Merriam-Webster dictionary definition) are certainly on the decline. Democracy itself is not a coherent ideology—it sets forth a value system, but not one that supports specific socio-economic and political programs. Indeed, the range of socio-economic systems chosen by different democratic countries is wide, ranging from the comprehensive welfare systems of Scandinavian countries to systems where government intervention remains highly suspect, although widespread, as in the United States. The concept of what kind of economic system best embodies the ideals of democracy furthermore can change over time within the same country, and nowhere more so than in the United States. Furthermore, democracy prescribes formal political processes such as elections, but does not promise that specific changes will take place as a result. Thus, democracy is a rather weak instrument of mobilization. Attempts to turn the idea of democracy into a more coherent ideology packaging together values, political institution and an economic model based on an unfettered free market are floundering, even in democratic countries as economic recession began to take hold towards the end of 2008.

There are, however, ideas with mass appeal and an ability to mobilize people into action in some countries—Islamism in Muslim and particularly Arab countries, and nationalism in many parts of the world. Neither most forms of Islamism nor nationalism are today integrated systems of values supporting well-defined political and socio-economic programs, however. Furthermore, the appeal of any ideology based on Islam is perforce limited to the Muslim world. Socialism has few adherents, although the problems that gave the ideology its underpinnings—poverty, inequality, and injustice—still exist.

44   *Marina Ottaway*

Indeed, coherent ideologies appear to have been replaced at present by fragmented ideals and causes—socialism has become anti-globalization and environmentalism, and the workers' movement has been replaced by young people demonstrating at G-8 meetings.[3] China presents to the world a model of economic development that has enormous appeal to many governments in developing countries, but not a political model stirring the imagination of the public and inspiring mass movement. Islamists are highly fragmented—with those advocating the reunification of the *umma* (community of believers) under the caliphate at one extreme and those advocating democratic political participation within individual nation-states at the other, with all sorts of positions in between. Without predicting the end of ideology—a prediction made in the early 1960s and promptly disproven by the wave of strongly ideological politics that spread even in Western countries by the end of the same decade (see Bell 1960 and Waxman 1968)—it is important to take note that, as of now, ideologies are weak A weak democratic ideology meets the challenge of other weak or fragmentary ideologies. The fight for democracy is political rather than ideological.

This chapter explores four issues: (1) the problems of Islam as an ideology; (2) the limits of nationalism; (3) the decline of socialism; and (4) the rise of boutique ideologies.

The complex challenge of Islam

Islamist organizations in all their varieties undoubtedly present one of the major challenges to democratization in the Arab and to a lesser extent in the Muslim world. Islamist organizations also present a domestic challenge to all major European countries, which have sizeable populations of Muslim immigrants or poorly integrated citizens of Arab origin.[4] The challenge, however, is much more political—or security-related in the case of violent organizations—than ideological. Most Islamist organizations do not have what could be called a coherent all-encompassing ideology, that proposes a social, economic and political model viable in the twenty-first century. The discussion that follows will focus predominantly on Islamist organizations in the Arab world, where they appear to be particularly influential because of the weakness of secular organizations and political parties.

Islamist organizations comprise an extremely broad spectrum that makes generalizations difficult. There are violent and non-violent groups, groups that advocate the Islamization of the state and those that advocate withdrawal from the state in favor of a transformation of the society. All forms of Islamist organizations have both political agendas and ideological aspirations, but not to the same degree or in the same form, thus they pose different challenges.

From the point of view of incumbent authoritarian regimes, all Islamist organizations, whether moderate or radical, are a challenge. Authoritarian regimes do not accept competition and Islamist organizations provide particularly strong competition because they speak a language the populace

Ideological challenges to democracy 45

understands easily and because they can relate to citizens on the basis of shared religious values. Such organizations also have many points of contact with the general public through their networks of charitable organizations and the mosques, and thus sometimes become the only viable opposition to the regime.

Moderate Islamist organizations are probably a greater political challenge to incumbent regimes than either radical Islamist groups or secular parties, because their appeal can be very broad. Religion is an important factor in the lives of most Muslims, and the conservative social values rooted in Islam are widely accepted. Moderate Islamist groups are thus not threatening, but familiar. This is not the case with extremist groups willing to use violence and advocating an interpretation of Islamic precepts and Islamic morality that goes well beyond what is practiced by most Muslims in their daily life. Acts of random violence appear to be particularly offensive: in Egypt, an attack on tourists visiting a Pharaonic temple in November 1997, which left over 70 people dead, had a marked impact on popular attitudes toward radical Islamists. Indeed, some al-Qaeda leaders went into exile and turned to an international war against "Crusaders and Zionists" after failing to garner enough support in their own countries for their radical agenda. Ayman al-Zawahiri, considered to be al-Qaeda's major ideologue and strategist, is a case in point.[5]

From a security point of view, radical groups undoubtedly present the major challenge not only to Arab regimes, but also to Western countries. The major danger here is not the possibility that such groups will seize power in any country—this appears a remote possibility at best, given the fact that most Arab countries, despite their governance deficiencies, have strong security apparatuses. The major threats to security reside instead in the constant possibility of relatively small-scale terrorist attacks. These attacks produce victims and cause fear; they also damage the country's international reputation, and undermine their tourism industry which is becoming quite important in some economies like Morocco, Egypt and Dubai, and possibly cause a loss of investments if a country becomes truly unsafe. For the West, too, the security threats posed by radical Islam are real, but by no means existential. Islamist terrorist organizations can do a lot of damage and cost a lot of lives—but even the detonation of a radiological "dirty" bomb in a major city would not mean the end of Western civilization, despite high human and economic costs.

Evaluating the ideological challenge to democracy posed by Islamist organizations requires a fairly detailed discussion of the varieties of Islamist visions set forth by various organizations. While this chapter alone cannot possibly do justice to the great diversity of the Islamist spectrum today, even in the Arab world alone, it will hopefully be adequate to explain in what sense political Islam does or does not pose an ideological challenge to democracy.

The most radical Islamist organizations propound a political model and values that are completely antithetical not only to democracy but also to the international system of nation-states that we know today. Among these

46 *Marina Ottaway*

radical groups are the organizations falling in the al-Qaeda spectrum that are directly engaged in terrorist activities, but also non-armed groups, including the Wahabi establishment in Saudi Arabia, teachers in the Pakistani madrasas and radical sheikhs everywhere, that preach to their followers the necessity of reforming Muslim states and societies through violent means in order to make them conform to Islamic principles. These groups do not accept existing regimes because they are not truly Islamic. Indeed, they do not even accept the legitimacy of the present states, which they consider part of an international order imposed on the Arab world by the colonial powers after World War I. Such an international order is unacceptable because it fragments the *umma*, the Islamic community, into a number of artificially created and separate Muslim-majority states. Instead, they advocate the reunification of the *umma* under a caliphate. Thus, they challenge not only the legitimacy of regimes, but that of the states as well. And a revived caliphate, in the extremely unlikely event it could be resuscitated, would not be a democratic state, where power is based on a popular mandate. Instead it would be a theocratic state ruled by people purporting to base their decisions on the law of God and the will of God.

There is no doubt that this political vision is antithetical to democracy. To become an ideological challenge, however, such a vision would have to attract many followers and influence their political behavior and there is no evidence this is happening. Indeed, not even all radical Islamist groups make the revival of the caliphate into an immediate, actionable goal. While no radical Islamist groups would probably reject the idea as a distant goal, their activities tend to be national or at best regional—there are now both an al-Qaeda in the Islamic Maghreb and an al-Qaeda in Mesopotamia, loosely affiliated with al-Qaeda, but operating as national or at most regional groups. In Algeria in the 1990s, the Front Islamique du Salut (FIS), an organization that did not recognize the legitimacy of the post-colonial Algerian state, nevertheless carried out its activities within the boundaries of that state, even participating in its elections in the hope of coming to power in a sweeping electoral victory.

Potentially, the strongest Islamist ideological challenges to democracy could arise from two sources that do not appear particularly threatening: first, moderate Islamist parties that participate in their countries' legal political process and accept most democratic tenets, yet hold back on others; and second, organizations that are purportedly apolitical and focus on transforming the society rather than the state, but also preach ideas that can only be seen as a challenge to democracy.

In many Arab and Muslim countries, there are Islamist political parties that have chosen to participate in the legal political activities of their country, working not only on the level of the nation-state rather than of the *umma*, but also within the existing institutional framework. Such organizations do not oppose the state or the political system, but only the government in power, as typical opposition parties do. Such parties exist in Morocco (the Justice and

Ideological challenges to democracy 47

Development Party or PJD), in Algeria (the Movement for a Society of Peace), in Jordan (the Islamic Action Front), in Kuwait (the Islamic Constitutional Movement), in Bahrain (the Wefaq Political Society), in Yemen (the Islah Party), and in Egypt (where the Egyptian Muslim Brotherhood is a banned organization but nevertheless finds ways to participate as a de facto political party, and at present controls 20 per cent of parliamentary seats). Other, smaller Islamist parties also operate in some of these countries. In addition, there exist Islamist parties that compete in elections but at the same time remain armed movements—Hizbollah in Lebanon, Hamas in Palestine, and all Shi'i parties and some Sunni ones in Iraq—but these parties will not be discussed here. It is these moderate parties and movements that might present an ideological challenge to democracy, depending on how they evolve.[6]

These participating movements, as they will be called here for short, are the product of a rethinking of Islamist political stances that took place within the Muslim Brotherhood in the past few decades—with the exception of Bahrain, where the major participating Islamic movement is Shi'i, all other participating parties are spin-offs of the Muslim Brotherhood in their respective countries. The rethinking was prompted by the dilemma the organizations faced: they had renounced violence, thus they could not use force to change the regime, and even less so change the nature of the state. Yet the ideas that dominated their political thinking precluded political participation in the existing, non-Islamic political system. By rejecting both violence and legal participation, the Muslim Brothers were condemning themselves to political irrelevance. By the 1990s, through a lot of internal discussions and also the rise of a younger generation of activists to positions of influence, many Muslim Brotherhood-related organizations came to the conclusion that it was possible for them to participate in the legal political system without violating their Islamic values. Disciplined and well organized, these organizations soon became the most important opposition groups in their respective countries, far surpassing liberal and leftist parties. They also became the most vehement advocates of democracy—they needed at least a modicum of democracy in their countries in order to be able to operate.

The rise and effectiveness of participating Islamist groups prompted consternation on the part of Arab governments unused to being challenged by effective opposition parties, leading to the adoption of repressive measures in many countries. The entry of Islamist parties into legal politics also triggered a debate, both among Arab secular intellectuals and in the West concerning whether these movements had truly embraced democracy or instead were just using democratic methods opportunistically with the goal of abrogating them if they came to power. The main fear was summed up in the often repeated idea that the elections in which Islamists participated would become "one person, one vote, one time" affairs—Islamists would participate, win, and immediately abrogate any semblance of democracy. Islamist participation also triggered an endless debate about the compatibility of Islam and

48 Marina Ottaway

democracy—an ultimately pointless debate because the answer depends on who interprets Islam and who interprets democracy.

The debates within the participating Islamist groups are much more interesting and well worth examining because they reveal the existence of positions even in the most moderate movements that do challenge democracy ideologically. Furthermore, these views could be influential because they are moderate, and in tune with the everyday thinking of many Muslims. The debates highlight two important issues: the divisions that still exist in all these organizations concerning participation; and the existence of a number of unresolved and controversial ideological issues.

There is no doubt that in all participating Islamist organizations there is a group of reformers truly committed to respecting the democratic process and believing in fully engaging in the legal political process. There is also no doubt that the reformers are still challenged by many, not only in the leadership but also among members, who are still doubtful about participation. Furthermore, the balance of power between the two groups varies depending on the political context. Reformers are strongest when Islamist parties are allowed to participate in a normal fashion—or at least, in the fashion that is normal by the standards of the country, without becoming the target of special obstruction—and achieve some concrete results. When the authorities become more repressive toward Islamist groups, openly hampering their political activities, reformers lose clout within the movements because participation appears futile.

In the early part of this decade, reformers appeared to be on the ascendancy, gaining influence as a result of the good electoral performance of their parties. In Morocco, Egypt, Jordan and Kuwait, Islamist parties performed well in elections, securing additional seats. As a result, the advocates of participation gained in stature and influence. The next round of elections, however, was not particularly successful. Islamist parties lost significant ground in Jordan and Kuwait, did worse than expected in Morocco, and met with so much government obstruction in Egypt that they withdrew from the municipal elections. Electoral losses were followed by an increase in the influence of more conservative elements—in some cases, as in Jordan, reformists in the leadership of the parties were ousted. In other cases, as in Morocco, most reformists maintained their positions, but faced increasing questioning in the party.

In a sense, this is normal democratic politics; in all parties, defeats are usually followed by a renewal of the leadership. However, in participating Islamic parties, such renewal of leadership can have a dramatic impact on political orientation because there are significant unresolved ideological issues, some "gray zones" on which it is difficult for parties to reach clarity because any clear position would alienate some parts of their constituencies. The rise and fall of particular factions thus can affect the movement ideologically.

The most significant of these gray zones concern the place of Islamic law, sharia, in the modern state, whether it should be the source of legislation or a source of legislation; the degree of acceptable pluralism; the position of

Ideological challenges to democracy 49

women; and tolerance for other religions.[7] Underlying most of the issues is a fundamental question about the source of governmental authority and legislation—whether the ultimate source is God or the people. The issue is ideologically thorny for Islamists. If sharia is the word of God, than sharia is bound to be above laws made by elected parliaments, whose duty then is not to legislate but to interpret how sharia would apply to certain contemporary situations—in other words, the parliament does not obey a popular mandate. Opinions on these issues differ among participating parties, and also within each of them. There is a liberal extreme, best represented by Morocco's PJD, whose leadership has embraced the position that the party must accept any law enacted democratically, as long as it can be reconciled with a somewhat nebulous Islamist frame of reference. At the opposite extreme are the hardline authors of a draft program for a political party the Egyptian Muslim Brotherhood aspires to form. The draft, emerging from within the Brotherhood and immediately becoming extremely controversial, called for the formation of a council elected only by religious scholars to vet all acts of the parliament for conformity with the sharia. This would void the concept of popular sovereignty. The position of most participating Islamist parties and movements falls between these two extremes, and is less clear-cut and grayer.

It is extremely difficult to judge where the followers of a participating movement stand on these issues. Leaders write and discuss their views openly, but of course the public does not. There are indications, though, that the most liberal positions—those that come closest to accepting the tenets of democracy—are not the most accepted and that the identification with Islam is stronger than the identification with democracy. Indeed, some leaders of participating Islamist parties worry that recent electoral set-backs by their parties indicate that the organizations have become more liberal than their followers are willing to tolerate. Positions on all these issues are in flux, but it clear that right now Muslims easily accept democracy as a method to choose leaders and hold them accountable, but are more hesitant in accepting the idea that sovereignty ultimately resides in the citizens, rather than in God.

In considering possible ideological challenges to democracy, it is also worthwhile exploring the implications of the spread of what can be called *dawa* (or proselytizing) Salafi organizations, which have dropped out of political activity, shelved indefinitely the political project of Islamizing the state, and currently devote their efforts instead to convincing individuals to lead their lives according to Islamic tenets, slowly reforming the society. Salafi organizations are committed to convincing Muslims to follow in the footsteps of the "pious ancestors" adhering to strict, old interpretations of Islamic doctrine and eventually to building an Islamic state. In other words, Salafis are the true fundamentalists. Purportedly apolitical, *dawa* Salafi organizations are growing in importance in many countries. Political Salafi organizations, which aim at Islamizing the state rather than just the society, on the other hand, have found it difficult to make an impact: their view of an all-embracing Islamic state is too far removed from the reality of the contemporary world.

50 *Marina Ottaway*

Furthermore, they do not want to become involved in the politics of states they consider illegitimate, because they fragment the *umma*, but do not have the capacity to overthrow them.[8]

Indeed, there are only two examples of Salafi movements participating in the legal political process of Arab states—in Algeria in 1990 and 1991, and in Kuwait from the restoration of parliament after the First Gulf War to this day. In Algeria, the FIS competed in the municipal elections of 1990 as well as in the first round of the 1991 parliamentary elections, and their success pushed the military to seize power, triggering ten years of internecine war. In Kuwait, Salafi groups routinely participate in elections. In other countries, Salafi organizations have sidelined themselves from the normal political activity, with a minority turning to violence and much larger number turning to dawa. Ideologically, Salafi groups devoted to *dawa* are not a challenge to democracy—they are not actively pushing an alternative political model, but postponing a discussion of the issue until after the society has been transformed. In the long run, however, *dawa* Salafis are likely to turn to politics again—Islamist organizations have always alternated between a strategy of transforming the society first and one of transforming the state first. When *dawa* Salafi groups turn to politics, they will challenge democracy through their rejection of a political system based on individual rights, which democracy is, and of the nation-state, which fragments the umma.

Islamism in all its forms has been a challenge to democracy, although a political and security rather than an ideological one. The issue is not that Islam is incompatible with democracy, but that in the political world of Islamic organizations as they are now, not as they might become, the convergence between Islam and democracy cannot be taken for granted. There are gray zones in the thinking of even participating Islamic parties. There is resistance by Arab governments to consider them legitimate players. There is resistance by many liberal Arab intellectuals to accept that Islamist movements may have, or can develop, legitimate democratic credentials. And finally there is to this day considerable skepticism in the West. All this shows that in the real world of politics Islamist movements continue to be a challenge to democracy, primarily a political challenge and only secondarily as an ideological one as well.

The persistence of nationalism

Nationalism remains an idea with considerable appeal in today's world. It has experienced a resurgence since the end of the Cold War, which has lifted the post-World War II freeze on borders imposed by the stand-off between the Soviet Union and the United States, allowing the long-pent-up demands of many minorities to have their own state to be manifested again.

Between the end of World War II and the end of the Cold War, nationalism appeared limited to the developing world, where colonized people revolted against colonial powers. By the mid-1970s, the days of anti-colonial nationalism were largely over, as colonial empires were almost completely dismantled. Anti-colonial nationalism was curiously respectful of the territorial subdivisions created by the colonial powers. People rose against foreign domination, but within the boundaries created by it. The result was the emergence of a large number of states around the world whose people had short common histories and weak common identities—countries whose citizens shared little more than the experience of colonial domination. The problems of weak nationhood were compounded by the weakness of the state. Many of the new states were "quasi-states" (Jackson 1993), owing their existence to international recognition and to an international system that temporarily froze the status quo in place, rather than to an effective capacity to maintain a monopoly over the means of coercion and to govern the territory.

With the end of the Cold War, the unthinkable idea of modifying state boundaries became a reality again. Many states, particularly those emerging from periods of authoritarianism, faced the growing nationalism of ethnic groups (or the sectarianism of religious groups), which in the most extreme cases led to large-scale violence and even the fragmenting of the state. This nationalism of sub-state groups became a major obstacle to democratization as in many countries nationalism trumped democracy, at least in the short run. The problem first exploded most acutely in formerly socialist countries, where newfound freedom produced not only demands for democracy but also for self-determination. Ethnic nationalism led to the disintegration of the Soviet Union into its constituent republics, many of which were in turn challenged by their minorities—Ossetians and Abkhazians in Georgia, Armenians in Azerbaijan, Chechens in Russia, for example. Yugoslavia was torn apart, initially by multi-party elections in which people voted according to their identities. In Burundi, elections triggered a spate of ethnic killings; in Kenya, parties representing rival ethnicities went into a frenzy of ethnic cleansing following the December 2007 presidential election, only stopped by international intervention and mediation. And in Iraq, elections since the fall of Saddam have accentuated divisions, as ethnic and religious identities were mobilized as instruments to control parliament, cabinet and provincial councils, thus gaining power. These are just a few examples drawn from the dozens of cases where nationalism has been trumping democracy since the end of the Cold War.

The viciousness of these conflicts, including widespread ethnic cleansing as the new national states tried to expel or eliminate minorities, has been recounted in many studies and will not be repeated here. What is important for this discussion is to note that sub-state nationalism challenged democracy by violating the fundamental tenet of universal citizenship—the equality of the rights of all inhabitants of a country.

The post-Cold War rise of nationalism spread, or threatened to spread, to all countries with mixed populations. Yet nationalism did not trump democracy in all such cases. Although invariably the multi-party elections that almost all countries started holding after the end of the Cold War provided the incentive for the formation of ethnic or religious parties, the explosion of ethnic nationalism was not inevitable and automatic: the variations depended on the determination and ability of political entrepreneurs willing to play on conflicting identities, no matter the human costs.

The nationalism of the post-Cold War period posed not only a political challenge to democracy—and incidentally to the international community's efforts at state reconstruction—but also an ideological challenge. This has not always been true of nationalism. European nationalism in the nineteenth century originally had a strong democratic component, as had American nationalism earlier. Anti-colonial nationalism was also not ideologically antithetical to democracy—nationalists demanded the right to self-determination for all citizens of the colony, not just some groups. The political reality was different—most anti-colonial movements proved not to be committed to democracy and many were dominated by members of specific ethnic groups, but they were not ideologically discriminatory. There was no Kikuyu nationalism in Kenya, for example, although Kikuyus dominated the independence movement. Post-Cold War nationalists, on the other hand, put forward ideas that were antithetical to democratic principles: in their eyes, the rights of the group were more important than those of the individuals, in clear contradiction to the principle of universal citizenship—"Croatia is the country of the Croats" proclaimed the preamble to that country's constitutions, adding, almost as an afterthought, "and of its minorities." Similarly, the political parties that competed in the post-Dayton Agreement (1995) elections in Bosnia in 1996 were defending first and foremost the rights of the group to which they belonged—and voters demonstrated that they shared their views by choosing not only parties representing their group, but the most radical parties among them. Nationalism, in other words, still remains a powerful idea that can gain followers and guide political action in contradiction to democratic ideals. It is not clear, however, whether nationalism can maintain its ideological appeal in the long run.

There are several reasons to doubt the long-term ideological appeal of nationalism in any one country. First, the ideology of nationalism is at its most powerful in the presence of an enemy. If independence is achieved and the country is not threatened, nationalists no longer have much to offer, because they mostly do not have a coherent set of ideas to guide the political and socio-economic life of the country, except perhaps for a vague image of a powerful and rapidly developing country, which is usually not realized. Successful nationalism eventually transforms into something else. It transformed into fascism and Nazism in Europe, it transformed for a period into socialism in many developing countries in the 1960s and 1970s. It is less clear to what extent it can also give way to democracy, turning into what authors such as Greenfeld (1992), Brubaker (1999) and Ignatieff (1993) have defined as "civic" nationalism. There are, to be sure, historical examples of such transitions from nationalism to democracy, including that of the United States—

Ideological challenges to democracy 53

although the transition to a full-fledged democracy as experienced in the United States would be considered intolerably lengthy today. In some European countries such as Germany and Italy, the nationalism that led to unification in the middle of the nineteenth century had a strong democratic component, but that component was soon superseded. It is more difficult to find contemporary examples, though. At present, nationalism appears much more likely to challenge democracy than to facilitate it.

The crisis of socialism: problems without ideology

The most important ideological challenge to democracy, beginning in the nineteenth century and until the end of the Cold War was posed by socialism, particularly by Marxist-Leninist socialism, as defined by the Soviet Union and exported around the world. It was the demise of socialist systems in Eastern and Central Europe and in the Soviet Union that led to rosy predictions about the triumph of democracy, even the end of history (Fukuyama 1992). And, indeed, socialism as an all-encompassing ideology trying to provide a single answer that will address all economic, social, and political problems appears finished at this point. To be sure, there are still some die-hards, including in the industrial democracies of the West, who believe in the validity of the Marxist-Leninist model and claim that what failed was not the model, but the Soviet corruption of it. But these supporters are few, probably decreasing in numbers and more engaged in obscure ideological diatribes than in winning over and organizing followers. Equally rare are the intellectuals engaged in a serious effort to re-elaborate socialism, and to rethink its strategies in ways in keeping with twenty-first-century realities.[9]

While the ideology has all but vanished from the realm of politics, the problems that fed socialist ideologies, particularly in the Marxist formulations, still exist. The poverty, inequality, exploitation, and social class cleavages that accompanied early industrialization and gave socialism its appeal are not as extensive in the West as they were in the past, but they do still exist. In the rest of the world, they are still pervasive, and they are becoming even more dramatic in countries beginning to industrialize or in those where the rate of urbanization has outpaced that of urban job creation. Even in the West, periods of economic crisis increase socio-economic grievances and their articulation, because those affected by crisis are not only the chronically poor, but also the newly poor who have lost their footing in the middle class.

However, the problems that gave socialism its broad appeal in the past do not have the same effect today. Responses appear much more fragmented. In the West, the economic crisis is leading many to question the validity of the unfettered free-market model that took hold with Prime Minister Margaret Thatcher in the UK and President Ronald Reagan in the United States in the early 1980s, and has influenced the policies of many industrialized countries ever since. But the questioning is not leading to widespread rejection of the market economy, and certainly not to the rejection of democracy. Rather, it is calling into question the dominant balance between free markets and government regulations—discussions on the topic tend to be much more technical than ideological. In developing countries, the most notable recent development has been the spreading of small, uncoordinated acts of protest, rather than the rise of mass movements for change. There are workers riots in Egypt and many acts of protest in China, for example, but they do not amount to the emergence of new, ideologically based movements. Populist leaders, like Venezuela's President Chávez, capitalize on the people's discontent, but socialist parties are moribund except where they are in power, as in China, and labor unions in most countries are becoming weaker.

Socio-economic grievances are not posing the ideological and political challenge to democracy that existed when strongly organized socialist parties were offering overall explanations for the problems people encountered and presented alternatives. A full explanation of why this is the case would require much more systematic research. Only a few hypotheses can be set forth here. Possibly, the reason why the problems of poverty and inequality do not lead to an ideological response is that problems are complex and citizens are better educated, and thus less likely to respond to simple slogans. More people are now aware of the failure of the socialist models guided by ideology, and of the economic and political misery they created. Finally, the stark political and economic choice between socialism and capitalism that socialist ideology proposed has been weakened by the emergence of other socio-economic models that have attracted attention and brought about results. In industrial democracies, the worst excesses of capitalism have been tempered by welfare state measures, which result in a modicum of redistribution through taxation and the provision of social safety nets in the form of pension plans, public education, free or subsidized health care and other forms of assistance.

Paradoxically, such welfare measures are to a large extent the achievement of moderate socialist parties operating in democratic political systems, which were able to introduce significant reforms without wrecking the economic engine. There are significant differences among countries in this respect: the United States falls far behind most European countries in the generosity of its welfare state provisions, while Scandinavian countries are ahead of most of the rest of Europe. And in many countries the balance between free enterprise and regulation is still contested, with the pendulum swinging back and forth. The world has moved toward deregulation in the past 20 years and is likely to move back toward more government intervention and regulation as a result of the global financial and economic crisis that broke late in 2008. What is clear, though, is that the stark ideological choice between capitalism and socialism that was posed in the nineteenth and early twentieth centuries has been replaced by a continuum of solutions, or a multiplicity of intermediate steps between the two extremes.

The rise of boutique ideologies

Old problems persist, but the old answers have lost their mass appeal. Rather than looking for single, all-encompassing answers, people appear to be turning to a variety of what can be defined as boutique ideologies—offering specialized ideological responses to specialized problems. The rise of boutique ideologies is more prevalent in well-established democracies, but a degree of ideological fragmentation is appearing elsewhere as well.

Boutique ideologies are not full-fledged ideologies in the sense of offering a body of integrated ideas that proclaim a value system supporting a socio-economic and political program. Instead, they only address one or a few problems seen as central to everything else. But they are ideologies in the sense of representing ideas and values in which their adherents believe passionately, and that guide their political and personal activities. The range of boutique ideologies is broad, encompassing ideas that can be classified as leftist, others can be classified as mainstream, and many that cannot easily be fitted into either category. Anti-globalization is a boutique ideology with clearly socialist roots, but without the broad focus of socialism, and it exists in both industrialized democracies and in developing countries. Environmentalism has become one of the refuges for disgruntled former socialists, particularly in the West, but the problems it addresses are in no way the problems that worried socialists. Human rights, even raised to the level of ideology, falls well into the center of the democratic mainstream. Animal welfare activists are impossible to classify into traditional categories of right and left. And some boutique ideologies, for example, feminism, come in both liberal and conservative versions.

Some boutique ideologies have become fairly well developed and integrated into mainstream politics, others operate on the margins. Anti-globalization groups have their international meetings, complete with documents and positions papers, although they seem to mobilize mostly around the meetings of international financial institutions and of the G-8, remaining dormant, or at least out of sight, the rest of the time. Environmentalists range from green political parties operating in a democratic fashion and fully committed to democracy—the green parties in Europe fall in this category—to organizations that disdain politics and turn to direct action to attain, or at least to publicize, their goals. Animal welfarists lobby parliaments to regulate the size of the cages in which chickens are raised; and lobbying is a traditional democratic activity although the specific demand is not. But some have also been known to burn down legally constructed buildings that in their opinion interfere with the habitat of some species.

Some boutique or fragmentary ideologies clearly challenge democracy: examples are the ideology of white supremacist groups and of the most radical fringes of the anti-globalization movement. But most boutique ideologies do not challenge democracy and in fact have a strong democratic content. The important question, however, is not whether specific boutique ideologies

56 *Marina Ottaway*

challenge democracy, but whether the fragmentation itself does so. Fragmentation does not appear to be a problem in countries where the democratic system is robustly implanted, and large, established political parties still perform the crucial task of aggregating interests to make individual votes count. In European countries and in the United States, groups embracing boutique ideologies simply add to the considerable pluralism that already exist, and they are in any case mostly very small fish in a large pond dominated by special interest groups and lobbies that operate without ideology but with considerable resources. Whatever disruption the more radical groups cause is usually easily held in check by existing institutions.

However, in countries where democracy is only weakly implanted, or, worse, where authoritarian governments still maintain their grip on power, ideological fragmentation may weaken democratic efforts, making it more difficult to develop a strong, coherent opposition. Evidence is so far mostly anecdotal—ideological fragmentation is a recent, post-Cold War phenomenon. For example, this author has been told many times, by civil society activists in several African and Arab countries, that they had considered joining a political party, but decided instead to form their own small non-governmental organization (NGO) devoted to a specialized cause. If this is indeed a widespread phenomenon, it could have repercussions for democracy, depriving political parties of members and even more importantly of potential leaders. It is worth keeping in mind that historically the rise of democracy has been facilitated by comprehensive, integrated ideologies with broad appeal, which sustained large political parties. Ideological fragmentation does not encourage such parties. In fact, it is more likely to be accompanied by a proliferation of NGOs or of fringe parties. Of course, the experience of the past may not have to be repeated in the future, but the historical evidence at least forces us to raise the question about the impact of ideological, and thus organizational, fragmentation on democratic transitions and on fragile democracies. This is not only an abstract question, but a policy one as well. The United States and European countries have been supporting NGOs in countries that are not democratic or are in the early stages of a democratic transformation, in an effort to energize citizens to become more active by engaging in causes important to them. The existence of civil society organizations increases pluralism, it is thought. It also encourages ideological and organizational fragmentation, and it could make democratic transitions more difficult. This is an issue that deserves more study since it has policy implications for those countries that have invested money and efforts in setting up and nurturing civil society organizations as part of their efforts to promote democracy.

Weak challenges to a weak ideology

Challenges to democracy as a political system remain strong and may even be getting stronger, and the wave of democratization that started with the fall of

Ideological challenges to democracy 57

socialist regimes may have run its course. This does not mean that that there will be no more democratic transformations or that the world will not experience new waves of democratization in the future, as it did in the past (Huntington 1991). At present, however, democratic transition appears to have stalled.

This stalling of democracy, however, is not the consequence of new, strong ideological challenges. Islamism in Muslim countries, and ethnic nationalism and religious sectarianism in countries with a diverse population can exercise strong appeals. But Islamist ideology is not well developed, except in the most extreme forms that have failed to develop mass appeal. Nationalism, today as in the past, is an ideology useful to mobilize people against something, rather than an organizational blueprint for a political, economic or social system. Socialism remains a defeated ideology, despite the fact that the problems of socio-economic inequality and injustice which gave the ideology its appeal persist and may even be worsening in some countries. And boutique ideologies, in their fragmentation, certainly do not present a serious challenge.

The weakness of the ideological challenges, however, does not mean that democracy has triumphed at the ideological level. This is something that is too often forgotten by governments and organizations seeking to promote democracy. There are aspects of democracy that undoubtedly have broad, although not universal appeal; and others have very little. For example, democracy understood as lack of government repression and as the citizens' right to hold rulers accountable appears to be broadly accepted. Democracy as a system that puts individual rights ahead of those of the community, or, at least assumes that the good of the community can be the result of individual choices, encounters resistance in many societies. The concept of universal citizenship is poorly accepted in divided societies, as is that of popular sovereignty in deeply religious ones. And many people around the world, including some in democratic countries, do not have a clear understanding of how democratic systems are supposed to work. For all these reasons, the ideological appeal of democracy is not as strong as democracy promoters would like to believe. It is true that public opinion surveys everywhere show that the majority of citizens believe that democracy is a good political system and that it would serve their countries well. It is equally true that further probing often reveals that what respondents mean by "democracy" is not necessarily what those who designed the survey meant (see discussion by Doorenspleet in Chapter 6).

Because democracy is a complicated political system, which includes some values that are universally understood and accepted and others that are far from being universally accepted in many countries, its ideological appeal is limited. In fact, in countries in transition, citizens are easily disillusioned, when their enthusiastic participation in elections does not bring about the expected material improvement. This ideological weakness is reflected in the fact that movements for democracy have historically been elite movements. This was true in the United States and it was true in Europe. It remains true

58 *Marina Ottaway*

in developing countries where the pro-democracy activists are mostly members of educated elite. Mass political movements have relied historically on ideologies that are much easier to understand, such as socialism and nationalism.

Today, democracy only faces rather weak challenges at the ideological level. While democracy itself remains a weak ideology, ideological challenges to it are also weak. This removes one obstacle to democratic transitions, but not the major one. Although ideological challenges to democracy remain weak, political challenges continue to be strong in many countries. The main obstacles to democracy today are found in the political rather than the ideological realm.

Notes

1 For more information on the rise of semi-authoritarian regimes, see Ottaway (2003), Diamond (2002), Levitsky and Way (2002) and Carothers (2002).
2 For more information on US promotion of democracy and in the Middle East specifically, see Ottaway (2008) and Ottaway and Carothers (2005).
3 The G-8 is the group of eight countries comprising the governments of Canada, France, Germany, Italy, Japan, Russia, the UK and the USA.
4 For an in-depth study of Islamist organizations and political Islam in the West, see Roy (2004).
5 For a profile of Ayman al-Zawahiri, see Wright (2002).
6 See Ottaway and Hamzawy (2008), which represents the culmination of several years of research on and dialogue with the parties under discussion.
7 For a detailed discussion of the main controversial areas of disagreement whithin Islamist movements in the Arab world, see Brown et al. (2006) and also the reply provided by a member of the Egyptian Muslim Brotherhood Guidance committee: Online. Available at: www.carnegieendowment.org/files/FutouhEnglishFullText_5_.pdf.
8 For a discussion of political Salafism in Algeria, see Boubekeur (2008).
9 See, for example, Panitch (2001).

4 The continuing backlash against democracy promotion

Thomas Carothers

In 2006, I and other writers called attention to an emergent international backlash against democracy promotion (Carothers 2006; National Endowment for Democracy 2006). The backlash entails growing hostility and resistance on the part of authoritarian and semi-authoritarian governments to Western, especially US democracy promotion programs and policies. Of course, Western democracy supporters have long encountered a closed door or heavy resistance in many authoritarian countries. This current phenomenon is about governments that once allowed external democracy assistance in their country forcing out or greatly restricting such activities, or it is about governments that never paid much attention to the possibility of such activities on their territory suddenly taking steps to block it.

The measures that governments employ against democracy assistance vary. In some cases, governments impose legal restrictions that force democracy aid groups resident in the country to leave or prevent those attempting to work from a distance to do so. Restrictions on the funding and activities of non-governmental organizations (NGOs)—NGO laws—are a favorite such instrument although laws and regulations relating to political parties and/or elections are also used. Some governments do not force out or completely block external democracy aid groups but harass them. The harassment may be crudely physical—beatings, thefts, and threats against representatives of such groups or against their local partners. Or the harassment may be legal or administrative, such as intrusive tax inspections, administrative fines and office space refusals. Harassment may also take the form of public criticisms or denunciations by government officials of democracy aid groups and their work.

The Russian government, under then President Vladimir Putin, was the initial leading force of the backlash but governments in other parts of the world, including Central Asia, East Asia, the Middle East, Sub-Saharan Africa, and Latin America, quickly joined in. In the past few years the backlash has continued and spread. Russia remains the paradigmatic case. In his last two years as president before handing over in mid-2008, Vladimir Putin stepped up his assertive campaign against Western democracy promotion. He denounced Western democracy aid providers in harsh, blunt

60   *Thomas Carothers*

language as political meddlers who violate Russian sovereignty. Shortly before the December 2007 Duma elections, for example, he denounced Western democracy aid in scathing terms:

> Unfortunately, some people in this country treacherously gather near foreign embassies, and are hanging around diplomatic missions in hopes of support from foreign funds and governments, not from their own people ... There are those confronting us who do not want us to carry our plans ... They need a weak and feeble state. They need a disorganized and disoriented society, a split society, so that they can carry out their dirty tricks behind its back.[1]

Russian authorities have harassed and expelled representatives of Western democracy promotion groups. They have made it difficult for Russian NGOs to receive Western funding and harassed many of those that do. Putin mounted a sustained attack on the election monitoring work of the Organization for Security and Cooperation in Europe (OSCE), imposing such restrictive conditions that the OSCE declined to send observers to the 2007 Duma elections and the 2008 presidential elections. Putin also sought to stir up a similar resistance to Western democracy promotion in other countries, personally warning leaders in China, Central Asia, and elsewhere about what he believed were the dangerous nature of such activities.

The backlash has also widened in two key regions: Central Asia and the Middle East. In Central Asia, Western democracy promoters are finding less and less room to maneuver. Most Western organizations have given up trying to support civil society in Uzbekistan in the face of the obstacles put up by the government there. Tajikistan presents similar difficulties. Although open to Western assistance in some areas, such as the economic domain, the Kazakh government has blocked political party aid and established heightened controls over civil society programming. Even Kyrgyzstan, which was relatively open to Western democracy assistance for many years, became a more difficult environment for such work in the period during its 2007 elections, elections that provoked conflict within the country over issues of fairness and openness.

The increased attention to the Middle East by Western, especially US, democracy promoters in recent years has produced a backlash in various parts of the region. In early 2007, the Iranian government arrested and imprisoned for several months two Iranian-Americans, one a staff member of the Washington-based Woodrow Wilson International Center for Scholars and the other a Tehran-based consultant for the Open Society Institute, accusing them of being part of US efforts to foment a "velvet revolution" in Iran. Both were released later the same year but the arrests had a powerful chilling effect on the willingness of Iranians to take part in any Western-sponsored activities involving Iranian civil society. Further crackdowns on Iranian intellectuals and civic activists have followed. The Egyptian government has blocked the efforts of some US democracy groups to set up offices in Cairo. The government of Bahrain backed away from its initial receptivity towards US democracy promotion earlier in the current decade to a more restrictive approach. Other Arab governments, such as in Algeria and Yemen, have also shown signs of increasingly cold feet about US democracy programs.

In Latin America, the florid criticisms by Venezuela's President Hugo Chávez of US democracy assistance activities have been taken up by some of President Chávez's regional allies. In September 2008, for example, Bolivia's President Evo Morales declared the US ambassador to La Paz *persona non grata*, accusing him and the US Agency for International Development of conspiring against Bolivian democracy by supporting groups in eastern Bolivia that have opposed the Bolivian government's policies concerning the use of the country's ample natural gas revenues.[2]

As the backlash continues, exploring the causes of it becomes more possible and also more important. The initial explanations—such as the view that the backlash is primarily due to a resurgence of authoritarianism in the world—have tended to be too unidimensional. A complex set of causal factors is clearly at work. The passage of time also permits some examination of the reactions of the Western democracy promotion community to the backlash. Examining these reactions leads to consideration of the question of norms—which international norms cover democracy promotion and whether some formalization of norms would be useful in attempting to limit the backlash.

The surprising afterlife of the color revolutions

Although the backlash against democracy promotion is the result of multiple factors, the "color revolutions" in Georgia, Ukraine, and Kyrgyzstan were clearly a major trigger. Even though these events were few in number, limited to one region, and produced only mixed pro-democratic efforts after their initial bloom faded, they resounded remarkably widely around the world.[3] Autocrats in many regions reacted, declaring that they would not permit such events to occur and warning both their own countries and outside actors against pushing in such a direction.

The color revolutions produced serious concerns and defensive reactions even in countries that do not match the political profile of the countries where color revolutions did occur. The color revolutions (and the similar case of the electoral revolution that ousted Serbian President Slobodan Milošević in 2000) took place in contexts that shared some important characteristics: (1) an incumbent government that was somewhat anti-democratic but not fully authoritarian, one that violated political rights but which did tolerate some active, significant opposition parties and some independent civil society, including, very importantly, at least one independent radio station or television station; (2) a leader who had been losing popularity and was perceived to be in political decline; and (3) a recent record of national elections which,

62 *Thomas Carothers*

even though manipulated by the incumbent government, did give opposition parties a chance to organize and compete (McFaul 2006). Yet the main countries pushing back against Western democracy assistance in recent years, such as Russia and China, have few or any of these features. They are more authoritarian societies, with relatively secure leaders, very weak or nonexistent opposition parties, fragmented, highly constrained civil societies, and either perfunctory or nonexistent national elections.

Why did the color revolutions cast such a wide spell, even in countries which do not fit the profile of a country ripe for such a cataclysm? In some places of course the power-holders accusing foreign actors of trying to stir up a color revolution in their country are not genuinely worried. They are simply using the color revolution "threat" as an excuse to stir up anti-foreign popular sentiment, to crack down on domestic political activists, or to block Western democracy promoters they find irritating even if not threatening.

Nevertheless, in many cases of pushback, the color revolution concern is real. The relevant power-holders probably do not feel that a civic uprising is imminent or even possible any time soon but they view it as a troubling prospect that they want to nip in the bud. Two interrelated elements of the color revolution phenomenon, or at least perceptions of the phenomenon, are central to this fear.

One of these elements is the specter of mass protests. The mass protests that occurred in the color revolutions were only one part of a larger chain of political events that led to the fall of the regime. Also critical were the active campaigns and electoral successes of unified opposition coalitions and the work of NGOs to scrutinize the elections through domestic monitoring campaigns and parallel vote counts. Yet due to their visibility and drama, the mass protests appeared to many observers as the essence of the color revolutions.

The specter of mass protests is inherently unsettling to authoritarian leaders. They erupt unpredictably and are extremely difficult for power-holders to deal with. Even authoritarians who believe themselves to be well liked by their citizens seem to harbor fears that just a few small streams of citizen discontent may suddenly coalesce into a surging river of protests. Some of the governments engaged in pushback, such as those in Russia, China, and Iran, either came to power through or have in their national history revolutionary movements that started with the concerted actions of small groups of activists, culminating in mass protests and other mass actions. Power-holders in these countries tend to connect the color revolution idea to such experiences. One Iranian-American who was questioned by the Iranian security services about his civil society work, reports that the Iranians said that they know all about color revolutions because their own revolution, the Islamic revolution, was all about civic resistance and mass mobilization.

The other element of the color revolutions that has contributed to such a wide, sharp defensive reaction is the belief prevalent in many quarters that outsiders, especially US groups, fundamentally drove these events. Studies that have assessed the actual weight of the role of outside actors in the color

The continuing backlash 63

revolutions reach the consistent conclusion that the outsiders' role is not determinative. It can be a valuable helping hand to domestic forces pushing for change, but it neither creates those forces when they do not already exist, drastically increases their strength, nor directs their actions.

Nevertheless, the tendency of many observers, especially power-holders in authoritarian or semi-authoritarian countries, to assume a much greater level of influence of outside actors and subscribe to the "made in the US" view of these events is not surprising. The idea of foreign-sponsored political influence and manipulation by determined, sophisticated, well-financed organizations funded by governments or private foundations in powerful, wealthy foreign countries is a fertile one. Nondemocratic power-holders themselves rely on behind-the-scenes efforts to try to manipulate political events in their own countries or neighboring ones. They naturally therefore tend to respect the power of what they see as parallel efforts by interventionist foreigners. Moreover, the idea of color revolutions as products of outside intervention fits into a familiar historical narrative in many countries where past US or other Western political interventions resulted in ousted leaders, such as the 1953 coup in Iran that ousted Prime Minister Mohammed Mossadegh.

It was not hard, for example, for many observers in the former Soviet Union and elsewhere to imagine that "the man who broke the Bank of England," namely the investor and founder of the Open Society Institute, George Soros, could break a weak government in a small, poor former Soviet republic if he chose to. Thus when Soros said in a 2004 interview, "I'm delighted by what happened in Georgia, and I take great pride in having contributed to it," and added that he would be happy to see similar events unfold in Central Asia, his words rang loudly for many in the region.

Western journalists eager to tell a dramatic story about the color revolutions have sometimes played up the role of Western democracy promotion groups. Even leaving aside paranoid fantasies and genuine historical narratives, it is not surprising that persons in a country confronting a growing swarm of hard-charging, experienced foreign organizations involving themselves in their elections, assisting their political parties, and funding and training politically-oriented civic groups are uncertain and often unsettled about what impact such actors have.

A damaging context

The color revolutions were enough on their own to spark concern in many quarters about Western democracy promotion. Yet several elements of the larger international context in which they occurred multiplied this effect. Most importantly, the color revolutions happened to take place in the period immediately following the US-led intervention in Iraq. In March 2003, the United States led an intervention that ousted President Saddam Hussein from power in Iraq. Seven months after the United States and its allies defeated Saddam, the "Rose Revolution" brought a pro-US leader in power in

64 *Thomas Carothers*

Georgia. A year later, the Orange Revolution did the same in Ukraine. Although this series of events was a coincidence, it did not look like one to many people. Instead it appeared to many that the color revolutions were an integral element of a new Bush global regime change policy—Washington would oust some governments by force, some through economic sanctions and diplomatic pressure, and some through quiet, well-crafted aid to political opposition groups, replacing them with compliant, pro-Western governments. More generally, Bush's extremely assertive and also relentless presentation of the Iraq intervention as the leading edge of his "global freedom agenda" undermined the legitimacy of US democracy promotion and of democracy promotion generally. In the minds of many people around the world, democracy promotion became a code word for military intervention and US hegemony. This greatly fueled the backlash, alarming people about what democracy promotion really is and allowing nondemocratic power-holders all over to justify restrictions on external democracy assistance as national self-defense.

This foreign policy dimension of the backlash has been most vividly exemplified by the case of Russia. During his presidency, and in the first year of his prime ministership, Vladimir Putin became increasingly suspicious of US policy towards Russia, in tandem with Russia's growing recovery of national self-confidence (fueled by the energy bonanza that greatly boosted the Russian economy). By 2007, Putin and the Russian security establishment generally were talking darkly about the growing threat of encirclement of Russia by pro-Western governments that sought to join the North Atlantic Treaty Organization (NATO) and do America's bidding. The fact that Western, especially US, democracy assistance was linked with the rise of pro-Western governments in Central Europe and the Baltic States throughout the 1990s and Georgia and Ukraine in this decade tempted Russians to view Western democracy promotion as a direct foreign policy challenge to Russia, and to react vociferously against it on those terms.

Other elements of the Bush war on terrorism beyond Iraq also contributed to the backlash. The US abuse of foreign detainees and prisoners in detention facilities and prisons in Iraq, Afghanistan, Guantánamo Bay, and elsewhere, as well as heightened war-on-terrorism encroachments on civil liberties within the United States further eroded the credibility of the United States as a symbol of democracy, and thus by extension, of US democracy promotion. These actions encouraged other governments, especially in the Middle East, South and South-east Asia, and Africa, to impose copycat restrictions on political and civil rights, in the name of fighting terrorism (Human Rights Watch 2003). These restrictions have often affected domestic civil society groups, sometimes reducing the scope for external funding or other support to these groups and thus adding to the growing chill on international support for civil society development.

A further element of the recent international context—one not at all related to the color revolutions and only very partially related to US policy—has also bolstered the backlash. This is the dramatic rise in the world prices of oil and gas that occurred starting in 2005 and lasted until the middle of 2008. High energy prices boosted the fortunes of an array of nondemocratic governments around the world, especially in the former Soviet Union, the Middle East, and Sub-Saharan Africa, reflecting the fact that most energy-rich countries are not democracies. These governments felt much more politically secure both at home and also internationally thanks to their burgeoning oil and gas revenues. They knew that energy-hungry Western governments were unlikely to react strongly to measures by them to block Western pro-democracy diplomacy and assistance. Their energy revenues also gave them plentiful funds to carry out political assistance programs of their own in their own neighborhoods, creating another kind of riposte to Western democracy aid (see Chapter 10 by Richard Youngs).

Reactions to the backlash

Faced with pushback, most democracy aid providers react with quiet persistence leavened by necessary tactical retreats. If they are blocked from setting up and legally registering an office in a country where they want to work, they will often try operating informally there. For example, the two US political party institutes, the National Democratic Institute for International Affairs and the International Republican Institute, have been prevented by the Egyptian government from opening offices in Egypt, but they nevertheless operate in the country informally, without legal registration but with the knowledge and tacit acceptance of the government. If democracy aid groups are forced out of a country, they sometimes continue their work from a neighboring country—using representatives there who travel periodically to the prohibiting country or bringing people over for training or other activities from the prohibiting country to the neighboring country. Some democracy aid groups, for example, carry out Belarus-related activities from Poland.

Democracy assistance groups hit with pushback do sometimes seek diplomatic support from their governments to try to maintain some access. In most cases, they do so quietly, wary of loud actions that might inflame nationalist reactions. An exception to this preference for quiet diplomatic support was a campaign by a concerned coalition of Western NGOs in 2005 to mobilize diplomatic and public pressure against the Russian government's plan to enact a highly restrictive new NGO law. In its initial form that law included provisions that would have prohibited foreign funding of Russian NGOs and made it impossible for Western NGOs to set up offices in Russia. The US government took up the cause, eventually raising it to the presidential level—President Bush expressed concern about the draft law in a meeting with President Putin late that year. The Russian government backed down partially, removing some of the more draconian provisions of the draft law though nevertheless enacting a law that increased the levers of control over Russian NGOs.

66 *Thomas Carothers*

Although democracy assistance groups have in some cases pulled back in response to the backlash, they have not changed their basic methods or practices. Most of the US groups that tend to carry out the more politically assertive side of democracy aid have not engaged in any substantial reconsideration or reformulation of their work. They have not done so both because they feel they are fully justified in pushing when they can on authoritarian and semi-authoritarian regimes (for reasons discussed in the next section) and that any pulling back would only be rewarding repression and resistance to democratic change. To the extent they see a need to change their methods in response to the backlash, they see it as arising with regards to communication about what they do—if concerned governments and public better understood what Western democracy assistance is in fact rather than in myth, their thinking goes, such governments would object less to it.

The backlash has affected US democracy aid providers more than European ones, both because US groups do more politically assertive work on the whole than Europeans and because of the strong tie between US foreign policy and the backlash. Nevertheless, European democracy assistance support is sometimes affected. In Russia, for example, not just US but also British and German groups are finding less room to operate or have come under pressure. The Uzbek government has pushed out not just US aid groups but Western ones generally. The discrediting of the concept of democracy promotion inevitably puts almost all democracy assistance under a harsher light. Although European democracy aid providers have not carried out any major shift in response, behind closed doors they talk about the need to emphasize alternative frameworks for their work. Human rights is one alternative, seen by some as preferable for being less openly political and also more firmly grounded in international legal agreements. Governance is another, valued for its more technocratic, less political image.

With regard to reactions to the backlash at the broader diplomatic level, rather than just within the democracy aid community, the picture is relatively straightforward. The Bush administration changed its policy course but not in response to the growing backlash. President Bush and his advisers did not acknowledge or even show any signs of being aware of the damage their policies did to the legitimacy of democracy promotion. This was part of their general unwillingness to recognize the numerous damaging consequences of the Iraq intervention, their Middle East policy generally, and some elements of the larger war on terrorism. The administration backed away during the last two years from most of its push for democratic change in the Arab world (although it pressed on in Iraq) but this was not a response to the backlash. Rather it was prompted by renewed concern (especially after the Hamas victory in the 2006 Palestinian elections) that political openings in the region might lead to gains or even takeovers by Islamist parties or forces, as well as the administration's desire to tighten security ties with its Arab autocratic allies to check Iran's growing weight in the region.

Faced with the backlash in its most concerted and assertive form—that is, from the Russian government—the Bush administration took a soft line. Although the administration lent support to the US NGO community on the issue of the Russian draft NGO law, the administration took an accommodating line generally towards Russia's authoritarian slide under former President Putin. As with China, Pakistan, Ethiopia, Kazakhstan, Saudi Arabia, Egypt, Jordan, and many other nondemocratic countries, US economic and security interests requiring good relations with the government greatly outweighed the administration's declared "global freedom agenda." In simple terms, the Bush line required little readjustment in the face of the backlash against democracy promotion because for the most part (with the exception of Iraq) Bush policy was already far more realist than its hyperbolic pro-democratic rhetoric suggested (Carothers 2007c).

On the European side, most governments were not giving any special rhetorical or substantive emphasis to democracy promotion and thus did not feel any special need for a course correction in the face of the backlash. European governments were of course divided over their willingness to take part in the Iraq intervention. But even those that took part (with the exception of Britain, under Prime Minister Tony Blair) did not sign on to the notion of a global freedom agenda. If anything, the majority quietly deemphasized explicit references to democracy promotion out of a desire not to be associated with the Bush regime's change in posture more generally.

During the past few years, several European governments have modestly attempted to rebuild a more openly pro-democratic policy line. The Swedish government has pointedly included democracy as an integral part of its development policy. It quietly worked to make democracy promotion one of the themes of its tenure of the EU presidency, in the second half of 2009. The Dutch government has tied democracy more closely to its development policy. In February 2008, British Foreign Secretary David Miliband gave a speech on democracy promotion in which he attempted to chart a post-Blair, and to some extent post-war in Iraq framework for British foreign policy in which democracy promotion would play a significant role. One can see these various formulations as efforts to respond to the backlash against democracy promotion by reasserting a commitment to the objective through a more explicit association with the widely legitimate goal of development.

The question of norms

The backlash and the reactions to it have drawn attention to the question of norms concerning democracy assistance. When and in what ways is it legitimate for governments to regulate, and if they wish to prohibit externally sponsored democracy aid activities on their territory? Or looked at from the other side, what right do democracy aid providers have to carry out their work in other countries?

68 *Thomas Carothers*

Despite decades of active democracy aid efforts in more than 100 countries, surprisingly little formalization of norms has occurred in this domain. In some ways the question of norms relating to democracy promotion can be compared to the question of norms relating to human rights promotion. Both domains are defined by a fundamental tension between national sovereignty and universal or at least externally legitimated values pushing against a country from the outside (see Chapter 2 by Laurence Whitehead). Many human rights activists distinguish their domain from that of democracy promotion with regard to the conflict with sovereignty. They argue that the universal legitimacy of the values they advocate is unquestionable, because human rights are enshrined in international legal agreements. In contrast, they assert, democracy is just one of various competing political ideologies. Democracy promoters respond by citing the work of some international legal scholars like Thomas Franck and Gregory Fox who posit an emerging universal right to democratic governance.[4] They also point to the presence of a right to elections in the Universal Declaration of Human Rights and to the democracy standards in regional agreements and norms, such as the Copenhagen Criteria (1993) of the European Union and the Inter-American Democratic Charter (2001) of the Organization of American States, as evidence that democracy is not just one of many competing political ideologies or systems, but the only one to gain such widespread normative adherence.

Human rights activists also argue that their work conflicts less directly than does democracy assistance with the sovereignty of the countries in question. Whereas human rights organizations generally concentrate on monitoring and reporting of developments in other countries, democracy promoters go into other countries and carry out activities (grant-making, technical assistance, advising) that directly seek to produce political change. The difference, they argue, is between an indirect and a direct approach to trying to foster change in other countries. Democracy promoters respond by pointing out that the difference between the two domains is not so distinct. Sometimes human rights activists go beyond simply monitoring and reporting. They may support local human rights groups, providing them with training, moral support, and funds. Thus they are sometimes hands-on actors trying to directly shape institutions and people in countries where they work. Moreover, they argue, whether an engagement seeks to promote change in another country indirectly or directly, the underlying point is that an external actor aims to encourage and stimulate change in how a government in another country acts toward its citizens.

The issue of norms relating to democracy aid largely remained implicit in the 1980s and 1990s. Most countries where democracy aid providers operated were moving out of dictatorial rule into attempted processes of democratization. Democracy promoters worked in these places with the permission and often encouragement of host governments or some parts of the government, and so the question of a challenge to national sovereignty was largely avoided. Democracy promoters did direct some work to authoritarian countries,

The continuing backlash 69

such as Burma and Cuba. In those cases the question of norms was simply a standoff—the governments in question denied external actors any access, or greatly limited the access on the grounds of national sovereignty, and democracy promoters did what they could.

Since the 1990s, the question of norms governing democracy assistance has become a more significant area of debate. As some governments reduce space that they previously gave to outside democracy promoters, they invoke their right to sovereignty to justify this curtailment. But because democracy promoters are already often present in their territory, arguments ensue about the rights of these democracy aid actors to keep doing what they have been doing. Many democracy aid providers operate in the belief that their work does not just rest on a permissive basis but on a normative one. Thus, for example, they see international election observers as having become such a customary practice that if a government refuses to accept observers, it is effectively violating a norm. Similarly, they view accepting at least some amount of external support for local civil society organizations as having become such a common practice in developing democracies as to have attained the status of a norm.

The arguments between the Russian government and Western democracy promoters over both election observing and civil society support are cardinal examples of this newly heightened attention to the question of norms governing democracy assistance. When Putin attacked the OSCE's election-observing work and imposed restrictive conditions that made OSCE observation of the 2007 Duma elections and the 2008 presidential elections difficult, Western democracy promoters counterargued that these actions contravened a customary normative practice. Similarly the Putin government's effort to impose restrictions on foreign support for Russian NGOs produced a norm-based exchange. Western actors asserted that the Russian government was violating customary standards among democracies. The Russian authorities countered that the regulations they wanted to put in place were no more restrictive than those in some established democracies, such as France.

A key issue in such normative debates about democracy assistance is that of nonpartisanship. Backlash against democracy aid often starts with the accusation that the outside actors have a partisan agenda. Governments attack international election observers for alleged political bias and denounce foreign support for civil society development as a method for meddlesome foreigners to back political favorites. Yet Western democracy aid providers generally insist that their work is nonpartisan, which means that it supports democratic change but does not favor any particular group or party contending for power.

The issue of partisanship comes especially to the fore in the most assertive democracy assistance efforts that center around elections in semi-authoritarian contexts such as in Serbia and Croatia in the late 1990s or Belarus, Georgia and Ukraine since 2000. These efforts seek to bolster the political forces challenging an entrenched strongman who is holding an election, and also those groups pushing for more credible electoral processes. These aid efforts usually include direct support (training, advice, and sometimes funds) to opposition parties as well as aid to civic advocacy groups monitoring the election and mobilizing citizen participation, and to independent media, which often has a distinctly anti-regime orientation. The normative arguments in favor of this more assertive aid, which looks highly partisan in the eyes of target governments, are complex.

Democracy promoters engaged in such work make two central arguments with respect to its normative justification. First, they assert that while they may be favoring some political actors over others, for example, providing training to a coalition of opposition parties but not to the governing party, they are not taking sides among democratic actors competing with one another but rather supporting democratic actors struggling against a non-democratic power structure. Such work, in their view, is distinct from partisan involvement and is intrinsically legitimate on the basis that democracy is the most legitimate political system.

Second, democracy promoters often justify their extensive and politically pointed engagement in electoral processes as not being an attempt to produce a particular outcome in the election but rather as trying to "level the playing field," i.e. to help foster a fair process. Given that the ruling powers have taken actions and created conditions that disfavor the opposition, they argue, outsiders are justified in providing some support to help make up for these disadvantages.

Underlying both these arguments is the idea that governments which fall short on democracy are entitled to less political sovereignty than democratic governments. Democracy promoters do not assert this in so many words, but those that engage in politically assertive work in semi-authoritarian or authoritarian contexts act on the basis of such a belief.

Those arguments find little sympathy among governments resistant to allowing such work within their national territory. They reject the distinction democracy promoters try to make between supporting democrats versus taking a partisan line, questioning the objectivity, as well as the right, of a foreign political organization to make such political judgments. Western democracy promoters, these governments argue, assign the label "democrat" instrumentally to those political groups they like or can get along with and "non-democrat" to those that they perceive may threaten their own interests in some way. Similarly, concerning the argument about leveling the electoral playing field, skeptical governments ask who gave foreign organizations the right both to decide what constitutes an uneven playing field and, having made such a determination, to intervene to level it.

Within the US democracy promotion community, these heightened normative debates have caused some persons to consider whether it might be useful for democracy promoters to try to formulate and formalize norms for their work. Such norms might, they believe, make it easier to resist backlash measures. Outside of the domain of election observing, however, few such efforts have yet advanced. Although the idea is appealing in some ways, it is probably not the bulwark against backlash that some persons might hope. If the broader community of democracy promoters did attempt to agree on norms for their work, for example, with political parties or civil society, the more politically assertive democracy aid groups would likely find other parts of the democracy promotion community prefer very cautious principles hewing strongly to absolute nonpartisanship that would constrain them more than they would like. Moreover, even if the community were able to agree on a set of norms, governments resistant to external democracy promotion would not feel bound by them, and would argue that they are self-appointed principles of action with no international legal validity.

Looking ahead

The backlash may ease somewhat over the next several years. The raw feelings about the color revolutions will presumably fade with time, especially if no similar events occur. In the US, the new administration of President Obama is seeking to rebuild the credibility of US democracy promotion, both by moving away from the Bush administration's regime change line and by cleaning up US human rights practices in the war on terrorism. The decline in oil and gas prices caused by the global financial crisis that broke in late 2008 has deflated some of the confidence and outgoing assertiveness of various authoritarian governments.

Yet even if the backlash fades, it is unlikely to disappear. Although it was spurred by fairly specific conjunctural conditions in the middle years of this decade, it was grounded in larger changes in the overall context of democracy promotion. These are changes that signal the end of the relatively enthusiastic, forward-moving period for democracy promotion policies and programs of the mid-1980s through the end of the 1990s. That period was framed by two crucial features: first, democracy was spreading rapidly and widely in the world, and, second, thanks to the end of the Cold War and the arrival of a period of greatly reduced geo-strategic rivalries among major powers, concerns over political interventionism diminished in many places. These two features helped propel democracy promotion forward.

In the twenty-first century, however, both those features ebbed. Democracy stopped advancing overall in the world. The Third Wave of democracy was replaced by a time of overall democratic stagnation. The number of electoral democracies was the same at the end of the opening decade as at the start—a sharp contrast to the upward line of previous decades. In such a context, democracy promotion becomes much more difficult. The most successful democracy support programs have almost always been those that build on the positive momentum of local actors. With such momentum lacking in most places, the task becomes much harder.

72   Thomas Carothers

In addition, the relatively quiet geo-strategic environment of the 1990s, featuring a dominant single superpower system, has given way to an increasingly competitive and at times conflictive multipolar system, characterized by tensions and challenges between the United States and various countries (for example, Russia, Iran, and Venezuela) and between other countries as well (Columbia and Venezuela, Russia and Georgia, Iran and Israel, and others). With what Robert Kagan (2008) describes as "the return of history," external political interventionism across borders has flared up as a source of concern, and it is harder for democracy promotion not to be pulled into that web of suspicion and hostility.

The backlash against democracy promotion is thus one symptom of a more daunting context gradually for democracy promotion in the decade ahead. At the same time that the Western policy community comes to grips and grapples with how to respond effectively to the backlash, it must also confront the larger imperative of finding new ideas and approaches to fit an international context for democracy work that has fundamentally changed from that of decades past.

Notes

1 Vladimir Putin, reported in *The Washington Post*, 22 November 2007, A27.
2 *The Wall Street Journal*, 10 September 2008.
3 The image of mass civic protests quickly became a symbol of the color revolutions. Lebanon's Cedar Revolution of 2005 is sometimes put in the category of color revolutions but it was different in a crucial way—it centered around resistance to foreign domination (by Syria) rather than a rejection of electoral results believed to be manipulated.
4 See, for instance, the contributions by Franck (1992) and Franck, Fox and others in Fox and Roth (2000).

5 Democracy assistance and the search for security

Nancy Bermeo

> The Soviet dissident Andrei Amalrik compared a tyrannical state to a soldier who constantly points a gun at his enemy – until his arms finally tire and the prisoner escapes. The role of the free world is to put pressure on the arms of the world's tyrants – and to strengthen the prisoners who are trying to speed their collapse.
>
> (President George W. Bush, Prague, 2007)[1]

Like the quotation above, this chapter is about the role that free countries play in pressuring dictators and in strengthening the opposition to dictatorship. It is also about 'arms', but departing from Amalrik's metaphor, it focuses on weaponry and military assistance. It asks how US military assistance initiatives interact with initiatives to speed the collapse of dictatorship. Do military assistance and democracy assistance work in concert or at cross-purposes?

Curiously, the growing literature on democracy assistance pays little attention to military assistance, despite the fact that these two aid initiatives interact in highly consequential ways. As a contribution to filling this void, this chapter argues that scholars and policy-makers should pay much more attention to what I call 'aid interactions' and that military and democracy aid interactions often work at cross-purposes.[2] Interactions with economic aid may be highly consequential too, but given space constraints, the focus in this chapter is almost exclusively on how military assistance initiatives affect democracy assistance initiatives. It also focuses exclusively on US aid policy because full statistical information on other major powers' aid policy is not publicly available.[3]

The analysis begins by situating the main argument in the literature on democracy assistance and explaining why the scholarly community has neglected the military–democracy aid interaction thus far. I then explain why we should not neglect this interaction in the future and what we learn if we investigate the interaction – even superficially. The lesson, briefly put, is that the United States often undercuts its democracy assistance efforts with its military assistance initiatives and that policy-makers must remedy this if democracy is to advance.[4]

74 *Nancy Bermeo*

The interaction and the literature

The failure to join discussions of military aid with discussions of democracy aid is due to three factors. First, it reflects the neglect of civil–military relations in the democratization literature more generally. Bruneau and Trinkunas concluded in 2006 that scholars writing on democratization have produced 'no literature' systematically analyzing 'the effect of foreign programs and relationships' on civil–military relations.[5]

The failure to join discussions is also an artifact of the subdivisions within the field of political science. The literature on military spending is generated by security specialists within the field of international relations while the literature on democracy assistance has been dominated by comparativists. The one group of scholars that bridges these divides focuses on post-conflict democracies, but their studies usually focus on small sets of single countries rather than on aid in general.

Finally, the neglect of the interaction between military aid and democracy aid derives from divisions in the state apparatus of the United States. Military assistance is associated with the Pentagon while democracy assistance is associated with the State Department. Though the White House provides common direction, policies are often conceived in separate policy communities and implemented by separate actors.

Happily, the neglect of aid interactions may be on the wane. As the wait for a fifth wave of democracy drags on, and a series of once-celebrated new democracies slides into soft authoritarianism, scholars and policy-makers are beginning to analyze democracy assistance programmes with a wider lens. Fukuyama and McFaul (2007: 41) have recently made the point that 'democracy promotion should be placed in a broader context' and called for a new Cabinet-level agency to coordinate aid for democracy with aid for economic development, poverty reduction and good governance. Actors at the US State Department are also aware of the need to think holistically: an official document entitled *Promoting Democratic Governance* concludes, 'To have an impact on the difficult and seemingly intractable cases, the United States and other donors must do more, *more coherently*, across a range of objectives' (USAID 2002: 52).

Finally, Finkel, Pérez-Liñán and Seligson (2007, 2008) have completed two extensive studies which evaluate the effects of democracy assistance programmes while controlling for other forms of aid. The awareness of 'aid interactions' is thus on the rise, but the interaction between democracy assistance and military assistance still begs more attention.

For example, the two recent studies by Finkel et al. raise a number of questions about democracy assistance that can only be answered with a focus on military assistance as well. The first study, released in 2007, assesses the effects of democracy assistance in 165 countries between 1990 and 2003. A second study extends the analysis forward to 2004, and includes further controls as well as other forms of aid. Both studies use state-of-the-art statistical techniques and are exemplary in their transparency.

The study of the period between 1990 and 2003 concludes that 'contrary to the generally negative conclusions from previous research', US democracy aid exerts 'a significant, albeit modest, impact on democratic outcomes' (Finkel et al. 2007: 435). The authors draw this conclusion after controlling for a whole host of 'confounding processes' including the trajectory the country might have taken without US democracy aid. The authors also control for the possibility that the effects they identify are an artifact of a US tendency to aid countries which are more likely to move in a democratic direction from the start. Though the study ends with a list of caveats, and reminds us that 'democracy programs may take several years to mature', its conclusion is unambiguous:

> There are clear and consistent impacts of USAID democracy assistance on democratization in recipient countries. An investment of one million dollars (measured in constant 2000 dollars) would foster an increase in democracy 65 per cent greater than the change expected for the average country in the sample for any given year.
>
> (ibid.: 436)

The second phase of the project examines more variables, including aid of various sorts, but draws a similar conclusion. Though including data for 2004 picks up the effects of the war in Iraq and therefore weakens the strength of the association identified in the first study, the second project's findings are also unequivocal. 'Once the "Iraq effect" is controlled for, democracy assistance has a positive effect on democracy at the same level as the previous study' (Finkel et al. 2008: 1). The study concludes; '[T]he 14 years of data we have analyzed here provide a robust basis for drawing the conclusion that USAID DG assistance in the post-Cold War period has worked' (ibid.: 68; italics added).

Those who support democracy assistance will embrace this conclusion with relief and hope that questions about the efficacy of democracy promotion are resolved, but even optimists will not deny that the projects open a series of other questions. First, how will democracy assistance work in a particular country? Second, as the authors of the studies state themselves, 'democracy assistance is still only a small portion of total USAID assistance' (Finkel et al. 2007: 436). Per capita, the dollar amounts transferred from the US to potential democratizers are so small that it is difficult to be certain about their causal weight in any individual case. In South Africa, for example, annual democracy assistance totalled well under $1 per capita in the three years prior to regime change. In Ghana, the comparable figures fell below 50 cents and in Indonesia and Kenya they fell below 20 cents (USAID 2006). What are the conditions under which such small investments might 'work'? Finally, 'the Iraq effect' can be controlled for statistically, but not politically. Even if we conclude that democracy assistance 'worked' before 2004, will it work in the future?

76 Nancy Bermeo

Interactions with military aid

All these questions call for closer attention to the larger contexts in which individual democracy assistance programmes operate. Though I shall not attempt to answer any of these questions here, I shall make the case that military assistance is a contextual factor that must not be ignored in our future discussions of democratization. The first and most obvious reason is military aid's relative weight.[6] Though democracy aid rose considerably in the period under study, military aid dwarfed democracy aid by a factor of over 11 to 1 in 2004 (see Figure 5.1). Even in 2000, the year before the coalition's invasion of Afghanistan, military aid outweighed democracy aid by a similar multiple. The massive difference in expenditure was even higher before 1997. It pre-dates both the War on Terror and the administration of George W. Bush[7] and is a long-standing feature of American foreign policy.

The second and more compelling reason to fuse discussions of military aid with analyses of democracy aid derives from what the research of Finkel et al. already suggests. Their aggregate level analysis concludes that the association between military aid and the effectiveness of democracy aid is strongly negative. Although the finding is discussed in only a few sentences, the 2008 study by Finkel et al. states:

> Democracy assistance is *less* effective when the U.S. provides larger amounts of military assistance. Our model suggests that, as countries receive larger amounts of U.S. military aid, the impact of USAID democracy assistance matters less and less, and among the few countries that receive larger than 1.1% of U.S. military outlays, the effect of DG

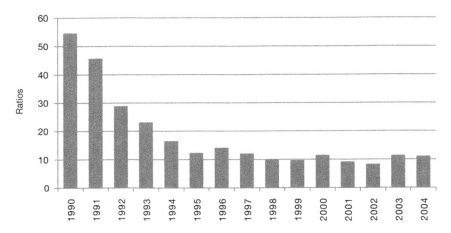

Figure 5.1 Ratio of US military aid to democracy aid
Source: USAID (2006), Finkel et al. (2008)
Note: Military aid is the sum of military assistance and security assistance.

Democracy assistance, search for security 77

assistance is statistically indistinguishable from zero. The pattern warrants further investigation, as countries with larger military investments from the United States sometimes receive significant amounts of DG assistance as well. Thus, substantial amounts of DG outlays appear to be targeted toward countries where their effects are more limited.

(2008: 67; italics in the original)

When does military assistance undercut democracy assistance?

Why would democracy assistance be less effective as military assistance rises? The answer requires us to distinguish between states and regimes and to compare the very different sorts of states that receive US aid. Democracy is a type of *regime*, meaning it is a type of 'formal and informal organization at the center of political power [that] determines who has access to political power and how those who are in power deal with those who are not' (Fishman 1990: 428). A *state* is the larger institutional context in which a regime exercises its power. The state 'is a (normally) more permanent structure of domination and coordination including a coercive apparatus and the means to administer a society and extract resources from it' (ibid.: 428). Military aid programmes everywhere target the coercive apparatus of recipient states, and because a state's coercive apparatus inevitably affects what the recipients of democracy aid can and cannot do, military aid is bound to interact with democratization projects. If a state is dominated by authoritarian leaders, it is likely to use its coercive apparatus in ways that work against democratizers. If a state is dominated by democratic elites, or if democratic elites control the forces of coercion, the coercive apparatus is likely to be helpful to democratizers instead.

If democratic (or even neutral) actors control a state's coercive apparatus, military assistance and democracy assistance may not be antithetical. Quite the opposite, strengthened state coercive capacity in this scenario is likely to be helpful to democracy. As Diamond reminds us, 'People can be robbed of their freedom by an overbearing political order and by the *absence* of order as well' (Diamond 2003: 315). Democracy cannot flourish in the absence of security. Those who seek either an opening to democracy or further democratization require the protection of armed forces if their voices are to be heard. This is why freely elected, decidedly democratic, executives such as Liberia's President Ellen Johnson-Sirleaf argued that a stronger association with the US military would not harm Liberian democracy but enhance its longevity instead.[8] We need only recall the role of French resources in the founding of democracy in the United States to illustrate that military aid and democratization can sometimes work hand in hand. The challenge is to give the right sort of resources to the right sort of actors.

One can imagine at least three plausible scenarios for the interaction of coercive forces and the actors who might use democracy aid. Under what we might call the *Rule of Law Scenario*, the state's coercive apparatus works in the interests of democratizing actors, using its monopoly of force to protect

78 *Nancy Bermeo*

whatever formal freedoms the system allows including protecting voters and civic organizations, enforcing liberalizing judicial decisions and guaranteeing that those who win fair elections are allowed to take office. In this scenario, military aid and democracy aid are most likely to work in tandem.

Under what we might call the *Rationalized Security Scenario*, the state's coercive forces work against the interests of democratizers. Using the need to preserve security as their rationale, the state's coercive forces constrain democratizing actors through direct coercion or through simply refusing to fulfil their obligation to protect.

Under a third, *Divided State Scenario*, fissures within a state's coercive apparatus make for inconsistent interactions between the state's armed forces and the recipients of democracy aid. One faction of the state's coercive apparatus may protect the recipients of democracy aid while another faction coerces them instead.

Of course, these three scenarios can be played out without any military aid at all. State elites use force to protect or oppress citizens without the resources of outside actors. But aid from outside actors can make some scenarios more likely than others and much depends on the nature of the recipient state. Unfortunately, US military aid goes disproportionately to authoritarian states which play out the Rationalized Security Scenario. The challenge of balancing US security goals with the expressed desire to advance democracy has been consistently resolved in favour of the former. The fifth wave of democracy may never rise if this irony and its implications are not understood.

The problem is evident not simply in the obvious case of Iraq but in US military aid programmes throughout the world. It precedes the George W. Bush administration and is not likely to be solved easily even if a new administration manages to end the war in Iraq.

What sorts of states receive what sorts of aid?

Aggregate spending data illustrate that the current mix of military and democracy aid favours the Rationalized Security Scenario and that the United States is in the ironic position of promoting democracy while funding autocracy. Figure 5.2 gives us information on dictatorships, democracies and hybrid regimes receiving democracy aid between 1990 and 2004.[9]

Figure 5.2 omits failed states and states that have recently been the target of armed intervention because these states cannot be classified by regime type. It thus excludes countries such as Afghanistan and Iraq and thereby understates the amount of aid going to nondemocratic regimes. Yet even with these exclusions, the data show that the dictatorships in this category received dramatically more dollars of military aid than either democracies or hybrid regimes. The military aid gap between dictatorships and democracies widened considerably after the terrorist events of September 11, but the gap itself precedes both the war on terror and the George W. Bush administration. The

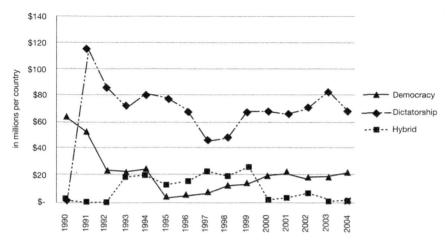

Figure 5.2 US military aid by regime type
Source: USAID (2006), Finkel et al. (2008)
Note: Military aid is the sum of military assistance and security assistance. Figures control for the number of cases in each category and include only cases that received both democracy aid and military aid in a given year. Egypt did not receive democracy aid in 1990, thus the graph understates the amount of military aid going to dictatorships in 1990.

differential decreased between 1990 and 1997 but began to rise in 1998, during the Clinton presidency. This fact suggests that the challenge identified here is not simply the outcome of which party controls executive power. Its roots are deeper.

Figure 5.3 shows that the pattern we see for military aid is duplicated for US arms sales. US arms sales to countries receiving democracy aid also go disproportionately to dictatorships. This pattern, too, precedes the administration of George W. Bush.

Figure 5.4, detailing European arms sales to countries receiving democratic 'governance aid,' suggests that the US arms provision pattern is not simply a reflection of demand.[10] Though UK arms sales also favoured dictatorships between 2001 and 2003, British, French and German arms sales to governance aid recipients have generally favoured democracies.

The disproportionate amount of US military aid (and weaponry) going to dictatorships is not offset by compensating amounts of democracy aid. Quite the contrary, dictatorships get considerably more military aid than democracy aid. The left column in Table 5.1 lists the recipients of democracy aid that began and ended the period under study as nondemocratic.

In well over half of the countries that remained dictatorships, military aid per capita outweighed democracy assistance per capita. In over half of all the countries that remained mired in dictatorship, military aid outweighed

80 *Nancy Bermeo*

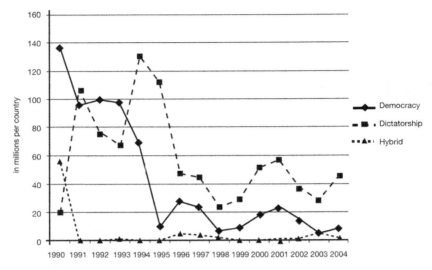

Figure 5.3 US arms sales by regime type
Source: SIPRI.
Note: Democracy Assistance recipients only.

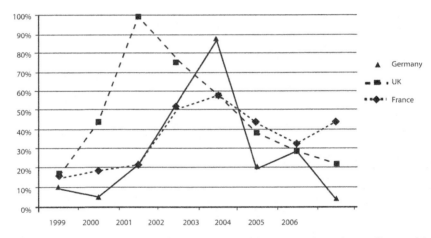

Figure 5.4 Proportion of French, German, and British arms sales going to dictatorships
Source: SIPRI, OECD.
Note: Governance Assistance recipients only.

democracy aid by a multiple of more than 2 to 1. The imbalance for the Arab states is especially dramatic.

The right column in Table 5.1 lists the pre-transition aid ratios of countries that became electoral democracies and remained democratic during the period under study. The ratios of military to democracy aid received by these

Democracy assistance, search for security 81

Table 5.1 Ratio between US military aid and democracy aid (in US$)

Countries that remained dictatorships		Countries that became democracies	
Bahrain	258.52	Mexico	108.10
Oman	245.17	Ukraine	6.98
Morocco	102.95	Senegal	5.15
Jordan	73.04	Yugoslavia (Serbia-Montenegro	3.99
Egypt	65.16	Dominican Republic	2.54
Cameroon	40.31	Thailand	1.97
Vietnam	18.86	Georgia	1.50
Tunisia	16.44	Indonesia	0.76
Yemen	6.66	Albania	0.64
Mauritania	5.31	Ghana	0.59
Swaziland	4.10	Kenya	0.43
Rwanda	2.09	Guatemala	0.32
Togo	1.38	Mali	0.29
Uzbekistan	1.33	Romania	0.28
Uganda	1.15	Bangladesh	0.26
Turkmenistan	0.62	Guyana	0.06
Kyrgyzstan	0.44	Mozambique	0.05
Guinea	0.38	Croatia	0.04
Kazakhstan	0.27		
Tajikistan	0.22		
Zimbabwe	0.21		
Sudan	0.18		

Sources: USAID (2006) the Greenbook, Finkel *et al.* (2008).
Notes: Military Aid is the sum of military assistance and security assistance. For every
$1 spent on democracy aid in Bahrain, $258.52 was spent on military aid. Countries
must receive both military aid and democracy aid in order to be included in this table.

cases (before their transition) differ dramatically from those received by dictatorships. Countries that became lasting democracies received a mix of aid with a significantly smaller military component and a significantly larger democracy component.

The contrast between the aid ratios for countries that remained dictatorships and the countries that became democracies suggests that different allocation patterns have different effects on regime change and that the aid 'mix' matters.

Table 5.2 offers us more suggestive evidence about the consequences of the aid allocation patterns just described. The first column shows that countries that became democracies received more democracy promotion aid than those that remained dictatorships, but the difference is neither dramatic nor surprising. The second column in the Table 5.2 compares average military assistance for countries that became democracies and countries that remained dictatorships. Here the difference is dramatic indeed.

Countries that made the transition from dictatorship to democracy between 1990 and 2003 received significantly *less* military aid before their transitions than countries that remained undemocratic. ($3.10 per capita vs. $71.71 per

82   *Nancy Bermeo*

Table 5.2 Average democracy, military and economic aid: countries that remained dictatorships vs countries that became democracies

	Democracy Aid (avg. per capita) (US{$})	Military Aid (avg. per capita) (US{$})	Security Assistance (avg. per capita) (US{$})	Agriculture and Economic Growth Aid (avg. per capita) (US{$})	Number of cases
Countries that remained dictatorships	2.95	71.71	0.67	35.13	22
Countries that became democracies	3.61	3.10	0.36	11.87	18

Source: USAID (2006) the Greenbook, Finkel *et al.* (2008).

capita) These figures suggest that military aid may have an independent and negative effect on the likelihood of democratic regime change and thus that increasing democracy aid without decreasing military aid may not boost democratization. Scholars and policy-makers who argue simply for increased spending on democracy assistance must keep this in mind.

They should also consider the interactions of economic aid and democracy aid. Even though the countries that remained dictatorships were no poorer than those which made the transition to electoral democracy, dictatorships were favoured in terms of economic aid. Table 5.2 indicates that countries that remained dictatorships received, on average, three times as much economic aid per capita as nations that remained democracies. The effects of this difference require more research, but if economic aid boosts the performance profile and therefore the legitimacy of dictatorships, economic aid may undercut the effect of democracy aid as well. An understanding of these differences requires extensive statistical work plus detailed case studies but it is clear that the mix of aid that the United States sends abroad has consequences we have yet to understand.

Aid interactions and human rights

As we explore whether aid interactions undercut the likelihood of democratic regime change, we should also explore how aid interactions affect the particular components of democracy assistance programmes. Finkel et al. have illustrated that the components of democracy assistance programmes do not 'work' in tandem. On the contrary, despite finding that democracy assistance 'works' in the aggregate, Finkel et al. have shown that 'USAID human rights assistance has a significant *negative* impact on the human rights' records of recipient states. '[R]eceiving rule of law funding directed at the improvement of human rights' and, specifically, at preventing states from 'abusing the personal integrity of their populations' actually correlates with an increase in human rights abuse (Finkel et al. 2008: 5 and 55; italics added).

Why would increased funding for the protection of human rights correlate with increases in human rights abuse? It is possible that the US directs a disproportional amount of human rights aid to countries with especially 'suspect' human rights records (and that the trend is one of reverse causation) but Finkel et al. (ibid.: 85) show that this hypothesis does not hold up to statistical tests. Moreover, even if this particular form of aid did go disproportionately to states with the worst human rights records, reverse causality would not explain the dynamic, temporal dimension of the association, that is, why human rights violations actually *increase*.

A focus on the interaction of aid initiatives suggests a more compelling explanation for this troubling association. The following, highly problematic, mix of incentives may be at play: aid for the development of civil society, political parties, and anti-corruption programmes encourages all sorts of political actors to engage in opposition activities and challenge ruling elites. Aid for human rights programmes and judicial development programmes encourages these same actors to use the judicial apparatus of the state as a vehicle for change, but this causes fissures in the state elite. These fissures threaten the anti-democratic forces in government who then use the coercive apparatus of the state to crack down on democratizing forces and protect their own power base. Anti-democratic actors have the capacity to initiate a crack-down precisely because military aid has bolstered the strength of the coercive apparatus and lowered the costs of repression and abuse. In the meantime, aid for free media and transparency has increased the likelihood that the abuses will be reported and recorded. One set of incentives leads people to exercise or demand their rights while another set of incentives lowers the costs of abusing the rights of these same actors. And so the incidence of recorded abuse rises. Recent events in Egypt under President Mubarak and in Pakistan under General Musharraf illustrate the scenario I have just described. How often this cycle of events has been played out elsewhere requires more research but it is a predictable outcome of the US attempt to meet the challenge of promoting national security while aiding democracy abroad.

Security interests and democratic ideals

The challenge of balancing the search for US security with initiatives to advance democracy abroad has been obscured by frames that present the two as consistently complementary.[11] Though former Secretary of State Condoleezza Rice (2005) argues against 'attempting to draw neat, clean lines between our security interests and our democratic ideals', security interests have trumped democratic ideals throughout US diplomatic history. Fukuyama and McFaul (2007: 29) are correct in asserting that 'The United States has never made democracy promotion the overriding goal of its foreign policy.'

Although the compelling evidence for the democratic peace argument suggests that a world of stable democracies would make the US (and other democracies) more secure, a worldwide project of democratization may not

84 *Nancy Bermeo*

have this effect. Democracy and democratization are not synonymous and the elections that mark the early phase of attempts at democratization do not always bring democrats to power. The electoral popularity of the Islamic Salvation Front in Algeria in 1992 and the more recent electoral victories of Hizbollah in Lebanon and Hamas in Palestine illustrate the point. Elections are the voice of the people and the sad truth is that a great many people now see the US as a security threat. The challenge of balancing security interests and democratic ideals under these lamentable conditions is particularly vexing.

The plurality of the security threat

The challenge of balancing security needs with democratization is further complicated by the fact that democracy is singular but security is plural. Although the advance of democracy takes place country by country in single territorial spaces, security is, intrinsically, a plural affair. It has domestic, regional and global dimensions. While the challenge of creating democracy is felt in only a subset of countries, the security challenge is felt by all states. Leaders, in both democracies and dictatorships, can credibly claim that their people are threatened by political actors within their state's borders, across their state's borders, and thousands of miles away. Today, with the 'war on terror', this inevitably multi-dimensional search for national security has created a confluence of interests between political leaders in democratic states (such as the US) and political leaders in authoritarian regimes. Today, as during the Cold War, regime elites in the US and regimes elites in dictatorships around the world can claim to be fighting a common enemy. But the common enemies today (as during the Cold War) have a more ambiguous identity than the enemies in conventional wars. As 'non-state' actors they often wear no uniforms and thus, the lines between friends, foes and neutrals, are not clearly marked. Deadly antidemocratic security threats abound, but democratizing actors who seek only a change in regime, or even an expansion of freedoms within an existing regime, can easily be framed as state security threats and silenced through intimidation, jailing or death. Ordinary people who witness the silencing remain silent themselves because political elites have led them to believe that the victims truly are security threats. Democratic states with their own security fears often remain silent too. Indeed, they often finance the silencing of the opposition. The pattern we see today recalls what was done during the fight against communism in countries as diverse as Iran in 1953 and Chile 1973. It is an old story, but it is a tragic story too and the many US actors who sincerely seek to assist democracy abroad must be mindful of its legacies and its lessons.

Looking backward

As we try to think more holistically (and historically) about how US aid should and should not be allocated, it is helpful (and possibly consoling) to remember that the third wave of democracy started in Portugal in 1974, years before formal democracy assistance programmes began. Portugal ousted its dictators because its military and its people (including its most competitive capitalists) no longer had the money or the heart to fight its colonial wars. Neither the US nor any other Western country provided Portugal's dictators with the military and material resources that the wars required.[12] Though aid to democratic forces poured in from West Germany and elsewhere after the dictatorship fell, the dictatorship fissured without much assistance from democratic outsiders. The regime was transformed precisely because the state's coercive apparatus was stretched beyond capacity. If aid from a third party had increased military capacity, it might well have prolonged the life of Portugal's dictatorship. In any case, the regime fell without 'democracy assistance'. The Portuguese case is not extraordinary in this regard. Nearly one-third of all electoral democracies formed after the end of the Marshall Plan and still existing in 2004 were formed prior to 1990 and thus prior to the current push for democracy assistance.[13]

Moreover, an analysis of the last six US presidencies reveals that the average annual rate of increase in the number of democracies around the world was higher under the Carter administration than under any other administration save that of George H. Bush (who assumed office just as the Soviet Union dissolved). Table 5.3 suggests that democratization advanced without formal programmes of democracy assistance, even during the Cold War.

Looking forward

The effects of aid interactions must not be exaggerated. The mix of military and democracy aid emanating from the United States has not, by itself, held back some natural tide of freedom. To make this argument, one would have to assume that the countries which have not democratized would have done so in the absence of US aid and that the process of democratization is always shaped decisively by the material resources of foreign actors. Both of these assumptions are dubious. The first requires us to ignore the facts that many

Table 5.3 Annual increase in democracies during six US presidencies

	New democracies (%)	New hybrids (%)	New dictatorships (%)	Countries in the world
Nixon/Ford	−0.32	1.90	0.00	158
Carter	1.39	0.62	−1.39	162
Reagan	0.60	−0.68	0.08	166
G.H. Bush	2.02	3.90	−3.23	186
Clinton	0.72	−0.98	0.65	192
G.W. Bush	0.29	0.15	−0.37	194

Source: Freedom House.
Note: On average, there were 2.02 per cent more democracies in the world each year G.H.Bush was president (1989–93).

86   *Nancy Bermeo*

people do not seek democracy and that many countries receive no aid at all. The second requires us to ignore cases such as Haiti in the 1990s where, despite low amounts of military aid and the second highest democracy assistance budget in the world, attempts to establish lasting democracy failed miserably. Clearly, other regime types have legitimacy in specific cases and even where democracy is the most popular option, democratization requires much more than material resources from abroad.[14]

Though the absence of the (possibly mythical) fifth wave must not be blamed on the contradictions of US aid policy alone, it is very likely that the overwhelming weight of US military aid works against democracy aid in many countries. In this more limited sense, the current mix of US aid does hamper democratization. If Finkel et al. are correct in their analysis, the mix has already undercut the positive effects of democracy aid in a broad range of cases. Table 5.4 lists democracy aid recipients which are also 'security priorities' (i.e. countries which rank in the top 15 of US military aid recipients).

Even a quick look at Table 5.4 shows that security concerns are leading the US to shore up the coercive apparatus of a number of dictatorships, as well as a number of electoral democracies seen as allies in the 'war on terror' or the 'war on drugs'.

The cases in the top half of Table 5.4 are those that receive over 1.1 per cent of the US military aid budget. This is the threshold at which Finkel and his colleagues found that democracy aid had no effect. My argument about the Rationalized Security Scenario suggests why. Sadly, this scenario might be extending to electoral democracies as well. The cases in the upper right-hand

Table 5.4 US security priorities receiving democracy aid, 2003–4

Non-democracies	*Democracies*
Afghanistan	Bolivia
Bahrain	Colombia
Egypt	Korean Republic
Iraq	Peru
Jordan	
Oman	
Pakistan	
	Bosnia-Herzegovina
	Ecuador
	Mexico
	Philippines
	Poland
	Turkey

Notes: Countries above the line received over 1.1 per cent of US military aid. This, according to Finkel *et al.* (2008), is the threshold at which democracy aid has no effect. Countries listed ranked in Top 15 in terms of US military budget allocation for 2003 and/or 2004. Israel is considered a security priority but does not receive democracy aid so is not listed.

quadrant are the electoral democracies which sit above the no-effect threshold. These, with the exception of South Korea, are seen as security priorities because of the war on drugs. Without more research, we cannot be sure that the dynamic is similarly negative in these cases, but given some of their checkered human rights records, it is doubtful that the massive amounts of military aid given to these regimes bolster only the Rule of Law Scenario.

Moving to the lower half of the Table 5.4, we find the cases which fall below the 1.1 per cent threshold but which still rank in the top 15 of US security priorities and could easily pass the threshold in the future. If aid interactions have the effects proposed in this chapter, we should be concerned that the effects of democracy aid will be undercut in these cases as well. Indeed, recent drops in the assessed quality of democracy in Ecuador, Mexico, and the Philippines raise the troubling specter of the Rationalized Security Scenario in states that are not dictatorships.[15]

More troubling than the amount of military aid extended abroad is its specific use. Though it is important to remember that US military aid funds a broad range of activities which are non-coercive (involving programmes such as civil construction, disaster relief and public health), the majority of military aid still goes directly to the coercive apparatus of recipient states. According to US government figures, military spending broke down into the following categories (in 2006); military assistance totalled US$12 billion, security assistance totalled US$4.7 billion and finally, the Foreign Military Sales Program (FMS) totalled US$20.9 billion.[16] The funds dedicated to the Foreign Military Sales Program are directed toward unambiguously coercive ends and they are on the rise. Figure 5.5, drawn from US government statistics, illustrates the point. The most recent figures detail spending only through August of 2008 but that year's figure already matched the high reached in 1993.

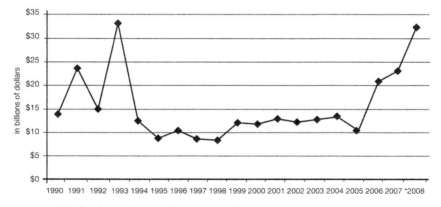

Figure 5.5 US foreign military sales, 1990–2008

Source: Department of Defense via Eric Lipton of the Washington Bureau of *The New York Times*.

Note: * 2008 figure is through 28 August 2008.

88   Nancy Bermeo

The 'war on terror' has eased former prohibitions on weapons sales to governments engaged in systematic human rights abuse and has also globalized the scope of US security concerns.[17] As a result, the number of countries receiving aid for weaponry has risen dramatically.[18] States which had once been barred from receiving arms transfers, such as Pakistan, Armenia, Azerbaijan and Tajikistan, were all receiving substantial transfers at the time of this writing. The number of countries receiving Foreign Military Finance (FMF) assistance jumped from 48 to 71 in the five years after 2001 (Berrigan and Hartun 2005). Table 5.5 records the countries added to the standard list of Foreign Military Finance recipients after 2002. By standard list, I mean countries that were already receiving FMS funds in 1997 – the decade before the current data were provided.

Countries in Asia and Africa with democracies which are frail at best are getting massive new injections of military assistance for the purpose of weaponry. Dictatorships and democracies which were not getting foreign military sales aid ten years ago are now having their coercive forces bolstered by the US. Between 2001 and 2003 alone, the US provided over 47 million dollars in FMS aid to Uzbekistan, 15 million dollars to tiny Djibouti, 17.5

Table 5.5 Additions to the standard list of US weapons aid recipients 2002–7

Middle East and North Africa	*Sub-Saharan Africa*	*Latin America and Caribbean*	*Asia*	*Oceania*	*Eurasia/ Europe*
Bahrain	Angola	Colombia	Afghanistan	Tonga	Armenia
Lebanon	Burundi	Ecuador	Cambodia		Azerbaijan
Oman	Cameroon	El Salvador	East Timor		Tajikistan
Yemen	Cape Verde	Honduras	India		Turkey
	Chad	Nicaragua	Pakistan		
	Comoros	Peru	Sri Lanka		
	Congo-Brazzaville	Suriname			
	Congo-Kinshasa				
	Gabon				
	Lesotho				
	Liberia				
	Madagascar				
	Mauritius				
	Mozambique				
	Rwanda				
	São Tomé and Príncipe				
	Seychelles				
	Sierra Leone				
	Swaziland				
	Togo				

Source: Foreign Military Financing Program US Overseas Loans and Grants (the Greenbook) (USAID 2006) 'Standard Ten Year Report'.

Democracy assistance, search for security 89

million dollars to Kenya, and 13 million dollars to South Africa.[19] More recently, between 2003 and 2006, Foreign Military Finance grants used to procure US defence articles and services, increased by over 375 per cent in Colombia and 260 per cent in El Salvador (USAID 2006).

Will strengthening the coercive forces of countries throughout the world enable the US to better assist democratic actors and promote the Rule of Law Scenario? The argument developed here suggests that, in many states, we should expect much less desirable outcomes. But there are arguments to the contrary and these merit attention too. Three counter-arguments loom large. First, and most powerfully, it can be argued that aid interactions are determined by unique local conditions and that the generalizations presented here may not apply in a given country. Second, it is possible that the more negative scenarios described here are necessary preludes to the Rule of Law Scenario and that military aid will yield more positive results with the passage of time. Finally, US influence within the coercive apparatus of a dictatorship may, in some cases, have a perverse up-side. The fates of President Ferdinand Marcos of the Philippines in the 1980s and of Pakistan's Pervez Musharraf, more recently, suggest that autocrats who have been sustained in power by aid-reliant coercive forces can easily lose their footing when the US threatens to withdraw support. The intransigent behaviour of the military in Myanmar (Burma), which now receives no aid from the US, highlights the association between *independence* and intransigence.

Despite the merits of these arguments, there are still at least three powerful reasons to believe that military aid and democracy aid often work at cross-purposes. First, in addition to the impressive effects identified by Finkel et al., the latest, systematic work on the effects of military assistance in general concludes that US 'military aid does not lead to any increases in the cooperative behavior of recipient states' (Tessman and Sullivan 2008: 4). In fact, scholars have recently pointed out that states receiving military aid may now be even less amenable to US influence than they were historically because the current strategic environment makes punishment for defection unlikely (Walt 2005; Mott 2002: 8). Though 'cooperative behavior', 'US influence' and democratization are not synonymous, the conclusions of these studies support the argument being made here by showing that military aid does not necessarily yield the rewards its advocates expect.

A second sort of evidence that should make us wary of aid interactions comes from historians. A great deal of historical work highlights the danger of regimes with high levels of military autonomy – a quality that military assistance bolsters. As Charles Tilly (2004: 200) reminds us, if militaries are autonomous, 'democratization does not advance'.[20] The political bargaining process that emerges from the state's needs to raise its own funds (and its own armies) for coercion and other functions has been a primary incentive for democratization for centuries. Military aid upsets this dynamic by allowing state elites to defend the status quo without having to secure resources from the citizenry. Military aid can easily function as a resource curse,

90 Nancy Bermeo

enabling dictators to protect themselves without extending rights to their citizenry.

One final reason to be wary of aid interactions derives from the fact that the legacies of military aid have a troubling longevity. The political parties that outsiders assist may disintegrate after a single election, and the civic groups that outsiders train may dissolve overnight, but the weapons that outsiders provide will last for decades. The challenge of truly assisting democracies abroad will not be met without a firmer focus on these grim realities and on the interactive qualities of all aid efforts. The US can, as George Bush suggests, 'put pressure on the arms of the world's tyrants', but as long as it continues to supply the weapons to their soldiers, the escape of those 'imprisoned by tyranny' may be delayed. These weapons may even be trained on new targets as time goes on. Pro-democracy forces in Afghanistan and Iraq know this tragic irony all too well.

Acknowledgments

The author thanks Nuffield College and the Department of Politics and International Relations at Oxford University for funding and Kris-Stella Trump and Joshua Woodward for research assistance. For helpful comments the author thanks Peter Burnell, Larry Diamond, Joshua Woodward, the participants in the Democracy's International Challenges Seminar in Brussels, as well as the audience at the panel entitled Democracy and Democracy Promotion Revisited at the 2008 meetings of the American Political Science Association. For a methodological appendix and a list of countries used for figures and tables, see the author's website (www.nuffield.ox.ac.uk/politics/Bermeo.htm).

Data sources

- US Democracy Aid figures from the Democracy Assistance Project by Finkel et al. (2008), available online at www.pitt.edu/~politics/democracy/democracy.html.
- European democracy aid figures retrieved from OECD's Creditor Reporting System, available at: www.stats.oecd.org. The aid category used is 'Policy Purpose: Participatory Development/Good Governance'.
- US Military Assistance figures retrieved from the U.S. Agency for International Development (USAID 2006), the Greenbook: 'U.S. Overseas Loans and Grants: Obligations and Loan Authorizations, July 1, 1945–September 30, 2006'. The category used is 'Military Assistance, Total'.
- Arms trade figures are information from the Stockholm International Peace Research Institute (SIPRI) Arms Transfers Database, available at: www.armstrade.sipri.org.
- Unless otherwise noted, all figures are listed in constant 2006 US. Where necessary, dollar figures have been converted using the Bureau of Labor Statistics CPI deflator.

Notes

1 See Bush (2007).
2 The terms aid and assistance are used interchangeably throughout the text for stylistic reasons. Unless otherwise noted, however, the statistical figures on US military aid include what the military classifies as military assistance and security assistance. For more details, see www.qesdb.usaid.gov/gbk/Reporting Concepts. html. I use the terms democracy aid and democracy assistance to refer to what the government officially calls Democracy and Governance Aid. This includes four sectors of activity: (1) Elections and Political Processes, including the development of political parties and legislative representation; (2) Rule of Law Programs including legal, judicial and human rights development initiatives; (3) Civil Society Programs including free mass media, civic education and labor organization programs; and (4) Governance Programs including, among other initiatives, transparency and anti-corruption projects and the promotion of decentralization and local government. See Finkel et al. (2008: 9–10).
3 Military aid figures for other countries are especially difficult to access.
4 Unless otherwise noted, I use the term democracy in this text to denote a regime in which voters choose their most important political leaders from among groups contesting competitive elections. Competitive elections exist when the media provide information about candidates and their platforms, when citizens can vote without being subjected to debilitating coercion and when candidates can campaign openly. This is a minimalist definition of democracy corresponding to what the literature typically calls 'electoral democracy'. I use this minimalist definition to underscore the point that military aid sometimes undermines not simply democracy in its liberal form but in its other, weaker, forms as well. Where it is necessary to quantify democracies and other regimes, I have conformed to political science conventions and applied precise decision rules to categorize an imprecise reality. Unless otherwise noted, in the quantitative sections of the chapter, I rely on the Polity IV data set using three Polity IV thresholds to classify regimes: democracies are regimes scoring 6 and above; hybrids score 0 to 5; dictatorships score below 0. The Polity Data can be found on line at www.systemicpeace.org/polity/polity4.htm. Reality is, of course, much more complicated than any simple scoring system.
5 See Bruneau and Trinkunas (2006). Larry Diamond and Marc Plattner published a series of short essays on civil–military relations in new democracies in 1996 (see *Civil Military Relations in Democracy*) but there has been a remarkable lack of attention to the subject since then.
6 The US National Research Council records that, 'direct funding for democracy assistance by the United States constitutes less than ... one-quarter of 1 percent of what is spent by the U.S. military'. US National Research Council (2008: 20).
7 G.W. Bush assumed the presidency on 20 January, 2001. Afghanistan was invaded on 7 October 2001.
8 Johnson-Sirleaf wanted the US to put its Africa Command in Liberia. She stated:

> If Africom aims to use its 'soft power' mandate to develop a stable environment in which civil society can flourish and the quality of life for Africans can be improved, African nations should work with Africom to achieve their own development and security goals.
>
> (Johnson-Sirleaf 2007)

9 These are the only years for which the data on democracy aid (as opposed to non-military aid in general) are available.
10 'Governance aid' is the European counterpart to what the US calls 'democracy and governance aid.' European governance aid figures were retrieved from OECD's

92 Nancy Bermeo

Creditor Reporting System, available at: www.stats.oecd.org. The aid category used is 'Policy Purpose: Participatory Development / Good Governance'.

11 When George Bush (2007) said, 'Expanding freedom is more than a moral imperative. It is the only realistic way to protect our people', he framed the security challenge and the democratization challenge as compatible. This framing was highlighted during the George W. Bush administration but it appeared during the Clinton years as well. For example, in his 1994 State of the Union address, Bill Clinton asserted that, 'Ultimately, the best strategy to ensure our security and to build a durable peace is to support the advance of democracy elsewhere' (Clinton 1994).

12 Kenneth Maxwell (1995) shows that the Nixon administration aided the Salazar regime surreptitiously for a brief period but the amounts involved were small.

13 The countries that began a successful transition to electoral democracy prior to 1990 include Argentina (1983), Bolivia (1982), Brazil (1985), Chile (1989), Colombia in (1957), Ecuador (1979), El Salvador (1984), Greece (1975), India (1950), Israel (1948), Jamaica (1959), South Korea (1988), Papua New Guinea (1975), the Philippines (1987), Portugal (1976), Spain (1978), Turkey (1983), Uruguay (1985) and Venezuela (1958). The dates listed are the years in which the cases achieved a +6 Polity Score.

14 According to official figures from USAID, Haiti's democracy aid reached a world high of nearly 8 US$ per person in the mid-1990s. Later only Serbia-Montenegro received more and its military aid/democracy aid ratio was less favourable.

15 According to the Polity index, Ecuadorian democracy moved in a more authoritarian direction in 2007. According to Freedom House, the average of the political rights and civil liberties scores for Mexico worsened by 1 unit (on a 7-unit scale) between 2003 and 2007. The comparable drop in quality for the Philippines was 2 units.

16 See http://qesdb.usaid.gov/gbk/ReportingConcepts.html

17 The 1976 Arms Export Control Act, which prohibited weapons sales to governments engaging in systematic human rights abuse, has been sidestepped with new legislation since September 11. According to Stohl (2008):

> Decisions to lift sanctions were made on a case-by-case basis. To date, the United States has completely lifted pre-September 11 sanctions on Armenia, Azerbaijan, India, Pakistan, Tajikistan, and the former Federal Republic of Yugoslavia (now Montenegro and Serbia). Since September 11, 2001, additional military assistance restrictions to Thailand and Indonesia have been waived.

18 For details, see the Federation of American Scientists (FAS) website at: www.fas.org/asmp/resources/govern/109th/AECA0106.pdf.

19 Available at: www.worldpolicy.org/projects/arms/reports/WatWTable3.html.

20 See also Tilly (1985: 183), North and Weingast (1989), and Mann (1988: 159).

6 Public support versus dissatisfaction in new democracies

An 'inside challenge'?

Renske Doorenspleet

Introduction

Let me start with the good news. At the moment, we are living in an era with an unprecedented number of democracies all around the world. The past 30 years have seen significant gains for the spread of democracy. In the beginning of the 1970s, not many people in Poland, Mali, or Spain would have dared dream of living in a less repressive country. In the 1980s, not many people in South Africa, Mongolia, or Czechoslovakia would have believed that their regime could soon be transformed into a more democratic one. Throughout most of the 1990s, democracy seemed to be an unreachable ideal in countries such as Indonesia. And yet, democratization came to these countries as well. The past few decades clearly were decades of reform; decades of change, often in the direction of more openness – not only of the economy but also of many political systems in the world.

More and more countries have become democratic – all in a relatively short period of time, although most of them after the end of the Cold War. Already in 1991, Dankwart Rustow claimed in an interview that:

> [This worldwide change] is probably as close to a truly global turning point as we've ever seen. The world is becoming more unified than ever before, and democracy has become a strong, possibly irresistible force. This is the first time in history there is no legitimate alternative to democracy.
>
> (in Moffett 1991)

Indeed, democracy was spreading to more and more corners of the globe, transforming political regimes in Eastern Europe, Latin America, and parts of Africa. Not only was this recent democratization wave more global and affecting more countries than earlier waves, there were also relatively fewer regressions to nondemocratic regimes than in the past. In other words, one can really speak about an impressive, explosive wave of democratization after 1989 (see also Doorenspleet 2000, 2005). In the years after Rustow presented this view, the democratic type of regime has become even stronger and more appealing: many countries democratized in the 1990s.

94   *Renske Doorenspleet*

Democracy seems to be irresistible, but whether it was and is the only legitimate type of regime is very debatable, as will become clear in this chapter. Despite the overwhelming mass support for democracy, actual satisfaction with the democratic regimes is very low. New democracies are full of a lot of so-called 'dissatisfied democrats': citizens who are strong supporters of the democratic ideal but are not happy with the way democracy is working in their country. This chapter investigates whether this phenomenon is a challenge for new democracies or not.

In the next section, it will become clear that democratic government has increasingly become dominant in the world. Not only the number of minimal democracies has grown but also liberal democracy is no longer a rare species. However, the main body of the chapter will focus on a possible challenge for new democracies: the gap between people's support and satisfaction. The third section will describe what we mean by the concepts of support and satisfaction, while the fourth section presents the findings of previous research, which, unfortunately, has primarily focused on developments in established democracies. The final section will therefore present the data for new democracies in the world, thereby showing that the same pattern is visible with a huge gap between support and satisfaction. Citizens seem to be highly critical of the way their version of democracy is actually working.

Does this create a challenge for democracy? The existing literature is not conclusive on this issue; some optimistic approaches assume that those dissatisfied democrats are 'critical citizens' wanting more democracy (Norris 1999a, 1999b) while other more pessimistic approaches assume that these citizens are disillusioned and confused (for example, Stoker 2006). As existing studies often rest on assumptions, a later section of this chapter will 'unpack' the actual identity of dissatisfied democrats by focusing on three completely different cases on three different continents: Panama, Benin and Hungary. It will become clear that dissatisfied democrats are not necessarily 'good' for democracy, and might pose a danger indeed. The characteristics of dissatisfied democrats differ across countries, and the patterns in new democracies are not always comparable to those in the established western democracies; hence the implications for the strengthening of democratic governance probably also vary.

Democratic dominance in the world

The number of transitions to democracy has been overwhelming since 1989: never before in history have so many authoritarian regimes collapsed and changed in a more democratic direction (see Doorenspleet 2005). Moreover, for the first time this wave of democratization was truly a global, not merely a local or regional experience. Not only in Eastern Europe, but also in parts of Africa, Asia, and Latin America the idea of democracy triumphed.

It is important to realize that the 'democracy' we are talking about, generally means a limited form of democracy, namely 'minimal democracy'.[1] On

Public support vs dissatisfaction 95

the basis of Dahl's ideas (Dahl 1971),[2] minimal democracy can be defined as a type of political regime in which: (1) there exist competition – institutions and procedures through which citizens can express effective preferences about alternative policies at the national level and there are institutionalized constraints on the exercise of power by the executive; and (2) there exists inclusive suffrage or the right of participation in selection of national leaders and policies. Conversely, non-democratic regimes are defined as those political regimes that fail to meet the first requirement of competition and/or the second requirement of inclusiveness (see also Doorenspleet 2000).

We should hence be cautious with our optimism about global democracy, since 'democracy' is often defined very narrowly, limited to 'minimal democracy'. The recent waves of democratization are, for the most part, waves of 'minimal' democracies and those democracies are not necessarily consolidated, nor do they always guarantee civil liberties or fulfil the more extensive requirements of an 'advanced' democracy (see Schedler 1998a, 1998b).[3]

Many of the new democratic regimes that emerged in the past two decades can be characterized by inclusive suffrage and competition but, at the same time, by a very low level of civil liberties and political rights (Diamond 1999; Zakaria 1997).[4] Minimal democracies are not necessarily liberal democracies. Turkey is a good example which combines a political system with competition and inclusiveness together with political repression prevalent in the Kurdish areas of south-eastern Turkey. Although in February 1991 the ban on speaking Kurdish in public was lifted, and Kurdish-language publications began to appear, the Turkish military intensified its repressive actions against the Kurdish population and in particular suspected terrorists. Turkey clearly was a minimal democracy, but certainly cannot be classified as a liberal democracy. In a compelling way, Zakaria (1997) argues that this distinction is crucial to understanding types of regimes nowadays, while also suggesting that the world had entered an era characterized by the rise of 'illiberal democracy'.[5]

Although Zakaria's ideas have been very influential, it is important to notice that freedom is still advancing and spreading over the world. While an increase in illiberal democracies seemed to characterize the mid-1990s, more recent research based on Freedom House data argued that a clear rise of illiberal democracy has not taken place now (Møller 2007). On the contrary, freedom has increasingly become a principal part of national and international politics. Not only more democracy, but also higher levels of freedom became the dominant trends in Western and East-Central Europe, in Latin America, and increasingly in Africa and the Asia-Pacific region (see Karatnycky 1999; Møller 2007). To be sure, it is true that countries in the Middle East have been largely untouched by trends of global freedom. Moreover, it is undeniable that many of the new liberal democracies remain fragile, and that freedom and liberties are under threat everywhere at the moment (in established democracies as well, particularly after 9/11). Finally, political reversals can certainly be expected, especially in the African continent (see also Chapter 1 in this book).

96 *Renske Doorenspleet*

Nevertheless, freedom has spread around the world since the 1970s (see Table 6.1). According to the Freedom House data, the number of free countries stood at 90 in 2007, representing 47 per cent of the countries in the world. Sixty countries qualified as 'partly free', which is 31 per cent of all countries. The data show that 43 countries are 'not free', representing 22 per cent of all countries.[6] More recent developments are a bit less rosy. Although the total numbers of countries designated as free, partly free, or not free have changed very little since 2006, within these broad categories there have been some negative changes in the last two years or so. Several countries that had previously shown progress toward democracy have regressed, while none of the most influential non-democratic regimes have shown signs of political opening.[7]

On the other hand, there are clear signs that minimal democracy does eventually have a positive effect on freedom. There has been a growing respect for civil liberties in most minimal democracies. Already in the last millennium Karatnycky (1999) pointed out that there was a clear decline in the number of minimal (or 'illiberal') democracies, and an increase in the number and proportion of the world's minimal democracies that are also liberal democracies. Recent evidence confirms this finding and, additionally shows there is no longer a growing divide between the liberal and illiberal worlds of democracy (Møller 2007). Whereas more than one quarter of the total number of democracies could be classified as minimal (or illiberal) democracies in the mid-1990s, this figure stood at around 8 per cent in 2005.

In other words, in regimes where civil liberties are restricted, the levels of competition and participation are also limited. On the one hand, regimes tend to be liberal, competitive and inclusive; and conversely there are regimes that are not liberal, not competitive and not inclusive at all. Mixed combinations have become rare (see Møller 2007). Compared with previous periods, freedom has become more important and prevalent in recently democratized countries in the world. At least that is the fact until very recently; however, given the most recent signs of stagnation and even decrease in the levels of freedom, a trend towards more illiberal democracies can be expected in the near future.

In sum, democratic government has increasingly become dominant in the world. There has been a world-wide increase of democracies. The rest of the

Table 6.1 The global trend of freedom: number of free, partly free and not free countries in the world

Year	Free	Partly free	Not free
1977	43	48	64
1987	58	58	51
1997	81	57	53
2007	90	60	43

Source: Puddington (2008).

Public support vs dissatisfaction 97

chapter will now focus on a possible challenge for new democracies: the gap between people's support and satisfaction. However, before doing so the next section will describe what we mean by these core concepts.

The concepts of support and satisfaction

What do we mean by support for democracy and satisfaction? Scholars in the field of democratic political culture generally agree these concepts are very complex, especially because citizens understand democracy both as an ideal political system and as a political system-in-practice (Dalton 2004; Klingemann 1999; Norris 1999a, 1999b; Shin 1999, 2006, 2007). According to Shin, this is particularly crucial in new democracies:

> To ordinary citizens who lived most of their lives under authoritarian rule, democracy at one level represents the political ideals or values to which they aspire. At another level, democracy refers to a political regime-in-practice and the actual workings of its institutions, which govern their daily lives.
>
> (Shin 2006: 8)

David Easton (1965, 1975) was the first who made a valuable distinction between support for the political community, regime, and authorities. Building upon this foundation, Norris (1999a: 10) used a fivefold conceptualization and drew a line between the political community, regime principles, regime performance, regime institutions, and political actors. The first level concerns diffuse support for the political community, which is usually understood to mean a basic attachment to the nation beyond the present institutions of government and a general willingness to co-operate together politically. The second level refers to support for the core regime principles representing the values of the political system; in other words, this level focuses on the support for the ideal of democracy. The third level concerns evaluations of regime performance, meaning support for how authoritarian or democratic political systems function in practice; this level hence focuses on the satisfaction with the regime. The fourth level focuses on support for regime institutions, and includes attitudes towards governments, parliaments, the executive, the legal system and police, the state bureaucracy, political parties, and the military. The final level deals with specific support for political actors or authorities, including evaluations of politicians as a class and the performance of particular leaders.

Shin (2006: 8–9) cuts the levels down to two and argues that we need to differentiate two broad categories: normative and practical. The normative or idealist level is concerned with democracy-in-principle as an abstract ideal, and refers largely to the psychologically loose attachment citizens have to the positive symbols of democracy. The practical or realist level is concerned with the various aspects of democracy-in-practice, referring to evaluations of the

98 *Renske Doorenspleet*

existing regime.[8] In my view, much confusion can be avoided by applying these distinctions.[9] In particular, Shin's distinction is very useful to tackle the main question of this chapter. The normative level largely reflects the idea of general support for democracy by the people, while the practical level can be captured by popular satisfaction with democracy.

So how do we find out what the levels of support and satisfaction are? Public opinion surveys are helpful sources of information to discover which norms, beliefs and opinion about political, social and economic developments prevail in a country. These studies of public opinion generate raw empirical data that is interesting for political scientists who try to evaluate people's opinion about the quality, stability and dilemmas of their recently democratized countries.

These periodic surveys, often called 'barometers', are nowadays being carried out in a growing number of countries. The analyses of this chapter will rely on the data from four different regional democracy barometers: the Afrobarometer, the East Asia Barometer, the New Europe Barometer, and the Latinobarometer. Despite some difficulties related to making comparisons using the different barometers, the barometers are rich sources of data about public opinion on the performance of regimes and the economy. For example, public opinion surveys have used several types of questions to assess the support for democracy. At the most abstract level, they have explored support for the idea of democracy in principle. Somewhat less abstract is the question, which all four regional barometers ask:

> With which of the following statements do you agree most? (1) Democracy is always preferable to any other kind of government. (2) Under certain situations, a dictatorship is preferable. (3) For people like me, it does not matter whether we have a democratic government or non-democratic government.

The respondents who rate democracy as always preferable to its undemocratic alternatives are considered to be supporters of the ideal of democracy. This question has often been used in order to measure people's support for the ideal of democracy. Satisfaction with democracy is usually measured by asking people: 'Generally, how satisfied are you with the way democracy is working in your country?' The answers to these questions give us – albeit often indirectly – insight into the democratic support and satisfaction of people living in new democracies.

The gap between support and satisfaction: research into the established democracies

Most analysts would argue that the success or failure of new democracies largely depends on the support by the citizens, which would lend legitimacy to the regime (see, for example, Klingemann 1999: 31). As a consequence, an

Public support vs dissatisfaction 99

extensive body of studies has focused on mapping, explaining and theorizing forms of political support over time and across countries. More particularly, scholars have focused on the levels of support for democracy, on the one hand, and satisfaction with how democracy is actually working, on the other.

The findings indicated that the satisfaction with democracy was quite low. This raises questions about the long-term health of democracy. Does it matter that people's satisfaction with democracy is low? For several decades, the dominant view among political scientists has been that it does matter. Starting in the 1960s, scholars emphasized that both support and satisfaction can be seen as indispensable elements for democratic systems. Only a high level of popular support can ensure that citizens accept and follow government policies; only a high level of popular support can guarantee the stability of the system (Almond and Verba 1963; Easton 1965). 'As money is to an economic system, so is political support to a political system. Support is the currency of democratic polities' (Rosenau 1974: 1; see also Easton 1975).

The view was that not only the lack of support, but also the lack of satisfaction and trust can easily weaken democratic institutions and lead to serious crises and breakdowns (Coleman 1965). According to Lipset, satisfaction is crucial: 'The capacity of the system to engender and maintain the belief that the existing political institutions are the most appropriate ones for the society' (Lipset 1981: 65). Since political criticism, institutional distrust and democratic dissatisfaction were widespread throughout the 1970s, several authors like Habermas (1973), for example, were very worried about the future of democracy, and predicted a legitimacy crisis for this type of regime. So, the dominant idea was that support and satisfaction bring stability, while lack of popular support and dissatisfaction lead to instability of the democratic system (see also Almond and Verba 1963). Weak support was associated with weak legitimacy and instability. As a consequence, people who were not happy with democracy in practice were seen as a threat to democracy, while supportive and satisfied citizens were considered to be 'good' for democracy.

Several writers predicted a 'crisis' of Western democracy (Habermas 1973; Crozier et al. 1975; Huntington 1981; see also Norris 1999a: 3–4). Although their ideological and theoretical approaches differed, their argument and diagnosis were similar: decreasing satisfaction and increasing demands of citizens lead to an overload of the state resulting in lower level of performance by the state. Habermas (1973), for instance, argued that the legitimation crisis could be explained by the fact that the governmental system was increasingly less successful in fulfilling the growing demands of citizens. One of the causes was lower economic growth; another, that the state has assumed an increasing number of functions. The same pattern was predicted for newer democracies in this period. O'Donnell, for example, argued that the process of democratization in Latin America produced rising public demands; these demands ultimately undermine economic development, weaken state management and issue in authoritarian rule (O'Donnell et al. 1986).

100   *Renske Doorenspleet*

In the 1990s, however, the dominant view started to change. The only evidence for the 'crisis' thesis was the cross-national decrease in attachment to political parties, but for the rest

> [There] is little evidence to support the various theories of crisis, contradiction and catastrophe. There are few signs of a general decline in trust, confidence in public institutions, political interest, or faith in democracy; nor is there much evidence of an increase in apathy, alienation, or faith in democracy.
>
> (Budge et al. 1997: 132)

Although people's satisfaction with democracy has always been rather low, the change in public opinion during the 1970s and 1980s in Europe was one of trendless fluctuations and certainly not a clear decline, so why worry (Norris 1999a: 5)? Moreover, the world-wide democratization wave after 1989 was hardly a sign of a crisis for democracy – quite the opposite (Huntington 1991). Democracy was not at risk.

In studies conducted in the 1990s, scholars found powerful and consistent evidence that support for democracy is high and stable over time. There are no major global trends suggesting that people are less supportive of the ideal of democracy (Klingemann 1999); popular commitment to democratic principles remained strong in (post)industrial democracies (Dalton 1999); more specifically there is no decline in satisfaction with democracy in Western Europe (Fuchs, Guidorossi and Svensson 1998). Fuchs and Klingemann (1998) showed that the citizens of West European countries have not withdrawn support from their democracies in recent decades, nor has their level of satisfaction decreased. 'For this reason alone, there can have been no challenge to the representative democracy of Western societies' (ibid.: 435).

High levels of support for democracy are still considered in the 1990s literature as important ingredients for consolidation of the new regime. The most widely accepted definitions of the consolidation of democracy connect it directly with legitimation, and hence people's support is seen as the essence of a regime's consolidation (see, for example, Linz and Stepan 1996; Diamond 1999; Bratton 2002). Thus, Linz and Stepan describe democratic consolidation as a process by which all political actors come to regard democracy as 'the only game in town' (Linz and Stepan 1996: 5). Diamond (1999) also argued that consolidation is indicated by acceptance by the overwhelming majority of citizens that democracy is the best form of government in principle and that it is the most suitable form of government for their country.[10] So, the ideas of democratic support and democratic consolidation are strongly linked in the literature. By supporting democracy, citizens give a democratic regime its political legitimacy.

Then again, scholars are now less alarmed by low levels of satisfaction, or, more significantly by a big gap between high support and low satisfaction. On the contrary, dissatisfied citizens are assumed to be 'critical citizens' (Norris

Public support vs dissatisfaction 101

1999a), who are no longer seen as a threat to democracy, but as a sign of a healthy democracy. Norris, who explicitly separates the dimensions of satisfaction and support and their respective impact, argues that 'We have seen the growth of more critical citizens, who value democracy as an ideal yet who remain dissatisfied with the performance of their political systems, and particularly the core institutions of representative government' (ibid.: 26). Moreover, just like Norris, Joseph Nye emphasized that we should not worry too much about declining confidence and satisfaction, because such critical citizens 'are good for democracy' (Nye 1997: vi). In addition, scholars like Klingemann argue that 'dissatisfied democrats can be viewed as a force for reform and improvement of democratic processes and structures' (Klingemann 1999: 32).

Ronald Inglehart also endorsed the claim that citizens are becoming more critical, and he offers an explanation. In *Modernization and Postmodernization* (1997), he argued that economic development, cultural change, and political change go together in coherent and, to some extent, predictable patterns. In times of economic crises or social change, people feel insecure and are likely to support authoritarian leaders. In more wealthy countries, though, people feel more secure, which ultimately 'reduces the tendency for mass publics to defer to authority' (ibid.: 8). In countries enjoying economic growth and development, people can 'afford' to change their materialist into 'post-materialist' values. Post-materialist people are more inclined to challenge leaders and have a more demanding standard for politics. These new post-materialist critical dissatisfied democrats can strengthen democracy. As Inglehart (ibid.: 9) states, 'The rise in postmodern values brings declining respect for authority and growing emphasis on participation and self-expression. These two trends are conducive to democratization ... But they are making the position of governing elites more difficult.' Inglehart strongly believes that postmodernization erodes respect for authority, but increases support for democracy (see also Inglehart 1999).

More recently, though, there seems to be a swing back again in the literature towards the more pessimistic view of the 1960s. Stoker (2006), for one, strongly disagrees with the view that dissatisfaction with democracy is just a reflection of rising citizen expectations and their willingness to be critical. He argues that the scale of discontent, disengagement and disenchantment from politics is such that the goals of democratic politics may be undermined by society's lack of faith in the system. Bratton and his co-authors while not seeing low satisfaction as necessarily a problem for the regime (Bratton et al. 2005: 81–4) still argue that satisfaction and support should be in balance (ibid.: 324–7). When levels of regime support and regime satisfaction vary too much and when the gap is too big, the consolidation of the regime is at stake.

In conclusion, there is still no consensus in the literature about whether democratic regimes need popular support and/or satisfaction. Moreover, there are a lot of hidden assumptions about the features of citizens living in a democratic state, and unresolved questions: for instance, what are the characteristics of a so-called 'dissatisfied democrat' (an individual who supports

102 *Renske Doorenspleet*

democracy but is not satisfied with this type of regime)? Up to the 1990s, scholars seem to assume that these people are critical and prepared to over-throw the democratic regime if necessary, and that they threaten the legiti-macy and stability of the democratic system. Scholars in the 1990s, in contrast, seemed to assume that dissatisfied democrats are critical citizens, with high levels of political knowledge and a lot of interest in politics, politi-cally active and well educated, prepared to defend the democratic values and keen to oppose the idea of strong leaders and authoritarian rule (for example, Inglehart 1997; Norris 1999a). Even more recent studies, however, assume that dissatisfied democrats are not confident or more assertive about politics, but simply more alienated and confused. Dissatisfied people living in democ-racies do not have enough knowledge about how politics is actually working, and their expectations about politics and the way democracy should work are 'hopelessly and spectacularly unrealistic' (Stoker 2006: 3).

A later section of this chapter will explore what the characteristics of dis-satisfied democrats actually are. Only by doing this can we determine which assumptions hold and what the profile of citizens living in a democratic state really is. Another contribution there will be to focus on the profile of citizens in new democracies, which has largely been an unexplored area till now.[11] But before investigating the characteristics of dissatisfied democrats, the next sec-tion looks at the levels of support for democracy and satisfaction in new as opposed to old democracies. Is the gap between support and satisfaction, which has always been so apparent in established democracies, found in newer democracies as well?

Empirical findings in new democracies

The general picture is not too gloomy. On the contrary. The empirical find-ings show that democracy rests in the hearts and minds of many people living in new democracies. Table 6.2 presents more detailed descriptive statistics based on data from four different regional democracy barometers: the Afro-barometer, the East Asia Barometer, the New Europe Barometer, and the Latinobarometer. The analyses show that intrinsic support of people in new democracies is quite high. On average, more than 64 per cent of the people living in new democracies support the general idea of democracy. In Benin, Thailand, Kenya and Senegal this percentage increases to around 80 per cent of the people. The highest is Senegal, where more than 87 per cent of respondents find democracy to be the best form of government and can be considered as supporters of democracy.

In general, not many people in new democracies defend the idea that a non-democratic government may be preferable. Just around 16 per cent agree that authoritarian government is better than any other form of government. So, although the evaluations of people from new democracies differ in this cross-national comparison, popular support for the ideal of democracy is generally quite high in new democracies.

Public support vs dissatisfaction 103

Table 6.2 Support for democracy in new democracies

Country (Year)	'Democracy is always preferable' (%)	'Sometimes authoritarianism is preferable' (%)	'It doesn't matter to people like me' (%)
Benin (2005)	82	7	11
Chile (1996)	57	20	24
Czech Republic (1992)	73	10	18
Guatemala (1996)	56	23	21
Hungary (1992)	72	8	20
Kenya (2005)	85	6	9
Lesotho (2000)	53	15	32
Madagascar (2005)	52	9	40
Malawi (1999)	67	22	11
Mali (2001)	61	16	23
Mexico (1996)	57	25	18
Mongolia (2001)	56	28	16
Mozambique (2002)	68	20	13
Namibia (1999)	71	14	15
Nicaragua (1996)	64	15	21
Panama (1996)	77	10	12
Paraguay (1996)	61	26	13
Poland (1992)	50	18	32
Senegal (2002)	87	5	8
Slovakia (1992)	66	11	24
South Africa (2000)	64	14	23
Taiwan (2001)	47	27	26
Thailand (2001)	84	11	5
Average in new democracies	66	16	19

Sources: Data are derived from the Afrobarometer (www.afrobarometer.org), Asian Barometer (www.asianbarometer.org), New Europe Barometer (www.abdn.ac.uk/cspp), and the Latinobarometer (www.latinobarometro.org).
Notes: The respondents who 'don't understand the question' and 'don't know' are treated as missing values. No answers to this question are available in the following new democracies: Bulgaria (1992), Croatia (1992), Lithuania (2001), Romania (1992), Slovenia (1992), and Ukraine (1992).

Hence, the findings seem to indicate that we should not be too pessimistic about the prospects of democracy in these countries. More and more countries have become democratic, more and more countries have achieved a relatively high level of political rights and civil liberties, and more and more new democracies are inhabited by a majority of people who fully support the ideal of democracy. However, the paradox of our present time is that, on the one hand, democracy is the dominant type of government in the world, while, on the other, there is considerable disenchantment with politics within the democracies. People like the idea of democracy and they support this type of regime, but they do not like the politics that go along with it. This paradox has been especially visible in the established democracies like the US (Nye

104 *Renske Doorenspleet*

1997: 1; Putnam 2000: 36–58), Britain (Stoker 2006: 33–5) and Western Europe generally (Schmitter and Treschel 2004), where trust, confidence and satisfaction with democratic government have declined and, probably related to this, voter turnouts have reduced. But the paradox is not confined to these democracies. On the basis of my own analyses of the available cross-national surveys, it is clear that satisfaction in new democracies is not very high either. On average, only half of the people living in new democracies are 'somewhat' or 'very' satisfied with democracy. This is significantly lower than the average of democratic support in new democracies, which stands at around 66 per cent (see Table 6.2). In other words, there is a large gap between support and satisfaction.

Of course, there are some important variations: in some countries, such as Mongolia, the Czech Republic and Thailand, satisfaction with democracy seems quite high. On the other hand, there are countries with a much lower satisfaction with democracy, such as Mexico, Madagascar and Lithuania. There are also regional differences. In Africa's new democracies, on average, 59 per cent of the people are satisfied with democracy – a figure higher than the world-wide average for new democracies but still leaving a noticeable gap between satisfaction and support (support for democracy being 10 percentage points higher than satisfaction). The fact that Africans support democracy while being dissatisfied with its achievements may be a sign that intrinsic support supersedes instrumental considerations (see, for example, Bratton and Mattes 2001). At the same time though, satisfaction with democracy is performance-driven in Africa. People's expectations about the economic future form an important explanatory factor. The higher the hope that democracy will deliver prosperity in the near future, the more likely are people are to be satisfied with their democratic regime of today (Bratton 2002). Well-educated people in particular remain sceptical that democracy will meet popular economic expectations; hence, education makes people harder to convince about the performance of democratic regimes (see ibid.: 12). Nevertheless, not only economic, but also political performance is important to explain satisfaction (see Bratton and Mattes 2001): if governments are not able to guarantee basic political rights, satisfaction with democracy will suffer.

In Latin America's new democracies, less than a quarter of the people are satisfied with democracy. Moreover, there is an extremely large gap between democratic support (which is quite high in Latin America) and satisfaction with democracy (which is very low). A United Nations Development Programme report (2005: 25) on democracy in Latin America also warns about this low level of satisfaction with democracy on the continent: 'The reality is that politics has major limitations and is in crisis. It lacks the capacity to address the problems to which citizens demand answers.' People in Latin America are simply not satisfied with how democracy is working.

While previous studies clearly showed that there is a gap between satisfaction and support in established democracies, then, the findings in this section indicate that the same pattern is visible in new democracies. There are a lot of dissatisfied democrats living in new democracies. However, it is not

Public support vs dissatisfaction 105

completely clear what the characteristics of these citizens are and whether they form a challenge for democracy or not.

Dissatisfied democrats: a challenge for new democracies?

So, who are the dissatisfied democrats in new democracies? Can they be seen as critical or confused citizens? Are they a protection for or a threat to democracy? In this section, three different new democracies will be compared from three different continents, to offer a representative picture of the profile of dissatisfied democrats.

Panama

Panama's history has been characterized by periods of political instability, frequent coups and rivalries among ruling families. From 1969 till 1989, Panama endured bouts of military dictatorship. On 20 December 1989, US forces invaded Panama in order to remove its former leader, General Manuel Noriega. A few hours before the invasion, Guillermo Endara was sworn in as the President of Panama during a ceremony that took place inside an American military base. Constitutional amendments passed in 1991 formally abolished the armed forces. The current constitution provides broad powers for the legislature with a lot of power for the president as well, who is both head of state and head of government, and created a multi-party system. Since the beginning of the 1990s, Panama can be classified as a democracy with a high level of competition, inclusiveness and freedom.

Analyses drawing on the Latinobarometer show that a vast majority of Panama's citizens support the ideal of democracy (more than 77 per cent), but many of them are not satisfied with the way democracy is working. Around 55 per cent of all citizens in Panama are so-called 'dissatisfied democrats' (people who support democracy but are not satisfied), which may form a challenge for this relatively new democracy. So, who are those dissatisfied democrats? And are they critical citizens?[12]

My own analyses show that they are not more critical and not more involved in politics than the rest of the population. This conclusion is based on ANOVA analyses. ANOVA is a general technique that can be used to test the hypothesis that the mean figures among two or more groups are equal, under the assumption that the sampled populations are normally distributed. To be more specific, this study uses the ANOVA technique to test for differences among four groups, namely the satisfied and dissatisfied democrats, and the satisfied and dissatisfied non-democrats. ANOVA analyses reveal that there are no statistically significant differences between the four groups on questions related to being interested in politics (F (obs.) = 2.4, $p > 0.05$), how often they follow the political news (F (obs.) = 2.6, $p > 0.05$), how often they talk about politics with friends (F (obs.) = 1.9, $p > 0.05$), and the desire to influence others of their own political opinion (F (obs.) = 2.2, $p > 0.05$). Table 6.3 presents the headline figures.

106 Renske Doorenspleet

Table 6.3 Cross-tabulation of support for democracy and satisfaction with democracy in Panama

Support for democracy	Satisfaction with democracy	
	No (%)	Yes (%)
no	16.8 (dissatisfied nondemocrats)	5.6 (satisfied nondemocrats)
yes	55.0 (dissatisfied democrats)	22.6 (satisfied democrats)

Benin

While dissatisfied democrats in Panama do not differ from the three other groups (satisfied democrats, dissatisfied and satisfied nondemocrats), the situation in Benin potentially looks different. French colonial rule in Benin ended in 1960. After several coups and countercoups, Mathieu Kérékou was brought to power in a 1972 military coup. He imposed a one-party state and followed Marxist-Leninist policies. After 1989, however, economic paved the way for multiparty elections. In 1991, President Kérékou lost the country's first democratic election and he handed power to Nicéphore Soglo. Since that time, Benin has been an inspiration of democracy and stability in Africa; protection of human rights has improved as well (Gisselquist 2008; see also Freedom House data).

Analyses drawing on the Afrobarometer show that a vast majority of Benin's citizens support the ideal of democracy (more than 8 out of 10 people), but – again – many of them are not satisfied with the way democracy is working. More than 30 per cent of all citizens in Benin can be classified as 'dissatisfied democrats'. However, research into whether they are more critical, or have other beliefs and attitudes that differ from the rest of the population, has yet to be done.

My own ANOVA analyses indicate – once more, just as in Panama – that dissatisfied citizens in Benin are not more critical or involved than the rest of the population. There are no statistically significant differences between the four groups on questions related to being interested in public affairs (F (obs.) = 1.1 $p > 0.05$), how often they discuss politics (F (obs.) = 2.2, $p > 0.05$), and the belief that politics and government are too complicated for them (F (obs.) = 0.8, $p > 0.05$). Table 6.4 presents the headline figures.

Although dissatisfied democrats are not really more interested or involved in politics in Benin, they do differ from the rest of the population since overall they are less prepared to obey the law and more inclined to support strong leaders. For example, there are statistically significant differences between the four groups in their belief that parliament or the president should make the laws (F (obs.) = 9.0, $p < 0.01$), that the president should be free to act or obey the laws and courts (F (obs.) = 7.6, $p < 0.01$), in their statements that they will only obey the government if they voted for it (F (obs.) = 4.0, $p < 0.01$), in their preference of immediate solutions to problems instead of following the

Public support vs dissatisfaction 107

Table 6.4 Cross-tabulation of support for democracy and satisfaction with democracy in Benin

Support for democracy	Satisfaction with democracy	
	No (%)	Yes (%)
no	11.5	4.1
	(dissatisfied nondemocrats)	(satisfied nondemocrats)
yes	30.5	53.9
	(dissatisfied democrats)	(satisfied democrats)

law (F (obs.) = 5.8, p < 0.01), in their belief that the constitution expresses values and hopes (F (obs.) = 5.0, p < 0.01), in their belief that courts should make binding decisions (F (obs.) = 9.6, p < 0.01), and in their opinion that people must pay taxes (F (obs.) = 22.5, p < 0.01).

The ANOVA analyses simply indicate there are differences between two or more group means; however, they do not tell us between which groups precisely the significant differences occurred. To find this out, a post hoc test must be done. The Tukey Test is a post hoc test designed to perform a pairwise comparison of the means to see where the significant difference is. It involves calculating a minimum difference between pairs of group means that must be exceeded for the group means to be significantly different.

Based on analyses of surveys done in Benin, Tukey tests reveal indeed that dissatisfied democrats differ from the other groups with regard to belief in the law and support for strong leadership. Compared to the satisfied democrats, dissatisfied democrats express significantly more support for the statement that the president – instead of the parliament – should make the laws. They also support the statement that the president should have freedom of action instead of following the laws and courts, which is in stark contrast to the opinion of satisfied democrats. While satisfied democrats prefer lawful solutions to problems, the dissatisfied democrats want immediate action and solutions. Compared to satisfied democrats, dissatisfied democrats also are more inclined to think that people must not pay taxes.

It is interesting to notice that dissatisfied democrats do not differ from satisfied democrats in their willingness to choose leaders through elections, while the rest of the population, namely the non-democrats, clearly prefer to abandon the idea of elections and to use 'other methods'. In addition, dissatisfied democrats do not want to try another form than democracy, but they think it is time to deal with the problems. Again, this is the same view as satisfied democrats have, while the non-democrats think it is time to search for a completely different form of regime.

In other words, dissatisfied democrats are widespread in Benin (with more than 30 per cent of the population), but they cannot really be seen as critical citizens. They do not significantly differ from the rest of the population with regard to their interest in and involvement with politics. On the one hand,

108   *Renske Doorenspleet*

they do not seem to form a threat to democracy in Benin. Together with the satisfied democrats, they are not inclined to support another form of regime for their country. Moreover, they seem to prefer elections above other methods of (s)election of leaders in their country. On the other hand, dissatisfied democrats might be a challenge for democracy after all, albeit in a less direct and more gradual way. They seem to support democracy, but a different and alternative form of democracy than the existing one; they want a democratic system with a strong president, in which immediate – but not necessarily lawful – solutions to problems are offered, and with less power for the rule of law, the courts and parliament. Dissatisfied democrats do not want a completely new authoritarian regime, but seem to desire an alternative form of democratic governance. They seem to want less instead of more democracy within the existing democratic regime, and more instead of less immediate action to solve the current problems of their new democracy.

Hungary

In the late 1980s, Hungary's economy was in sharp decline, and the Hungarian Socialist Workers Party came under intense pressure to accept reforms. Ultimately, the party congress dissolved itself, and Hungary held its first free, multiparty parliamentary election in 1990. Subsequently, voters have elected representatives to the 386-seat unicameral National Assembly under a mixed system of proportional and direct representation, while the Hungarian parliament elects both the president and the prime minister. Parliamentary elections are held every four years, and Hungary is now consistently classified as a liberal democracy.

Analyses on the basis of the New Democracies Barometer show that the vast majority of Hungary's citizens support the ideal of democracy (almost three-quarters of the people). Nevertheless, again, many are not satisfied with the way democracy is working. More than a quarter of all citizens in Hungary can be classified as 'dissatisfied democrats'.

Hungary is slightly different from the other two new democracies in that there are differences in political interest and involvement between the four groups of citizens. For example, there are statistically significant differences between the four groups in their level of interest in politics (F (obs.) = 15.3, $p < 0.01$), in their belief that people influence government (F (obs.) = 6.1, $p < 0.01$), and in their belief that people understand politics (F (obs.) = 8.5, $p < 0.01$). Post-hoc tests reveal that there are statistically significant differences between satisfied and dissatisfied democrats. Satisfied and dissatisfied democrats are generally more interested in politics than the citizens who do not support democracy. Unlike satisfied democrats, dissatisfied democrats generally belief that people can influence government. This finding is interesting because it suggests that dissatisfied democrats are not disillusioned at all and still think politics can be influenced, despite the fact that they are not satisfied with the way democracy is working in their country. Table 6.5 presents the headline figures.

Public support vs dissatisfaction 109

Table 6.5 Cross-tabulation of support for democracy and satisfaction with democracy in Hungary

Support for democracy	Satisfaction with democracy	
	No (%)	Yes (%)
no	14.5 (dissatisfied nondemocrats)	14 (satisfied nondemocrats)
yes	26.8 (dissatisfied democrats)	44.6 (satisfied democrats)

Hence, dissatisfied democrats in Hungary seem to be critical citizens indeed, which differs from the cases of Panama and Benin. Moreover, drawing on analyses of surveys done in Hungary, Tukey tests reveal that dissatisfied democrats differ from the other groups with regard to belief in the law and support for strong leadership. For example, compared to the satisfied democrats, dissatisfied democrats show significantly more support for the statement that unfair laws may not be obeyed, and that strong leaders are better than parliament.

In other words, dissatisfied democrats are widespread in Hungary (almost 27 per cent of the population), and they can be seen as critical citizens with a lot of interest in politics and the optimistic belief that people can influence politics. In contrast to satisfied democrats, however, they prefer strong leaders above parliamentary rule and think the law may sometimes be disobeyed.

Findings compared and future research

The three case studies have shown that support for democracy is high and widespread. At the same time satisfaction with democracy is much lower than democratic support in these new democracies. Still, three important differences among the cases must be emphasized.

First, the number of dissatisfied citizens varies across countries. While there are around 55 per cent dissatisfied democrats in Panama, the percentage is much lower in Benin (around 30 per cent) and Hungary (almost 27 per cent).

Second, dissatisfied citizens are not necessarily critical citizens. The profile of dissatisfied democrats is dependent on the country. In Hungary, they seem to be critical indeed, with a high level of interest and involvement in politics. However, in Benin and Panama, dissatisfied citizens are not more critical or involved than the rest of the population.

Third, whether dissatisfied democrats may pose a challenge for democracy is context-specific and strongly dependent on the specific country. Are dissatisfied democrats more extreme in their beliefs compared to the rest of the population, and can we expect them to rise up against the new democratic regime and seek alternatives? The surveys in the new democracies seem to show that dissatisfied democrats differ from the other groups: in both Benin

110   *Renske Doorenspleet*

and Hungary they appear to want a democratic system with a strong president, where immediate but not necessarily lawful solutions to problems are offered. In addition, they demand less power for law, courts and parliament. However, they do not prefer an alternative to democracy, but more probably a different form of democracy. As the characteristics of dissatisfied democrats vary across new democracies, so the consequences for the regime will probably differ too.

These findings lead us to other questions which future research should address. First, the issue whether dissatisfied democrats are more common in specific groups within the country is relevant but goes beyond what the available data can tell us. The analyses in this chapter suggest that dissatisfied democrats do not necessarily strive to adopt competing ideologies to democracy, but more an alternative adjusted form within the democracy itself. However, we do not know whether there are crucial differences between different (ethnic, social, or religious) groups in new democracies. Such knowledge is important, since in divided societies the picture could be quite complex: when some dissatisfied but easily organized ethnic, social or religious groups do embrace a competing ideology to democracy (authoritarian rule, say) and yet the great majority of people strongly support the existing democracy, or want an alternative adjusted type of democracy, then collective action problems might occur. The greater capacity of the former group to mobilize could constitute more of a threat to democracy than the latter. Future research should divide the dissatisfied democrats into different groups to see whether there are differences. In-depth case studies discovering what people really want, how they envisage the alternative form, and why, would be complementary.

Second, it is likely that there are not only differences among new democracies as illustrated in this chapter, but also that there are differences between new democracies, on the one hand, and established democracies, on the other. The new democracies are mostly poor or developing, while the established democracies are richer and more developed, making these two groups probably non-comparable to a large extent. Most of the existing literature on dissatisfied democrats is on the post-materialist democracies (see Norris 1999a; Inglehart 1997), while knowledge on this topic in poorer new democracies is scanty. Completely different processes and mechanisms might be at work here. In rich countries, dissatisfaction could reflect a different attitude from dissatisfaction in the poorer democracies, where it might be a sign of dissatisfaction with worsening circumstances such as lack of personal security, as well as poor material conditions or gross social and economic inequality. On the other hand, in a globalizing world, all governments – irrespective of the type of regime – may face increasing difficulty in meeting popular aspirations, resulting in a lowering of satisfaction everywhere. While this might be true, it could be argued that dissatisfaction poses more of a threat to new democracies where democracy is more vulnerable and where there is not (yet) a strong democratic political culture – both at the elite and mass level. In any

Public support vs dissatisfaction 111

case, it would be useful to differentiate among categories of countries (new versus old democracies; rich versus poor) where the different interpretations should be applied.

Third, more research is needed to 'unpack' the concepts of both support for democracy and people's satisfaction with how these regimes are working in practice. A preliminary issue here is that we need to know more about what people mean by democracy and hence what they are actually supporting. While the Afrobarometer includes questions like 'what, if anything, does "democracy" mean to you?', comparable open-ended questions are unfortunately absent from the other barometers: they should be introduced there, to enable more insight into this issue and more comprehensive cross-regional comparisons. A different research issue meriting closer attention is development of a better understanding of the concept and measurement of dissatisfaction. Dissatisfaction can be a function of people's disappointment because of unfulfilled expectations. Expectations in new democracies are likely to be very dynamic: probably people start from a very low base of satisfaction with previous regimes (see, for instance, Bratton et al. 2005: 82), while satisfaction is high just after the transition phase and then declines as people learn more about the actual performance of democratic governments. We also need to know where the expectations are coming from. Some scholars have challenged the theoretical validity of the concept of satisfaction (see Rose et al. 1998: 149), because it is uncertain whether respondents are dissatisfied with the political regime, the institutions or the government performance. However, there is clear recent evidence that people generally refer to government performance, at least in Africa (see Bratton et al. 2005: 83–4); thus, when people are not satisfied, they are not content with how the government is managing job creation, inflation, education, health care and crime control. Still, more research has to be done to understand people's dissatisfaction. A final issue is that we need to think more about what matters most: a (low) level of satisfaction, or the gap between satisfaction and support. The literature suggests that although low satisfaction is not necessarily a problem for the regime, the consolidation of democracy will be put at risk when the gap between support and satisfaction is too large (ibid.: 320–7). This chapter has followed this dominant view, but it would be interesting for future studies to investigate whether low satisfaction can also pose a challenge for democracy, and to what extent.

Finally, there may well be a role for agency here. What can political leaders do to manage people's dissatisfaction? Contributors to the literature on established democracies argue that democracies are certainly able to react adequately to the problems they face (Fuchs and Klingemann 1998; Norris 1999a; Norris 1999b), for example, by restructuring the political institutions into either more consensual or more majoritarian ones. In consensus democracies that have, among other things, proportional electoral systems and many political parties, people feel better represented and they are more satisfied with democracy than people living in more majoritarian democracies

112 *Renske Doorenspleet*

(Lijphart 1999). It is, however, questionable whether institutional reform is the best solution and would really work everywhere; certainly in the context of new democracies, improving the actual performance of the democratic governments could well be more effective. Politicians should probably work on enhancing performance, such as controlling crime, reducing unemployment and inflation, improving education and health care (see Bratton et al. 2005: 83–5). Success here will not only improve their own image, but also increase people's satisfaction with the democratic system, especially because satisfaction with democracy and government performance appear to be strongly related (ibid.: 83–4). The problem is of course that often there is no clear incentive structure for all the politicians to be concerned about increasing the level of satisfaction in society. If politicians take advantage of the same dissatisfaction to get elected against their rivals, there will be hardly any incentive to see dissatisfaction eliminated.

To sum up, the case studies in this section have shown that, on the one hand, the support for democracy is widespread, but that, on the other, there is a considerable gap between support and satisfaction. Moreover, dissatisfied citizens are not necessarily critical citizens; their characteristics vary across countries. In addition, the question whether dissatisfied democrats may pose a challenge for democracy is country-specific as well. However, we simply do not have enough knowledge about the views of people, the role they (can) play in new democracies, and what has been called the 'inside challenge' for democracy.

Conclusion

Is the wave of democratization now in retreat, or just treading water? This chapter showed that the recent world-wide waves of democratization have been impressive, and that a significant number of authoritarian regimes have made a transition to democracy. Not only towards a 'minimal' type of democracy, but in the majority of cases also towards an increasingly more advanced form of 'liberal' democracy. So, in this sense we should indeed be careful not to exaggerate the importance of recent setbacks.

This does not mean, however, that the future of democracy looks only bright and hopeful. Democratic regimes face an important challenge nowadays. A paradox of our present time is that, on the one hand, quantitatively speaking, democracy is the dominant type of government around the world, and there is substantial popular support for the ideal of democracy, while, on the other, there is considerable dissatisfaction with democracy within democracies, the new democracies included. People like the idea of democracy and they support this type of regime, but in general their satisfaction with democracy is much lower.

What does this mean for the legitimacy of a new democratic regime? This chapter tried to unwrap the specific characteristics of dissatisfied citizens but no general pattern can be detected. The characteristics of dissatisfied citizens

Public support vs dissatisfaction   113

are largely dependent on the specific country. In some countries, such as Hungary, they are critical citizens and seem to confirm the optimistic ideas of political scientists in the 1990s. In other countries, such as Benin and Panama, dissatisfied democrats are not more interested in politics than the rest of the population and are not necessarily 'critical citizens'. Moreover, dissatisfied democrats can have different values which may pose a danger for the new democracy. For example, dissatisfied democrats in Benin do not agree that people must obey the law. They will only obey the government if they voted for it, and prefer immediate solutions to problems instead of following the law. In Hungary, the same pattern can be detected: dissatisfied democrats prefer strong leaders and immediate but not necessarily lawful solutions to the current problems in their lives. In other words, the empirical findings do not support the idea that dissatisfied democrats are always 'good' for the new democratic regimes; on the contrary, they may form a risk for its consolidation and they are not automatically a helpful resource for democracy.

Hence, while democracy is still the dominant type of regime in the world, the main challenge for democracies probably does not come from enemies outside the nations. Instead the main challenge comes from democracy's own citizens (see also Dalton 2004: 1), who support the ideal of democracy but have grown dissatisfied with how democracy is working in practice. Low satisfaction could be problematic for the legitimacy of new democratic regime. There is a gap between principle and practice. To deal with this gap is increasingly important, especially if there is a decline in freedom around the world in the near future. Dissatisfied democrats are not always critical citizens, nor are they necessarily a 'safe source' for democracy.

However, it is important to emphasize that there are fundamental cross-national variations that must not be overlooked. These findings are important: a one-size-fits-all-story does not look appropriate. Moreover, dissatisfied democrats are not necessarily critical citizens, but they often want instant solutions and strong leaders. They seem to have high expectations about what the new democratic regime can do for them and their country, preferably in a firm and rapid way. The expectations and beliefs that people have about democracy and the extent to which those expectations are met could have profound political consequences. If expectations are frustrated, the legitimacy of the young regime may be in jeopardy, resulting in a weaker democracy that then erodes or is undermined even to the point of breakdown and collapse, or alternatively gradual replacement by a more authoritarian form of rule. Therefore, satisfying people's expectations will be a challenge for many new democracies in the near future.

Notes

1 See Doorenspleet (2000). Dahl (1971) emphasizes there is no country in which democracy's defining conditions are perfectly met; he proffers the term 'polyarchy' for systems where the conditions are sufficiently met, and uses the term 'democracy' for the ideal type.

114 *Renske Doorenspleet*

2 Conceptualizations of minimal democracy, especially those in the field of quantitative research on democracy and democratization have been strongly influenced by Dahl (1971).

3 Despite the recent global resurgence of 'minimal' democracies, this does not means endorsing the thesis of an 'end of history' associated with Fukuyama (1992).

4 These minimal democracies have often been defined as electoral democracies or alternatively illiberal democracies, see Diamond (1999); Zakaria (1997).

5 Moreover, Zakaria claims that regimes which introduced constitutional liberties prior to political rights of inclusive participation during elections are more likely to consolidate their liberal democratic system. In the past, this path was often followed by European states, especially during the 'First Wave'. First freedom, then participation – that is seen as the best path for stability. In contrast, regimes in which liberties and competition were introduced only after the political rights of participation are less likely to become stable democracies. First, participation, then freedom – this is seen as a risky route to be taken: 'Constitutional liberalism has led to democracy, but democracy does not seem to bring constitutional liberalism' (Zakaria 1997: 28).

6 The number of Free countries did not change from the previous year's survey. The number of Partly Free countries increased by two from the previous year. Not Free countries declined by two from 2006. The number of people living under Not Free conditions stood at 36 per cent of the world population, with half of this number belonging to just one country: China.

7 See data from Freedom House 2008 (www.freedomhouse.org) and the Polity Project 2008 (www.systemicpeace.org/polity/polity4.htm). More importantly, reverse trends or interruptions have been detected recently in several politically important countries such as Russia, Kenya, Egypt, Nigeria, and Venezuela, where sustained democratic declines could have broader regional if not global consequences.

8 This distinction is somewhat but not fully comparable with the widely used distinction between intrinsic and instrumental support for democracy. Intrinsic support means that people value democracy as an end in itself, while instrumental supporters see democracy as a means to other ends, such as improvements in living standards and reduction in poverty.

9 Factor analysis suggests that people make these distinctions, and there are divergent trends over time in support for different levels (see Dalton 1999; Klingemann 1999). Norris (1999a: 13) argues that:

> One reason for the confusion in the literature between those who see a pattern of declining confidence in established democracies and others who see only trendless fluctuations is the reliance on different indicators relating to different levels of support. It is rational and consistent, for example, for citizens to believe in democratic values but to remain critical about the way democratic governments actually work in practice, or to have confidence in political institutions but no faith in politicians, or to disparage most politicians but to continue to support a particular leader, or to trust each other but not elected officials.' It is important to make these distinctions clear.

10 Diamond (1999) suggests that the concept of democratic consolidation can be measured along two dimensions – beliefs and behaviour – and on at least three levels. At the higher level are the country's elites, the top decision-makers and political activists. For Diamond, a democracy may be considered to be consolidated if the elites accept the legitimacy of democracy, and if they respect each other's right to compete peacefully for power, and obey the democratic laws and mutually accepted norms of political conduct. At the intermediate level, a regime is democratically consolidated if all politically significant parties, interest groups and

Public support vs dissatisfaction   115

social movements endorse the legitimacy of democracy and of the country's specific constitutional rules and institutions. At the lower level, the level of the mass public, consolidation is indicated by acceptance of the overwhelming majority of citizens that democracy is the best form of government in principle and that it is the most suitable form of government for their country. In other words, democracy is consolidated when citizens and leaders alike conclude that no alternative form of regime has any greater subjective validity or stronger objective claim to their allegiance.

11 Some important exceptions are, on Africa's new democracies, the work of Michael Bratton; on post-communist new democracies, for example, Hofferbert and Klingemann (1999); on new democracies in Central and Eastern Europe, Mishler and Rose (1999); on South Korea, Rose, Shin and Munro (1999).

12 Unfortunately, the concept of 'critical citizens' has not been defined well or measured in previous studies (such as Norris 1999a, for instance). In this chapter, the concept is measured by a bundle of different questions like whether people are interested in politics, whether they follow the political news and how often, whether they talk about politics with friends and how often, whether they want to influence others of their own opinion or not, and whether they feel powerless or not (i.e. belief that politics and government are too complicated for them). These are only proxies; more precise concept formation and operationalization of this term require more attention in the future.

7 External sources and consequences of Russia's "sovereign democracy"

Michael McFaul[1] and Regine A. Spector

For nearly a half century, ideological struggle between the United States and the Soviet Union shaped international politics. The two countries adhered to antithetical visions about how domestic polities and economies should be organized. Soviet leader Mikhail Gorbachev ended this ideological competition by renouncing class struggle as the defining element of international politics and instead proposing a new Soviet commitment to "universal human values" as the cornerstone of a new world order (Gorbachev 1987). Soviet withdrawals from Angola, Afghanistan, and eventually even Eastern Europe demonstrated Gorbachev's resolve to create a new basis of relations between the East and West (Mendelson 1993). Gorbachev's move towards Western economic and political practices led to the end of the Cold War.

Russian President Boris Yeltsin embraced democracy and markets, first as an "ideology of opposition" while challenging Gorbachev and Soviet power, and after the collapse of the Soviet Union, as a blueprint for revolutionary transformation inside Russia. Implementation of these ideas produced mixed results, but few in the early 1990s questioned Yeltsin's ideological commitment to a Western model of democracy and capitalism. In turn, Soviet and then Russian foreign policy changed from a commitment to ideological struggle and power balancing against the West and the United States to a doctrine of integration into Western institutions and an embrace (however shallow) of Western norms and ideas, including democracy. Yeltsin sought to join Western multilateral institutions such as the G-7, the World Trade Organization, the European Union and even the North Atlantic Treaty Organization (NATO).

Almost two decades after the collapse of the Soviet Union, integration has stalled (Kagan 2008). During the 1990s, the Russian public's disappointment with the results of democracy and Western integration created opportunities for political leaders with anti-democratic orientations. The most militant of these ideological entrepreneurs—fascists and neo-communists—never assumed control of the state, nor did those firmly committed to democracy and Western integration. In this ideological vacuum arose Vladimir Putin and his allies in 2000, promoting a vision for Russia and its role in the world they called first "managed" then "sovereign democracy." Under Putin's leadership,

Russia's democratic institutions and practices, which were already weak, have significantly eroded. And integration with the West is no longer the central goal of Russian foreign policy.

Some explain Putin's new foreign course as a return to Russia's natural place in the world—a great power seeking to balance against the other great powers in the international system. Without question, part of Russian behaviour can be explained in these classic realist terms, especially during the past several years when President Bush's foreign policies have eroded America's prestige in many countries around the world.

However, a closer look at Russian international behavior reveals that President Putin has not limited his policies to traditional spheres of military buildup internally or alliances with other countries to seeking to counter American power. A subtle ideological dimension has reemerged, designed and implemented by Russian elite. Under the slogans of managed democracy and sovereign democracy, Putin has championed a non-Western form of government inside Russia and begun to develop a strategy for exporting this model in its near abroad. In addition, Russia has adopted a more assertive foreign policy in the rest of the world, seeking legitimacy and equality in global affairs. Windfall revenues from energy exports up to 2008 have transformed Putin's exercise of Russian international influence from an idea pushed by a few consultants close to the Kremlin into a major component of Russian foreign policy.

This chapter first traces the origins of the Russian domestic political trajectory, focusing on the influence of electoral revolutions in neighboring states. Second, we show how perceptions of Western involvement in electoral changes in these countries emboldened the Russian leadership to further erode democratic institutions within Russia in the name of promoting a "sovereign democracy." Third, we argue that this shift within Russia has had significant implications for Russian foreign policy both in countries neighboring Russia and in the world more broadly. Finally, we conclude with implications for international relations and global order.

Russian reactions to and involvement in the colored revolutions

The collapse of communism in Europe and the Soviet Union did not lead smoothly to the consolidation of democracy throughout the region. Nearly 20 years since the fall of the Berlin Wall in 1989, some countries in the region are liberal democracies, others are consolidated autocracies, and some fall somewhere in between (for explanations of this variation, see McFaul 2002; Hale 2005; Darden and Grzymala-Busse 2006).

The leaders in a group of "in-between" countries, beginning in Serbia in 2000, followed by Georgia in 2003, and Ukraine in 2004, rigged presidential and parliamentary elections, which prompted prolonged protests in capital squares leading eventually to changes in power (McFaul 2005; Bunce and Wolchik 2006a). Multiple factors caused these revolutions (see McFaul 2005).

118   *Michael McFaul and Regine A. Spector*

Civil society organizations such as youth groups (Bunce and Wolchik 2006b; Demes and Forbrig 2006), private media outlets, and independent election monitoring organizations[2] exerted pressure on the ruling regime (Ackerman and Duvall 2005). State organs that supported the incumbent regime, such as police and security services, disobeyed orders to disrupt crowds and ultimately sided with the opposition (Bennendijk and Marovic 2006; Way and Levitsky 2006). Elite political and business figures perceived the incumbents to be weak, ultimately uniting in their opposition to the regime (see Hale 2005, 2006).

While Western scholarship focuses on domestic drivers of these revolutions, Russian analysts and propagandists locate the origins outside Russia: the purported threat lay in organizations that implemented agendas of foreign countries (such as the United States) through the promotion of democratic institutions. Scholars and analysts generally agree that Western governments, non-governmental organizations, and foundations played a role in these revolutions, albeit one that facilitated and conditioned the events, not necessarily causing them.[3] Western influence targeted the sharing of knowledge among activists about how to lead strategic non-violent resistance movements, the funding of parallel vote counts and exit polls to expose fraud, and the promotion of alternative media outlets to facilitate the spread of knowledge and communication (Bunce and Wolchik 2006c; Beissinger 2007). Without knowledge and financial resources, the opposition could not have induced change. Yet these resources alone could not have caused the revolutions; a whole host of other conditions were necessary (Bunce and Wolchik 2006a).

Russian officials, however, clearly assigned a more direct role to Western powers in inspiring and aiding these revolutions. During the Serbian revolution in 2000, the year Putin became President, he found himself in the midst of an internal Russian debate about whether to recognize the results of the Serbian presidential election, in which the opposition candidate Kostunica declared himself winner of over 50 per cent of the votes. While Western policy was united in support of Kostunica, the Russian position was mixed. On the one hand, Russian Foreign Minister Igor Ivanov and others such as Russian nationalist Vladimir Zhirinovsky and Communist Party MP Gennadiy Zeleznev saw no serious voting irregularities and clearly supported incumbent Milošević (Lennard 2000a, 2000b, 2000c).[4] Most Russian officials had vehemently opposed the bombing campaign by NATO forces against the Milošević regime in Kosovo in 1999 and some, therefore, saw the 2000 events as a continuation of American interference in Serbia's domestic affairs (Heintz 2000; Goldier and McFaul 2003: Chapter 9). In part, they were right (Carothers 2007a).

This perspective contrasted with a position that was put forth gingerly by President Putin and supported by MP Vladimir Lukin and Yabloko leader Grigoriy Yavlinsky. Soon after the election, Russian President Vladimir Putin (via German Chancellor Gerhard Schroeder) indicated his possible acceptance of a Kostunica victory, and offered to help to resolve the election crisis by hosting both candidates (Milošević and Kostunica) in Moscow for discussions (Lagnado and Evans 2000).

Russia's "sovereign democracy" 119

Putin's strategy prevailed. By 2 October 2000, Russia conceded that Kostunica had won the election in the first round; the international media touted this as a "major change in Russia's position" (Harris and Vinci 2000). The Russian media conveyed a sense of disappointment with the whole ordeal, criticizing the inconsistent response and lamenting Russia's "danger of losing the remains of its authority" (York 2000).

Putin articulated a much more critical response to the Rose Revolution in Georgia in the fall of 2003.[5] In the aftermath of the November parliamentary election, opposition groups in conjunction with international observers such as the Organization for Security and Cooperation in Europe called the election a failure, rigged in favor of the pro-Presidential "For a New Georgia" party. As leader of the opposition, Mikhail Saakashvili claimed victory over then President Eduard Shevardnadze.

Russia's role appeared distanced—although not disinterested. The Russian Duma elections were just a few weeks away in December 2003, and the Russian political elite kept a close eye on events in Georgia. Russian President Vladamir Putin announced his support for Shevardnadze over pro-Western Saakashvili, despite the tense relations that Russia and Georgia experienced throughout the 1990s as Georgia's foreign policy lurched clearly towards the West.[6] Members of the Russian elite condemned the use of public protest as a means of political change in the country, keenly aware of a return to civil war and street violence Georgia experienced in the early 1990s (Interfax 2003). They also explicitly implicated foreign influence, in particular the US, in the conflict (Volkova 2003a, 2003b).

After almost three weeks of protests, Shevardnadze resigned after intense diplomatic go-betweens with all sides involved. Saakashvili's political entrance shocked Russian leaders, both because of the manner in which he seized power and because of the adulation he received from the West. The election was likely fraudulent, but Saakashvili's method of replacing Shevardnadze was also undemocratic; the West focused on the former and not the latter. For Russian leaders, the political ascent of US-educated and pro-Western Saakashvili symbolized a loss of influence over what Russia considers a vital strategic neighboring country (Karumidze and Wertsch 2005).

The 2004 elections in Ukraine aroused even greater fear within the Russian elite about American intentions and activities. During and immediately after the 2003 Georgian Rose Revolution, newspapers were abuzz about the potential "spread" of this revolutionary wave to Ukraine, the next regional country to hold an election. As with Serbia and Georgia, Russian interests in preserving the incumbent leader dominated the country's foreign policy goals in Ukraine. President Kuchma aspired to construct a system of "managed democracy"—formal democratic practices, but informal control of all political institutions—similar to Putin's in Russia.[7] Putin wanted the model to succeed and had aided Kuchma in the years before the 2004 Ukrainian presidential election by providing subsidized gas. Ukraine's geographical proximity and significant Russian-speaking population facilitated the flow of ideas

120 *Michael McFaul and Regine A. Spector*

and resources about Russia's regime alternative to the Western model of democracy.

Russian public relations companies had worked in many post-Soviet countries since the 1990s, however, a variety of people and organizations—including members of the Russian presidential administration—were particularly active in the 2004 Ukrainian elections supporting incumbent Viktor Yanukovich (Wilson 2005; Petrov and Ryabov 2006).[8] In 2004, Russian PR professionals created the "the Russian House" in Kyiv which organized public events to emphasize Russia's positive and pivotal role for Ukrainian economy and security. To help Yanukovych, Putin personally traveled twice to Ukraine in the fall of 2004. Russian state-controlled television channels with wide coverage inside Ukraine portrayed Yushchenko as an American puppet and Yanukovych as patriot. At the urging of the Kremlin, Russian businesspeople contributed to Yanukovych's campaign.[9]

While a Russian-sponsored election-monitoring group observed the Ukrainian vote and declared the first and second rounds free and fair, mass protests erupted after the second round of the election. Putin tried to strengthen Ukraine's "managed democracy" by quickly acknowledging Yanukovych as the winner in the presidential vote, even before the official results were released. Throughout the standoff during the Orange Revolution, Putin stood firmly on the side of Yanukovych, flatly denouncing the idea of rerunning the elections (Williams 2004).

Yet Putin's first major attempt at exporting managed democracy failed miserably. Some have called the Kremlin's clear support for the losing candidate "the Kremlin's greatest foreign relations blunder since 1991" and "a scandalous humiliation" (Petrov and Ryabov 2006). The Orange Revolution only confirmed suspicions and growing beliefs since 2000 that Western powers intended to pull these countries away from Russian spheres of influence (Markov 2005). By the end of 2004, high-level members of the presidential administration, journalists, and politicians alike were vocally drawing parallels between the Orange Revolution and the previous revolutions, and attributing them to a grand US agenda to "weaken Russia's influence throughout the post-Soviet space" (FBIS Report 2004).[10]

The failure of Russian foreign policy fed the fear of a "wave" of revolutions spreading across the post-Soviet region. Harsh criticism and strong reprimands by the international community, in particular European election monitoring organizations concerning the validity and fairness of the Russian parliamentary elections in 2003 and presidential elections 2004, only heightened the perceived fears of domestic overthrow engineered by outside forces.

Russia responds: erosion of democracy within Russia

Russian attribution of the role of the West in promoting the colored revolutions hastened the demise of already fragile democratic institutions within Russia.[11] Russia's post-Soviet leaders left a shaky foundation for institutions

Russia's "sovereign democracy" 121

of liberal democracy to flourish: in October 1993, Russia's first post-1991 president, Boris Yeltsin, ordered the parliament to be bombed and then pushed into place a "superpresidential" constitution, in December 1993. This inordinate concentration of power in the executive branch of government provided the conditions for emasculation of other pillars of government that check executive power (Fish 2001). Throughout the decade, Yeltsin and regional governors also manipulated elections using techniques that would be emulated and "perfected" in the Putin era (Wilson 2005: 39). That Russians' first experience with democracy coincided with one of the greatest economic depressions of modern history not surprisingly eroded popular support for democratic ideas. By the end of the 1990s, especially after the financial collapse in August 1998, Russians were tired of revolution and demanded stability.

The task of providing stability fell to Vladimir Putin, who was chosen to be the country's next leader by Kremlin insiders. Putin benefited tremendously from structural forces, most importantly the 1998 financial crash, which compelled tight fiscal policy and responsible monetary policy. This, in combination with a devalued rouble, generated positive economic growth in Russia for the first time since independence.[12] In addition, Putin came to power as world energy prices began to soar, fuelling economic growth and government revenues.

Putin took advantage of a positive economic environment and his enormous presidential powers outlined in the 1993 constitution to implement liberal economic policies and illiberal political reforms. Putin implemented a 13 per cent flat tax, a major reduction in the corporate tax, land reform, and the creation of a stabilization fund. Simultaneously, while Putin did not radically violate the 1993 constitution or cancel elections, the democratic content of formal democratic institutions eroded considerably after 2000.[13]

Putin undermined the power of Russia's regional leaders, the independent media, big business, both houses of parliament, the Russian prime minister, and independent political parties and civil society organizations. At the same time, he increased the role of the Federal Security Service (FSB), the successor to the KGB, in governing Russia and wielded the power of state institutions such as the courts, the tax inspectors and the police for political ends. The complete spectrum of changes in democratic institutions has been recounted elsewhere at great length; Table 7.1 summarizes them.

Why did Putin pursue these changes? Part of his motivation was to rebuild the country. In particular, Putin believed that the "oligarchs" as a group of people—who had engaged in asset-stripping, insider privatization, crony capitalism—were a threat to Russian national interests and the cause of an increasingly fragmented state.[14] As such, beginning in the early 2000s with the initial purging of individuals like Boris Berezovsky and Vladimir Gusinsky, and culminating in the 2003 parliamentary elections, an anti-oligarch message dominated the political space (Wilson 2005: 108–10). The arrest of Yukos chairman Mikhail Khodorkovskii just one month before the 2003 elections served to solidify the message and draw support to the presidential party, United Russia.[15]

Table 7.1 Major events/trends in Russian media, non-governmental organizations and elections (2001–7)

Date	Media	NGOs	Elections
2001	February: crackdown on oligarchs: NTV (formerly owned by Gusinsky) taken over by Kremlin via Gazprom and ORT (formerly Berezovsky) taken over by Kremlin via Abramovich.	November: Putin meets with thousands of leading NGOs in a Civic Forum (although with important ones absent) in an attempt to control and manage civil society, following on a June 2001 meeting with a smaller group of NGO leaders.	June 2000: changes to election of Federation Council members. July: Law on Political Parties passed: need 10,000 members and branches in at least 50 regions, with each branch having a membership of at least 100.[1]
2001	Introduction of censorship in Chechnya, judicial persecution of mass media, introduction of special services control over mass media.		
2001	Worldwide Day of Mass Media freedom. Putin got into the list of the 10 first mass media adversaries[2]		
2002	January: A court decision shuts down TV-6 (Berezovsky-owned majority), one of few independent television networks; staff continued operating as TVS under new licence. Many at TV-6 had come from NTV.	December: Peace Corps officially unwelcome in Russia.	December: Proposals to amendment of Electoral Law of 2001 requiring 50,000 citizens at 45 branches with 500 members in each branch by January 2006.
2002			The changes are brought into the Law on referendums that prohibit the conduct of referendums in the last year of presidential plenary power (Vishnevskii 2006).
2003	June: TVS (formerly TV6) shut down.		December: Parliamentary elections in which United Russia (formerly Unity) wins.
2004			March: Putin wins second presidential term September: Putin abolishes direct elections of oblast governors and presidents.
2005–now			The enlargement of federation subjects. By 2008, the number of subjects was reduced from 89 to 84.[3]

Table 7.1 (continued)

Date	Media	NGOs	Elections
2005	June: State-owned Gazprom buys popular daily *Izvestia*; *Nezavisimaya gazeta* was bought by Petr Aven and Konstantin Remchukov (Derepaska's manager). The newspaper becomes more "politically correct" (Rostova 2005).	May: Heightened suspicion and crackdown on NGOs. December: Duma passes new laws for NGOs requiring lengthy re-registration process by October 2006 and heightened monitoring of financing and activities.	July: Electoral Law passed in advance of the next 2007 elections. The elections will take place only by party lists. At that time, all 450 Duma members will be elected via party lists in a single nationwide constituency under proportional representation. (Unified Russia gets an advantage.) The threshold to win seats is increased to 7 percent of the total vote.[4]
2006	October: Politkovskaia murder (in total 13 journalists murdered during Putin's tenure) July: Amendments that broaden definition of extremism to include criticism of public officials, targeted towards journalists.		October: Creation of new official "second party" called "Just Russia" which includes Rogozin's Rodina, and the Party of Life, the Party of Pensioners and Rodina. November: Electoral law changed to prevent foreign funding of parties and other aspects of electoral campaigns. It became prohibited for the parties to nominate members of other parties. The small parties lose the chance to unify their efforts (Vishnevskii 2006). New changes to the Law on main warrantees are adopted: the minimum barrier of the election attendance is abolished; the registration of candidates accused in extremism activity is prohibited, the propaganda of some candidates against other candidates in the TV air is prohibited (ibid.). Gosduma gave Putin the right to use FSB abroad.[5] The law restored the institute of property confiscation.

(continued on next page)

Table 7.1 (continued)

Date	Media	NGOs	Elections
2007	July: More amendments on extremism and expanded scope for law enforcement officials.	August: Some charities pushed out of Russia, others temporarily suspended.	October: Russia prevents OSCE election observers in December 2007 parliamentary election.
2008			March 2008 presidential election – Medvedev wins.
2008	Justice Minister Konovalov wants to improve monitoring of NGOs. In 2007, 8,351 requests to close down NGOs were sent to court.[6]		

Sources: Co-reporters David Atkinson (UBK) and Rudolf Bindig (Germany), The Report on the EU Parliament Assembly "The fulfillment of duties and obligations of Russian Federation. Document 10568, 2 June 2005." The Committee of Fulfillment of Duties and Obligations Made by States-Members of EU. (Committee on Monitoring); Anna Plotnikova, "'Kommersant': 'Komu bi nas ni prodali, pokupatelem vse ravno okazhetsa Vladimir Putin,'" News Vocom. www.voanews.com/russian/archives/2006-08/2006-08-31-voa3.cfm?renderforprint=...1/27/2007; "Zhurnal 'Novoe vremia' smenil vladeltsa," November 13, 2006 www.e-planet.ru/cgi-bin/news.cgi?id=475; Gazetu.Ru prodaut "Alisheru Usmanovu?" www.strana.ru/print/298895.html.; Anastasia Dedukhina, "Prof-Rambler," 31 October 2006. www.expert.ru/articles/2006/10/31/rambler/.; Ren TV pereshla pod control druga Putina, Grani.ru, grani.ru/Politics/Russia/p.120665.html 04/23/2007.

Notes:
1 Vladimir Putin, *Rossiyskaya Federatsia Federalnii zakon O politicheskih partiah* www.putin2004.ru/service/law_info/4006C90B
2 *Putin v spiske vragov pressi*, www.news.bbc.co.uk/hi/russian/news/nesid_1310000/1310878.stm
3 *Okruzhnaya poruka, Rosbalt*, 2008-05-19, www.rosbaltnord.ru/2008/05/19/485237.html
4 www.newsvote.bbc.co.uk/mpapps/pagetools/print/news.bbc.co.uk/hi/russian/press/newsid.
5 *Gosduma dala presidentu pravo ispolzovat za rubezhom FSB I vosstanovila institute konfiskatsii imushchestva*, 5 July 2006 www.newsru.com/arch/russia/05jul2006/gosduma_print.htm
6 "Russian Justice Minister wants to improve monitoring of NGOs," JRL 5-29-2008

Russia's "sovereign democracy" 125

Putin's focus on eroding oligarchic power has prompted a second explanation for his political crackdown—economic self-interest. Redistribution of important assets away from 1990s oligarchs to state companies and organizations run by a new cohort of "*silovarchs*"—Putin's close advisors and friends in the security services—continues (Triesman 2007).

A third factor imputes external events, specifically the colored revolutions, for domestic political changes. Instead of "home-grown" oligarchs as Russia's main threat, the purported danger shifted to being engineered from abroad after the colored revolutions. The Orange Revolution in particular generated hysteria inside the Kremlin, and spurred the clear articulation of fear—whether real or inflated—about a colored revolution inside Russia. In response, officials invented the concept of "sovereign democracy" (Krastev 2006). In its original form, the managed democracy model preserved democratic procedures and allowed for marginal political parties, media, and civil society to operate while preserving the main levers of political power, including first and foremost national television, in the Kremlin's hands. In the wake of the colored revolutions, Kremlin officials and their allies viewed civil society representatives as Western surrogates and recast their political project as the defense of "sovereign democracy."

The term's creator, deputy chief of presidential staff, Vladislav Surkov, identified the country's potential loss of sovereignty in the form of US influence of domestic political trajectories as a grave threat to Russia (Surkov 2006). By the fall of 2006, the pro-Kremlin party, United Russia, fully endorsed the concept of "sovereign democracy" (Saradzhyan 2006). In addition to the many press articles about "sovereign democracy," the concept was featured in books (Krastev 2006), academic conferences, textbooks, and rallies and speeches (US Open Source Center 2006).

Concrete policy changes subsequently followed. The three most prominent moves by the Russian government aimed at preventing a colored revolution in Russia included: reducing the opposition's scope to maneuver during the 2007–8 electoral cycle, restricting the activities of non-governmental organizations in Russia, especially those with foreign funding, and creating pro-Kremlin youth movements.

A national election won by the opposition precipitated the colored revolutions in Serbia, Georgia, and Ukraine. Consequently, Putin and his aides took extraordinary measures to make sure that Russia's fledgling opposition parties and leaders had no chance to compete in the 2007 parliamentary election or 2008 presidential election. In the December 2007 parliamentary vote, the Kremlin manufactured a respectable turnout and then helped to attract 64 per cent of the popular vote for Putin's party, United Russia.[16] The 2008 Presidential election went as planned with Dmitri Medvedev winning by a landslide. Throughout the electoral campaigns, several opposition candidates were excluded from the list of parties, President Putin enjoyed massive airtime on Kremlin-controlled television stations, opposition newspapers were confiscated, and government officials pressured their employees and directors of

126 Michael McFaul and Regine A. Spector

large companies to vote for United Russia. International and domestic election monitor organizations—key actors in the colored revolutions—were not allowed to observe the election.

In addition to managing electoral processes, the Kremlin also tightened the role of non-governmental organizations, which had played an important role in the colored revolutions. Legislation came into force in April 2006 mandating new requirements for non-governmental organizations (NGOs) in an attempt to monitor their work. These include new paperwork and documentation for all employees and members of NGOs, annual reports documenting the location and amount of financing and the purposes for which it was used, and disqualifying "undesirable" or "extremist" foreigners from founding and leading NGOs (International Journal for Non-for-Profit Law 2006). In addition to these formal requirements, the law gave government agencies a broader mandate to monitor and review NGO documents at any time, and make arrests and accusations more easily.[17]

This legislation resulted in a tightening of NGO space in the country. In 2005, the number of rejections in NGO registration was 1,918 and by 2007, the figure had risen to 11,000.[18] In parallel to these tighter controls on independent NGOs, the Kremlin devoted massive resources to the creation of state-sponsored and state-controlled organizations. On 16 March 2005, the Kremlin announced its Public Chamber Project, which built upon earlier attempts to control civil society organizations in the country (Petrov 2006). A central objective of these initiatives is to counter Western influence on Russian society, as President Medvedev explains:

> The support of NGOs remains our indisputable priority. You know that until 2006, the main part of such organizations was financed from abroad. I don't think that any developed western country could admit such a total foreign capital investment into its "third sector." This is why we decided to make apportionment of our own capital to support Russian structures of civic society. This decision was naturally determined. Now every year we spend more and more money to support such kind of noncommercial organizations on the account, among other sources, of the state budget.
>
> (Medvedev 2008)

Activists loyal to the state work for the Chamber, NGOs loyal to the state receive its money, and the government can safely support its activities without fear that they will disrupt its own agenda.[19]

The third focus of Kremlin efforts to manage and control Russian domestic politics led to the creation of state-led youth movements explicitly formed to counter those such as Otpor in Serbia, Kmara in Georgia, and Pora in Ukraine that had played a mobilizing role in those countries. Harkening back to the Communist Party's Youth League, the Komsomol, the Kremlin created its own pro-government youth movement (Nashi meaning Ours) in early 2005

Russia's "sovereign democracy" 127

to prevent an Orange Revolution scenario in Russia's elections of 2007–8.[20] Funded directly by the Kremlin and Kremlin-friendly businesses (such as Gazprom), the group has established branches in cities and regions across the country, boasting over 100,000 members as of 2007.

This and other such youth organizations serve multiple purposes.[21] First and foremost, they mobilize youth to attend government rallies, protests, and events, especially those important to the Kremlin. In the December 2007 parliamentary elections, a branch of Nashi was recruited to spread a "get out the vote" campaign and to assist in election monitoring (Nowak 2007).

Second, they serve as a forum to inculcate nationalist ideology to youth, and encourage patriotism and loyalty to the Russian regime. The ideas of "sovereign democracy" are promoted in conferences and summer camps held by the groups; for example, the 2007 summer camp extravaganza for Nashi members was attended by many members of the presidential administration and other ministries. Numerous interviews with youth members indicate the importance of "continuing on a course of stability" and providing the foundation for a "powerful and independent Russia," implying that color revolutions and other domestic political disturbances would disrupt these objectives (Arnold 2007).

Third, they provide a stepping stone to future government or business careers by building informal networks and relationships. In one perfect example: the founding leader of Nashi, Vasily Yakemenko, now works for the government's State Committee for Youth Affairs (Waldermann 2007).

Finally, Nashi and other youth groups help to promote Russian foreign policy interests by staging protest rallies outside embassies of governments in conflict with Russia.[22] The creation of such state-supported youth organizations was a pre-emptive strategy on the part of the Russian elite to prevent the role of independent opposition youth movements from mobilizing people who would engage in anti-government activities.

Russian pushback abroad

The electoral revolutions, in particular the Orange Revolution, gave new impetus to restrict democratic processes and practices within Russia. In addition, Russian foreign policy has become more assertive, culminating in the military invasion of Georgia in summer 2008.

Russian leadership redoubled efforts to strengthen ties with governments and non-governmental actors in the near abroad by convening several formal and informal meetings with officials throughout the region to discuss colour revolutionary threats and advise regional elites on these issues (Agence France Presse 2003). For example, in 2005, the European Forum brought together over 150 politicians, academics and experts from countries across the post-Soviet region in an effort to analyze the color revolutions, recruit potential counter-revolutionary forces, and promote a counter-revolutionary ideology (Chavusaw 2005).

128   *Michael McFaul and Regine A. Spector*

To counter NATO, the European Union, OSCE, and other Western clubs, Moscow became more animated in strengthening pro-Russian multilateral institutions, including the Commonwealth of Independent States (CIS), the Eurasian Economic Commonwealth, the Collective Security Treaty Organization (CSTO), and the Shanghai Cooperation Organization (SCO). Through the SCO, Russia and China conducted joint military exercises for the first time in 2005. Russian officials also have floated the idea of creating an international peacekeeping force through the CSTO (Blagov 2008). To different degrees, these organizations expressed their suspicion and disdain for colored revolutions.[23]

The Russian government also has engaged more intensely in seeking to shape international attitudes about democratic development in the region. While a purported "norm" of international election monitoring has emerged over the past few decades, recent events in Russia indicate that this norm is highly contested (Kelley 2008). Even before the Orange Revolution, Russia spearheaded the creation in 2002 of an alternative election monitoring organization to counter Western organizations such as the OSCE's Office for Democratic Institutions and Human Rights (ODIHR), which it believes have played an integral role in sparking the electoral revolutions. This organization has certified "fair and free" Russia's own elections since 2003–4 as well as the elections of CIS member states. As an OSCE member, the Russian government also launched an attack on ODHIR's election monitoring efforts.

To further dilute the legitimacy of organizations such as Freedom House that assess the internal activities of countries, including Russia, the Kremlin initiated its own ratings systems about democracy and governance organized by Moscow State Institute for International Relations (MGIMO) political scientist Andrei Melville. On their scale, Russia comes out higher than the US.

Russian organizations and foundations closely affiliated with the Kremlin also have become involved in funding NGOs in other countries. In 2007, President Putin issued a decree creating the Russkiy Mir (Russian World) National Foundation. Official statements on the Foundation's creation describe the Foundation as a Russian analogue to the British Council and the Alliance Française. That well-known political strategist Vyacheslav Nikonov—a consultant to Yanukovich in the 2004 presidential election in Ukraine—heads the foundation with an annual budget of US$20 million (Finn 2008).

In parallel to these efforts to strengthen ties with Russian allies both with governments and non-governmental actors throughout the former Soviet Union, President Putin and his government tried to weaken if not undermine the victors in the colored revolutions. In Serbia, Putin resisted all attempts to negotiate a solution for Kosovo, a stance that helped to split the domestic coalition that brought down Milošević in 2000. Out of frustration, several European countries and the United States decided to recognize the independence of Kosovo in April 2008, a move that deepened ties between Moscow and Serbian political forces opposed to Kosovo's independence

Russia's "sovereign democracy"   129

In Ukraine, Putin initially took tough action, cutting off gas supplies on 1 January 2006 when the Ukrainian and Russian officials failed to negotiate a new price. Putin's plan backfired, however, because of Western reaction to the disruptions in gas flowing into Europe, compelling Russia to restore exports levels the following day. The action, however, sent a sobering signal to Ukrainian politicians about their country's dependency on Russia.

Moscow targeted its most aggressive actions against colored revolutionaries toward the government of Georgia. Tensions intensified after the 2003 colour revolution, when Russia "punished" Georgia with embargos, travel blockades and other measures in attempts to destabilize the country; it also granted South Ossetians Russian passports, stymied potential settlements over future status of Abkhazia and South Ossetia, and ensured control over the breakaway regions with its not so neutral peacekeepers.

While earlier attempts by Saakashvili to re-exert influence within Georgia—for example in the region of Ajaria in 2004—did not elicit negative Russian reaction (George 2008), the continuing spread of the colour revolutions, the declaration of Kosovo's independence, and the pressure for a US missile defense system in Eastern Europe changed the regional and international context.

In the spring of 2008, tensions between Moscow and Tbilisi escalated over Abkhazia. After Kosovo declared independence, the Russian government hinted that it would recognize certain administrative responsibilities of the Sukhumi-based authorities, which was seen as a provocative step toward formal diplomatic recognition. Tensions continued to escalate in May 2008, when Russia increased the number of peacekeeping forces deployed in Abkhazia and a Russian MiG-29 fighter plane shot down an unarmed Georgian drone aircraft that was being flown over the Black Sea in order to observe troop movements inside Abkhazia. President Saakashvili stated that Russia was preparing for war (Saakashvili 2008).

War indeed broke out. On the eve of 7 August, Russian troops and tanks rolled into pro-Russian separatist regions of Georgia in response to a Georgian offensive on 7 August to reclaim territory in South Ossetia that it lost after separatist wars of the early 1990s.[24] A propaganda war between Russia and Georgia ensued about the causes of the conflict and the intentions of Russian military response: while control over Abkhazia and South Ossetia was one goal, Russia also sought to delegitimize Saakashvili. The conflict over South Ossetia was the first instance of Russian hard power being deployed to change a regime since the Soviet invasion of Afghanistan in 1979.

Russian foreign policy assertiveness goes beyond military occupation and territorial control. Russia has supported statements by leaders in countries within the CIS such as Belarus (RFE/RL Newsline 2007), Armenia (Fuller 2008), and Kazakhstan (Yermukanov 2006)[25] that threats to domestic instability and unrest come from outside the country, not from within. Most dramatically, Uzbek President Islam Karimov blamed foreign involvement in fomenting demonstrations in Andijon in May 2005, which he brutally ended by gunning down hundreds of innocent civilians.[26] In the wake of this tragedy,

130   *Michael McFaul and Regine A. Spector*

Karimov ousted American armed forces from an air base established in Uzbekistan after September 11. Although Karimov eventually sought to repair his relations with the United States, Uzbekistan's foreign policy orientation has remained much more pro-Russian, especially in the sphere of energy, a reversal considered by Kremlin officials as a great diplomatic victory (Najibullah 2008).

In Kyrgyzstan, Russian political influence steadily increased, especially after the ousting of President Askar Akaev in March 2005. The new president, Kurmanbek Bakiev, has faced numerous protests in Bishkek since his election in June 2005, perhaps the most serious at the end of 2006 when a show of tanks and teargas disbursed a growing crowd. President Bakiev called Moscow in the midst of the crisis, and clearly received tacit if not overt approval to use force to protect his rule (Spector 2006).

In addition to Russian activities in the former Soviet Union, Russia seeks to be recognized as a legitimate and equal actor in the world community. Extending the reach of Russian media is a significant component of this perceptions battle. RIA Novosti, the Russian government news agency, opened a think tank in Washington to counter the Moscow Carnegie Center, sponsors an English language weekly called Russiaprofile.org, and hosts an annual conference, the Valdai Forum, to expose foreigner journalists and academics to Russian officialdom. Started in 2007, the Russian state-sponsored television network, Russia Today, now broadcasts in the United States and Europe. *Rossiyskaya Gazeta*, a government-owned newspaper, funds monthly supplements in *The Washington Post* in the United States called "Russia: Beyond the Headlines," and sponsors similar paid advertising inserts in Britain, Bulgaria, and India. The Russian government also has hired a public relations firm in Washington, Ketchum Inc, "to help the government tell its story of economic growth and opportunity for its citizens," according to Randy DeCleene, an executive at the firm (quoted in Finn 2008). Finally, the director of the New York office of the Institute for Democracy and Cooperation, Adranik Migranyan, seeks to reduce Western criticism about Russia's special kind of democracy.[27] These actions amount to a considerable effort on the part of the Russian government to exert ideological influence abroad.

Conclusion

Increased Russian assertiveness does not signify the return of the Cold War. The prospect of military combat between Russian and American soldiers remains remote. And both countries are integrated into the same global capitalist system. Yet the era of democratic change inside Russia, and Russian integration into the community of democratic countries, has ended. As the Russian regime has become more autocratic, tensions between Russia and United States have increased. Rather than joining the West, Putin now sees balancing against the West, and the United States, in particular, as the central objective of Russian foreign policy (Gaddy and Kuchins 2008). Rhetorically,

Russia's "sovereign democracy" 131

the United States has emerged once again as Russia's number one enemy. This reorientation has implications for Russia's policy towards its neighbors, where the Russian government has pursued more interventionist policies designed to support pro-Russian leaders and interests.

Does this project have long-term potential? One key country to watch is China. To the extent that a "China model" is emerging—one that focuses on modernization and integration into the international economy while keeping a tight hold on the domestic political system—there is evidence that some Russian elite believe this to be an appropriate and legitimate developmental path.[28] Chinese leaders, in turn, embrace ideas about the importance of defending sovereignty, which explains their notable silence over Russia's military forays in Georgia and the recognition of Abkhazia and South Ossetia. While both countries still have greater stakes in their relations with the United States and Europe than with each other, it not inconceivable that ideological harmonization between Russian and Chinese foreign policy and public relations strategists could grow.

From the Russian side, a few signs are worth noting. First, in his inaugural overseas visit upon being sworn in as President in 2008, Dmitri Medvedev chose to go to Kazakhstan and then China, not to the West.[29] In an important speech to big business in Krasnodar in early 2008, Medvedev referenced Chinese companies as a model for Russian counterparts (Belton 2008). Finally, Russia is looking to China, Norway, Singapore and other Middle Eastern countries as it contemplates the establishment of sovereign wealth funds to manage its reserves.

A final factor that will shape the future of Russia's sovereign democracy concept is American power. In the 1990s, the United States emerged as the world's undisputed superpower while Russia looked weak in the aftermath of Soviet collapse and subsequent economic depression. In 2008, according to the Kremlin, the tables turned: the United States is bogged down in a financial crisis and unwinnable wars in Afghanistan and Iraq, and is discredited in the eyes of the world as a unilateral actor and violator of human rights. If American centrality in the international system continues to wane, multilateral relationships not anchored by the US will provide more opportunities for Russian (and Chinese) influence (Barma and Ratner 2006; Khanna 2008). To the extent that alternative nodes and relationships in the international system are emerging, the US and the West may have decreasing leverage and legitimacy in its democracy promotion agenda, and Russia may find its goal of pursuing "sovereign democracy" more tangible.

Notes

1 Michael McFaul is writing in a personal capacity. The views expressed in this chapter do not reflect US government policy.
2 For the role of the media, in the Georgian case, TV station Rustavi-2, and Ukrainian TV Channel 5 played a more significant role than TV played in the Serbian revolution. See Karumidze and Wertsch (2005) and Prytula (2006).

132 *Michael McFaul and Regine A. Spector*

3 For more on the role of Western actors in Georgia's revolution, see Fairbanks (2004); Wheatley (2005: Chapter 7). For more on the role of Western actors in the Serbian revolution, see Krickovic (2001). For more on the role of Western actors in the Ukrainian revolution, see Sushko and Prystayko (2006) and McFaul (2007). In general, see Bunce and Wolchik (2006a; 2006c).
4 Zeleznev called the pro-democracy crowd "high on alcohol and drugs" and predicted that the new government would be "illegitimate and weak."
5 For a detailed recounting of the politics, intrigues, and process of the Rose Revolution, see Wheatley (2005: Chapter 7).
6 See interview with Aleksei Malashenko in Karumidze and Wertsch (2005: 89–90).
7 On the Russian model, see McFaul et al. (2004).
8 Russian PR experts who worked for Yanukovych included Marat Gelman, Sergei Markov, Vyacheslav Nikonov, and Gleb Pavlovksy.
9 McFaul's interview with Sergei Markov (Moscow, September 2005).
10 For more examples of such statements, see Herd (2005).
11 While the causes and dynamics of the electoral revolutions have received significant attention, the responses to these elections by others in the region and around the world have been less studied. For two exceptions, see Spector and Krickovic (2007) and Hale (2006).
12 Ironically, it was Prime Minister Evgeny Primakov and his Communist minister for the economy who presided over Russia when tight "neoliberal" fiscal and monetary policies helped to spur Russia's first post-communist growth.
13 A different, that is to say more democratically inclined, leader could have come to power by the same accidental means that Putin did, been as lucky with devaluation and rising energy prices, and nonetheless pursued policies to strengthen democracy. The role of rents from energy exports often has a corrosive effect on democratic practices. For elaboration, see Fish (2005). However, the "resource curse" does not inevitably produce autocracy. For elaboration, see Haber and Menaldo (2007) and Dunning (2008).
14 On this penetration, see McFaul (1998).
15 For more on these elections, see Hale et al. (2004).
16 The two others parties that crossed the 7 percent barrier to win seats in the parliament – the Liberal Democratic Party of Russia and Just Russia—are loyal to the president.
17 The law was passed on 19 January 2006 officially as, "On Introducing Amendments into Certain Legislative Acts of the Russian Federation," but is known in common parlance as the "NGO Law" (Kommersant 2006a, 2006b).
18 Doklad o resultatah I osnovnih napravleniah deyatelnosti Ministerstva ustitsii Rossiyskoy federatsii na 2009–11.
19 For a full review of the Public Chamber's impact since its inception in 2005, see Petrov (2007).
20 Molodezhnoe dvizhenie Nashi, Manifest, www.nashi.su/ideology. See also Corwin (2005) and Kostenko and Romanov (2007).
21 Now under different names and on different regional levels, a range of youth organizations exist. Besides Nashi there are pro-Kremlin and pro-Unified Russia Rossia molodaya (Russian Youth), Rossiyskii souz molodezhi (Russian Union of Youth), Molodaya gvardia (Young Guard), Novie ludi – Povolzhie (New People), Mestnie – Samara (Locals), and others.
22 For example over the past two years, such protests have been staged outside the British and Estonian embassies over various foreign policy disagreements with these two countries.
23 "The Backlash Against Democracy Assistance," a report prepared by the National Endowment for Democracy for Senator Richard Lugar, Chairman of the Committee on Foreign Relations, US Senate, 8 June 2006, p. 7. See also Radyuhin (2005).

24 For a detailed timeline of these events, see Cornell, Popjanevski, and Nillson (2008).
25 Dariga Nazarbaeva, Kazakshtan's President Nazarbaev's daughter, stated:

> Popular unrest in Kazakhstan may be triggered not by the poverty of the population or by some other economic reasons, but by the passivity of pro-presidential parties in the face of the danger of "export of democracy" to Kazakhstan by outside forces.

26 For more excerpts from local newspapers and TV stations, see Kimmage (2005); Hill and Jones (2006).
27 "Russian NGO to Monitor US Democracy," 26 January 2008, Available at: www.theotherrussia.org/2008/01/26/russian-ngo-to-monitor-us-democracy.
28 For more on this ideological challenge posed by China, see Barma and Ratner (2006).
29 Accompanying Medvedev were important Russian businessmen, including Vladimir Yevtushenkov, the billionaire chairman of AFK Sistema, which has interests in telecommunications, technology, real estate and retail; Mikhail Pogosyan, Chief Executive (CEO) of Sukhoi Aviation Holding Co.; Valery Okulov, CEO of Aeroflot, Russia's largest airline; and Andrei Kostin, CEO of VTB Group, the country's second largest bank group. See Nasar (2008).

8 Democratizing one-party rule in China

Shaun Breslin

Questioning the compatibility of economic liberalization with continued political illiberal authoritarian rule is not just a matter for academic debate; it has been a key concern of the Chinese leadership itself almost from the very start of the economic reform process in 1978. But despite the predictions of some theorists, this does not seem to emerge from a fear that a new middle class will rise to challenge the Party for political power – indeed, rather than fear the emergence of the middle class, the Party leadership wants as many Chinese as possible to join its ranks. This is partly because the emerging new rich classes in China are very close to the political structure (and often still part of it) and in many ways are beneficiaries of authoritarian rule. It is also because of the importance of patriotism/nationalism in contemporary Chinese politics, which not only legitimates those actions and policies that are portrayed as being in the national interest, but also leads to liberal democracy often being equated with foreign imperialism and hegemony.

Rather, the concern for China's leaders is that the growth of inequality, corruption and environmental degradation could undermine the Party's position. They are also aware that many Chinese are frustrated with the actions of individual local leaders, and of a fairly widespread popular assumption that party–state officials serve their own self-interest first rather than serving the people. Since 2004 in particular, the need to reform to ensure regime stability if not survival has turned the focus on the importance of democratization. But in these Chinese discourses, the call for 'democracy' and 'democratization' do not refer to the move towards competitive multi-party democracy through which one-party rule is challenged. On the contrary, democratization is seen as a means of strengthening and re-legitimating one-party rule by creating a more transparent, open and consultative political system increasingly based on (and constrained by) legal structures.

As such, this chapter focuses on the demand and supply of political reform in China, and what it means for observers of democratization. It suggests that Fukuyama's (1992: xiii) belief that 'liberal democracy remains the only coherent political aspiration' may be mistaken. While it is difficult to gauge the real demand for liberal democracy in China as those who demand it fall foul of the power of the state, it appears that the primary aspiration in China

Democratizing one-party rule in China 135

is 'the national project' – restoring China to a perceived rightful position in the global order. The aspiration is for the emergence of indigenous forms of governance based on China's unique circumstances that guarantee Chinese independence and facilitate national regeneration and resurgence. Of course, these ideas are not universally held, and the political system itself has done much to construct the way in which this aspiration has been construed. At the very least, we can say that the primacy of liberal democracy is challenged in contemporary China, and China's resurgence is resulting in the questioning of the western model in other parts of the world.

Demanding democracy and limits on freedoms

The People's Republic of China (PRC) is a self-declared 'People's Democratic Dictatorship' where 'state power is in the hands of the people and serves the interests of the people' (State Council 2005). Article 35 of the PRC Constitution states that 'Citizens of the People's Republic of China enjoy freedom of speech, of the press, of assembly, of association, of procession and of demonstration.' However, this does not mean that the people are free to do what they want. Although there are no longer formally 'counterrevolutionary crimes' in China (since March 1997), the legal code still protects the Chinese Communist Party (CCP) from challenges to its authority. These include not only actions that might 'split the state; subvert the political power of the people's democratic dictatorship and overthrow the socialist system', but the even more amorphous reference to crimes that 'undermine social and economic order'.[1] In essence, not only is promoting democracy subject to prosecution under law, but so too are many actions that might fall short of promoting a democratic alternative. Despite the relatively more open and predictable political situation today, raising grievances still runs some risk of straying into the realms of not just illegitimate dissent but also illegal actions punishable by law.

And although the events of 1989 in Tiananmen Square have not been repeated, that precedent remains a potent example of other ways of silencing opposition, and the lengths that the leadership were (if not still are) prepared to go to restore order and quash protests. Nor is the 'June 4th incident' the only example. Wei Jingsheng who called for democracy to be the fifth modernization during the democracy wall movement in 1978–79 was jailed, briefly released in 1993, re-arrested and jailed, and only finally freed and exiled in 1997. More recently, attempts to create a China Democracy Party in 1998 were squashed at birth and its members arrested (Wright 2002). In the run-up to the 2008 Olympics, the authorities became increasingly nervous about the possibility of protests spoiling the carefully choreographed image of modern China and pre-emptive detentions seem to have been approved for those who might become 'trouble' during the games (Watts 2008). So one straightforward explanation for why democratization has not flourished in China is that the state does not want it to, and does what it can to punish its proponents.

136 *Shaun Breslin*

Everything is relative: the extension of rights and freedoms

Although the legal system can be and is used to protect the current system from perceived threats, the nature of Chinese authoritarianism has vastly changed from not just the Mao era that ended in 1976, but also from the first decade of reform. While the current Chinese system might appear repressive when compared to politically liberal societies, it looks remarkably liberal – much more free – when compared to even a relatively recent past. And in assessing the progress of political reform in China, it is essential to retain a sensible expectation of what can be expected by thinking about what has changed to date.

In the 1980s, Chinese were not free to work where they wanted, live where they wanted or even buy much of what they wanted. Access to decent jobs remained contingent on having the right political credentials, while other jobs were allocated by administrative fiat (the 安排 anpai system). For most urban residents, the work unit or danwei 单位 was not just the source of employment, but also provided accommodation, food tokens to be used in their canteens (typically different canteens for different levels with very different qualities of food), and approval for those whose turn had come to buy high demand goods such as bicycles, or those who wanted to travel. Visiting somebody at a different work unit usually entailed being signed in and out, and marriage before the approved ages required work unit approval; even then, there was no guarantee that the unit(s) would provide married living accommodation. In the late 1980s, tens of thousands of married couples lived in different cities because they could not get joint accommodation or one of the partners couldn't change their hukou 户口 – the system whereby individuals could only live in the place where they were officially registered. Eating at restaurants outside the workplace was possible, but entailed the use of ration cards and the ability to get served in the two to three hours that most places were open. Entertainment options were strictly limited and the state wanted to control what you read, what you watched and what you listened to. And as we shall see, dissatisfaction with this system was at least part of the reason why students took to political activism in 1989.

Authoritarian one-party rule today is very different. In terms of the formal legal system, Minxin Pei (2003) notes that norms have emerged in China that – whilst falling far short of democratization – nevertheless represent a significant difference from previous eras. For example, while torture of dissidents does occur, the torture of their family members 'has become almost taboo', allowing them to campaign on behalf of their family member's rights relatively free from the fear of suffering the same fate. Li and O'Brien (1996) point to the importance of the 'administrative litigation law' which came into operation in October 1990, providing a key means of redressing grievances against the state. To be sure, local government officials have found myriad ways of stopping people taking them to court – not least by not telling them

Democratizing one-party rule in China 137

what their rights are in the first place (O'Brien and Li 2004). But where there is a good knowledge of what is legal and what is not, then peasants have a remarkably good record in using the legal system to protect their rights. Peerenboom (2007: 20) has also pointed to the strengthening of legal forms and the much more predictable and transparent workings of People's Congresses (at various levels) and government agencies.

So the legal protection of rights is far from perfect, but it has greatly improved from the 1980s, and is a sign of not just toleration, but in some places the promotion of the legal system as a check and balance on the authority of the state. The same can be said about the election system – it isn't perfect, but much changed and more people have a chance to influence the way their lives are run than ever before. For example, villagers in China are experimenting in choosing one of their own as a form of 'political manager' to coordinate and oversee political issues, while competitive elections are allowing non-party members to seek and win representative office.

Furthermore, popular pressure can and does change things; perhaps most famously in Fanglin in 2001. After an explosion at a local school killed over 40 children, Premier Zhu Rongji first claimed the explosion was the result of a suicide bomber. The true story that the schoolchildren were making fireworks only emerged as a result of a concerted campaign by local families and the local press in the face of considerable official opposition. The media is also taking a high profile role in exposing official corruption and providing at least some form of check on the exercise of power.

An arguably more important change is the creation of a legitimate private space. Chinese *homo economicus* are free to choose and free to buy from an increasingly wide range of outlets without the state being particularly interested at all; the main constraint is now cost. Jobs are no longer allocated but gained through merit – though personal connections and outright corruption play an important role in many cases as we will discuss in more detail later. China even has two state ministers who are not party members (though good political credentials of course remain important). Workplace-assigned accommodation is not so much no longer compulsory as almost impossible to find – even state-owned enterprises have privatized much of their stock and tried to reduce the burden of housing their employees where possible. People can watch a range of TV programmes and films that have no political content at all, and choose from an almost overwhelming array of 'popular culture' magazines. Eating and drinking where you want is up to you, and people even have more choice to marry who they want – even to have sex before marriage or even to live together without getting married (though it still offends the moral sensibilities of many).

Now, of course, there are constraints. The state still controls the flow of information and retains controls over suspect political literature and culture. It also maintains strong surveillance over the internet to check for politically suspect activity. Compared to the West, this is still a restrictive political system. We should also be very much aware that these freedoms are not

138   *Shaun Breslin*

available to all. The options open to younger urban middle groups are simply not affordable for many millions of less well off urban dwellers whose priorities and goals are more basic. These options are also denied to many millions more in the countryside. And we should also note that periods of opening often give way to periods of stricter control and less tolerance, as was the case in the run-up to the Beijing Olympics.

But while it may not appear very dramatic when compared to the West, the creation of a private sphere in China is hugely significant. Where the state once interfered in all parts of everybody's lives, it has now withdrawn and allowed a private space that people can occupy as individuals – and within which they can do much as they like. There is one very important caveat. This freedom and private sphere exists only if people accept the political status quo and do not engage in any overt political activity that the state deems to be illegitimate. Whereas the Maoist state wanted every Chinese citizen to participate and be politically active, the contemporary state encourages apoliticism, and rewards citizens with a private sphere if they keep to their side of the bargain.

But it is not just about taking a step back from interfering in all aspects of the daily lives of individuals. For much of the post-Mao period, the unwritten social contract between the party-state and the people was built on three other pillars. If the people don't compete with the Party in the political sphere, the Party will provide the people with, first, material advancement and, second, stability. It will also defend China's national interests in a hostile and dangerous international environment. These three pillars have changed somewhat in recent years under the leadership of Hu Jintao and Wen Jiabao, with a renewed emphasis on equity, social welfare and 'democratization' (it is still too soon to tell whether this represents a new pillar of legitimacy or rather changes to the existing three). So this chapter will now proceed by considering these bases of legitimacy, and what they mean for democratization in China.

Bases of legitimacy for authoritarian rule

Legitimacy and economic growth

The first, perhaps most obvious of all, is legitimacy through economic performance. Attaining growth, raising living standards and pulling millions out of poverty have been key components in justifying the abandonment of the Maoist paradigm and the transition from socialism. However, while historical success is important, so too is the idea that much still needs to be done before even the basic task of economic reconstruction has been attained. Three decades of economic reform might have created as many as 80 million 'new rich' Chinese (Goodman and Zang 2008: 1) – just over 6 per cent of the population – but at least as many people still live on less than US$1 a day: poverty by most calculations. Twenty years after Zhao Ziyang argued that China was

Democratizing one-party rule in China   139

only in the 'primary stage of socialism', Wen Jiabao (2007) was still using the same idea to explain why the current system needs to be maintained for the foreseeable future:

> China is at the primary stage of socialism, and will remain so for a long time to come. The primary stage means a stage of underdevelopment, which manifests itself, first and foremost, in the low level of the productive forces. Therefore, we must unswervingly take economic development as the central task and go all out to boost the productive forces.

Thus, the socio-economic agenda will remain the primary focus of party policy for some time to come (and the socio-political agenda will have to wait).

The Chinese Communist Party and the bourgeoisie[2]

For the poorest of the poor, the task is to survive. For many of those who have been pulled out of poverty, the task is now to move from 'subsistence-plus' to become part of the 'middle class' (sometimes translated in English language publications as 'middle income class'). This became a state-sponsored aspiration through President Jiang Zemin's (1993–2003) emphasis on creating a 'xiaokang 小康' society where the majority are 'less affluent than "well-off" but better off than freedom from want'. Post Jiang, the Party has explicitly used the term 'middle class' (zhongchan jieji 中产阶级) instead, but whether it be the creation of a xiaokang or middle-class society, the promise remains the same: it will provide a political and economic structure in which all citizens can become relatively well off if the people do not challenge the Party for political power.

In essence, key party leaders feel that the current social structure is not stable. Economic reform to date has created a small but very wealthy elite, a slightly bigger but still relatively small middle income class, and a massive base of poor and relatively poor. The task now is to create an 'olive-shaped' (橄榄性 ganlanxing) structure – a small distribution at the top and bottom, with the vast majority in a large middle section (Wang 2004). But while the Party portrays itself as the only force that can bring about this class transformation, is it sowing the seeds of its own demise by creating a middle class, which some democratization theorists view as an essential prerequisite for democratization?

For the time being at least, there does not appear to be any real competition from the emerging new middle or bourgeois classes for political power; and at the risk of oversimplification, five main reasons can be given. First, we need to consider the size of these new groups/classes.[3] There are various different ways of defining what it means to be middle class as well as different methods of calculating size. The highest figures are based on a survey of nearly 6,000 urban residents by the Chinese Academy of Social Sciences, which found that just under half now consider themselves to be in the middle

140　*Shaun Breslin*

class (Lu 2004). However, Li Chunling (2004) is highly sceptical of these findings, arguing that the figures are necessary to laud the success of party policy in generating wealth and promoting a new xiaokang society. Li concludes that only 2.8 per cent of the entire population – just over 35 million people – were really members of the middle class in 2004 (Chua 2004). While this might represent the lowest plausible calculation, the general point that it is easy to overestimate the true size of the middle class is important and well made.

Second, not least because the process of transformation is still very much ongoing, there is no solidity among emerging groups. It might be more than a decade since Goodman (1998: 40) argued that it is difficult to identify 'a single identifiable social interest or propensity to action', but the basic argument remains true today. Even among those who think of themselves as middle class, there are self defined distinctions between different types of middle-class citizens. The majority placed themselves in either the fourth or fifth of ten possible ranks of who gets most from the distribution of 'social resources'. State and social administrators were considered to be the main beneficiaries in the first rank, private business owners second, and management personnel in the third rank (Lu 2004).

Third, this suggests that the Chinese middle class differs from European understandings because it contains within it not only intellectuals, managers and professionals, but also 'middle and lower-level cadres on the payroll of the party–state' (He 2003: 89). As such, the new middle class is not necessarily separate from the State but rather part of the state and dependent on it. Why should the middle class challenge the state for power when many of the middle class are part of the State apparatus and dependent on continued state power for their positions of relative privilege? Thus, expectations that an emerging middle class will challenge existing elites for political power need to be modified to take into account this symbiotic, not confrontational, relationship. Indeed, for Tsai (2007), we should throw away the focus on the middle class when considering political transformation in China as it complicates more than it can hope to explain.

Much of the non-state sector in contemporary China has its origins in the party–state sector that spawned it. Particularly at the local level, party and state officials have used their political positions to increase their economic potential and bargaining power. Dickson (2003) focuses on the children of party state officials and those officials who have 'put to sea' (xiahai 下海) – leaving formal political office to join the private sector. For Walder (2002), Li and Rozelle (2003) and others, the focus is on forms of 'insider privatization' that have resulted in what Ding (2000) calls 'nomenklatura capitalism'. Having been spawned by the political system, these new entrepreneurs utilize their links with that system to ensure that they do well in the private sector.

But the coalescence of political and new economic elites is not just a one-way process. Private entrepreneurs in China find it difficult to make headway

Democratizing one-party rule in China 141

unless they have a good relationship with the party–state elites. Even those who have no formal contacts with the party–state are essentially dependent on strong support from local authorities in order to survive. Successful 'private' local enterprises usually succeed thanks to the protection and aid afforded to them by local state elites. In an economy where land, raw materials, transport and finance capital are still in relatively short supply, occupying a gatekeeper role (or knowing somebody who does) has an important economic premium. As such, a form of business-local state is an essential prerequisite for successful economic activity. So the fourth in the list of five explanations is that, notwithstanding the liberalization of the Chinese economy, the State remains hugely important. As Gallagher (2007) argues, the private sector cannot really challenge the existing power holders when it is largely dependent on those same power holders for access to capital and markets. In short, while there is a growing private sector in China, this sector only flourishes because of its close relationship with the State. It is private, but it is not independent and 'most entrepreneurs feel that the system generally works for them' (Tsai 2007).

The fifth explanation takes a slightly different slant on the same basic idea and argues that new elites don't need to compete with the Party because the Party acts on their behalf. On the 80th anniversary of the creation of the CCP in 2001, party leader, Jiang Zemin called for private entrepreneurs to be allowed to join the Communist Party. Despite concern from within the Party, the Party Constitution was amended at the 16th Party Congress in November 2002 to add Jiang's theory of the 'Three Represents' (sange daibiao 三个代表) to Marxism-Leninism–Mao Zedong Thought–Deng Xiaoping Theory, as the Party's guiding principle. The following year, the PRC Constitution was also amended to not only include the 'Three Represents' but also to commit the state to guarantee the right to have and inherit private property As a result, the CCP now formally represents not just the Chinese proletariat, but also China's advanced productive forces, China's advanced culture, and 'the fundamental interests of the overwhelming majority of the Chinese people'. As a consequence, the CCP is no longer just the vanguard of the proletariat, but of the 'Chinese People and the Chinese nation'. Membership is now open to 'any advanced element', including private entrepreneurs.

However we want to term it, one of the features of the Chinese reform process is the transformation of relationships between existing state actors, and the changing basis of their power. There is a symbiotic relationship (at the very least) between state elites and new economic elites. They have effectively co-opted each other into an alliance that, for the time being, mutually reinforces each other's power and influence, not to mention personal fortunes. What we see, then, is a process of reformulation of class alliances within China and the reformulation of the class basis of CCP rule. As such, demands for democratization are diminished by the relationship between 'old' and 'new' elites, and further reinforced by the two other pillars of legitimacy – stability and nationalism.

142 *Shaun Breslin*

Legitimacy, stability, and nationalism

Providing stability might not sound like the most ambitious goal for a government – it really should be the bottom line of any government. But in the Chinese case, it is important for two reasons. First, memories of the most disorderly years of the Cultural Revolution (1966–69) might be fading, but remain alive to an extent. Certainly, in 1978, simply not being the old party and not being the Gang of Four and not pursuing leftist policies was enough to provide a considerable degree of support for Deng Xiaoping. Emphasizing the difference between old and new polities has remained important ever since, as the Party has changed from being what Zheng Shiping (2003: 54) terms a 'revolutionary party' based on class struggle and mass mobilization to a 'ruling party' based on stability and order.

Second, while the chances of a return to a Maoist radical past have now disappeared, the potential for disorder remains alive. Perhaps more correctly, it is kept alive as the discourse of potential instability, and the Party's claim of a unique ability to prevent the slide into chaos, has been carefully constructed and maintained by the Party itself. This emphasis on the need for stability is at the heart of the *White Paper: Building of Political Democracy in China* (State Council 2005). On one level, stability is seen as an essential prerequisite for economic growth. On another, rapid economic growth in itself creates the need for strong authoritarian control to maintain stability in the face of increasing inequalities and social tensions.

The need for a strong state to oversee and regulate China's rapid transformation is an idea that appears to have gained considerable purchase in Chinese society. As Zheng Yongnian (2008: 4) notes, 'More and more people, many of whom were liberals in the 1980s, have grown suspicious of democracy. Some of these people have even openly opposed democracy.' And the fact that the strong state model seems to have worked in generating considerable economic growth and success is clearly important here. The flip side of the coin is the apparent association of democracy with at least instability and even disorder and chaos, and of the relative lack of success of developing democracies when compared to China. As such, there is more than just a little element of national pride that China's way of doing things – economic liberalization without western-style liberal democratization – has worked; and that the 'Beijing Consensus' (Ramo 2004) is now being proposed as an alternative to the 'Washington Consensus' as a model for developing states. So in this respect, the success of the strong state model is intrinsically linked to the importance of nationalism.

In some respects, calling this phenomenon 'nationalism' is problematic. What we see in China seems to lack sufficient coherence and guiding principles to be counted as an ideology as such – it is not a 'science of ideas'. But in the way that it is promoted by the Chinese state as a programme and guide to action, then perhaps it does deserve the epithet; though the Chinese authorities prefer the term 'patriotism' – literally 'love the country'

Democratizing one-party rule in China   143

(aiguo zhuyi 爱国主义) – rather than nationalism (minzhu zhuyi 民族主义). Perhaps the best way of addressing the problem is to consider two different types of nationalism in China.[4] The first is a state-sponsored ideology with a set of coherent ideas intended to influence the populace, legitimate the authoritarian political system, and provide a theoretical guide to action. The second nationalism is a catch-all term for a wide range of popular sentiments that lack internal coherence, but share basic assumptions about the nature of the international environment and the goal of restoring China to a perceived rightful position of a 'great power'. These state and popular nationalisms have a lot in common in terms of their perceptions of the nature of international relations, and their objectives for national resurgence and regeneration. They also communicate with each other in a two-way feedback system – the official nationalist ideology might have inspired, legitimated and motivated popular nationalism, but the state now also finds itself having to respond to popular nationalist aspirations.

Official nationalism and democracy

In terms of official policy, the promotion of nationalism has important implications for democratization. In fact, while this chapter emphasizes three pillars of legitimacy, the other two could be conceived of as subsets of the overarching 'national project'. For example, from the very beginning of the reform process in 1978, the need to adopt a new polity was justified and legitimated by the need to build a strong China that could resist (and even oppose) the existing hegemonic global order (Hughes 2006). For Gallagher (2002: 344), breaking the old social contract between the workers and the state that led to unrest and ultimately the end of communist rule in Eastern Europe was accepted in China 'because it is justified in nationalistic terms – it will save Chinese industry from the threat of foreign competition'.

Furthermore, there is a carefully constructed relationship between nationalism, democracy and western imperialism. Even the strongest proponents of liberal political reform in China argue that it is not something that can come quickly, and is certainly not something that should be imposed on China from outside. For example, Yu Keping (2003) argues that China needs 'incremental democracy' (zengliang minzhu 增量民主) that evolves as China evolves. Society needs to develop, and the form of democracy that China will end up with needs to 'fit' with these societal changes. As such, there are no models that can be a template for China because all societies are different (and should thus have different forms of democracy). Others are more blunt in arguing that the West is trying to impose its form of democracy on China to prevent China from rising. This forms part of a longer process of anti-Chinese activity that can be traced back to the subordination of China by force in the Opium Wars in the nineteenth century. As the official Communiqué from the Fourth Plenum of the 16th Central Committee (2004) put it, 'The strategy of foreign forces to break up and westernise China has not changed.'

144   *Shaun Breslin*

Moreover, the last time that the West imposed its norms and cultures on China in the second half of the nineteenth century, it resulted in the loss of the most basic and fundamental democratic right – national integrity was destroyed by foreign domination. As such, it is not just that western democracy is non-Chinese or even anti-Chinese, it is actually anti-democratic in that it abrogated Chinese sovereignty in the nineteenth and twentieth centuries, and threatens to deny the right to develop a domestic indigenous Chinese form of democracy today (State Council 2005). So the essential starting point for democracy is independence and sovereignty, in order that the people of a country can rule themselves. By re-creating the nation state free from external control, the 1949 revolution achieved this basic democratic right. Having fought so hard to win this 'democracy', the CCP will do what it can to stop outsiders undermining independence and sovereignty. According to this interpretation, the revolution becomes less to do with class conflict than a struggle for national independence – and Mao's position as 'father of the nation' rather than architect of radicalism is similarly redefined and re-emphasized.

This idea that western democracy might be a means of containing China is compounded by a feeling that democracy and rights are not universally applied – that China is the subject of western double standards. It is being treated as akin to a pariah state by countries that themselves do not conduct all of their own affairs in keeping with democratic principles (Peerenboom 2007: 165). The US in particular is pushing China to democratize when the West did not do anything comparable at a similar stage of its political and economic evolution. Moreover, the West (and again largely shorthand for the United States) does not adhere to its own supposed fundamental principles of democracy. It frequently abrogates liberal democracy at home (China now produces its own annual report on human rights abuses in the US) and also overseas – for example, in abrogating the fundamental democratic and human right of sovereignty in Iraq.

Popular nationalism, the national project and criticizing the State

This understanding that the West either simply does not understand China or is deliberately trying to attack and hurt the Chinese people is shared by wide sections of the Chinese populace. Clearly, this popular sentiment does not exist in a political void: education, government statements, the media and even the entertainment industry, all play important roles in promoting the official position. But at times, as Shen (2007) has demonstrated, the state finds itself criticized by the people for not acting as it should to protect Chinese interests and to impose Chinese supremacy. Notably, internet discussion groups, bulletin boards and blogs have become the main means by which this criticism is articulated – so the spread of the internet has become a force for criticizing the state as many predicted; however, not to demand greater democracy, but instead greater nationalist resolve.

Democratizing one-party rule in China 145

Demanding that the Party do more for the national project has been at the heart of at least two of the major waves of criticism in the post-Mao era. The second of these in the mid to late 1990s was manifest in the publication of several best-selling works that portrayed the US as mistakenly attempting to impose its inferior norms and values on China, and calling for China to resist the global hegemon. Most famously, the highly popular *China Can Say No* (Song et al. 1996) railed against the US as the self-imposed creator of international norms, and the self-imposed adjudicator of right and wrong. China was a great civilization which should resist American hegemony and strive to exert itself over the global hegemon.[5]

The 1999 publication, *China's Path Under the Shadow of Globalisation* called for a much more aggressive (or at least assertive) response to any US attempt to harm China's interests (Fang et al. 1999). And although this book was self-consciously written as a continuation of the 'say no' literature, by focusing on the potential impact of economic globalization in China's entry negotiations to the World Trade Organization (WTO), it represents something of a link to the third wave of critical writing associated with the 'New Left'. While originally referring to a relatively small group of critical writers, the term 'New Left' is at times used as an umbrella term for all of those who criticize the negative consequences of economic liberalization (not all such writers welcome the term because it has connotations with previous periods of leftism in China and suggests an untrue desire to return to the radical Maoist paradigm).

The main focus of these critical thinkers is the negative consequences of economic reform, and those people who have been left behind as China's economy grows. But this is linked to nationalism, in as much as growth has been facilitated by integration with the global economy, and the global economy is seen as being dominated by foreign interests. In particular, China's accession to the WTO in 2001 provided a focus for those critics who thought that the government was allowing China's interests to be superseded by those of (foreign) neo-liberalism and the West. For Lu Di (2002), liberalization of the media means that transnational media corporations are now penetrating China – seen as part of a cultural invasion, enforcing foreign values on China with the same intentions as the British troops that enforced change on China through the Opium Wars.[6]

In highlighting the growth of inequality and other societal issues, New Left writers are obviously concerned about what this means for those affected. However, the more fundamental concern is what this means for China – for the national project. If this can be termed a movement, it is a movement that is essentially concerned about how best to serve to promote Chinese interests in a dangerous international environment and how best to promote the resurgence of China. And for some of these writers at least, this is something that can be best achieved by a strong state and the sort of Listian-inspired development that inspired German industrialization under Bismarck and Japanese modernization in the 1920s and 1930s (Han 2000).[7] Although the

146 *Shaun Breslin*

majority of writers do not specifically engage with List's work, these ideas are redolent in much of the broader New Left literature and in many of the popular sentiments articulated by taxi drivers and in restaurants in China. The strong state can defend China in a hostile international environment and also put in place much-needed state welfarism and social safety nets, and redirect wealth from the new rich to the new (and old) poor.

However, the state also needs to be reformed. China needs democracy – but not liberal democracy. There is a demand for the system to become more responsive to the interests of the new and old poor rather than the new rich. It is not state power per se that is the problem, but the relatively closed and self-serving nature of Chinese state power, and its over-emphasis on generating growth rather than distributing the benefits of growth more equitably. People also want the party–state to get its own house in order; to deal with outright corruption and the relationship between political power/influence and economic gain more broadly (even when it is not illegal). Democratization, then, is an essential component of the national project and preventing liberalism – even worse, foreign liberalism – from harming the Chinese people and undermining Chinese power.

In order to understand these later waves of criticism it is important to consider the early intentions of those who became involved in the original wave that led to Tiananmen in 1989. It is incredibly difficult to say anything definitive about the extent to which this was a democracy movement, for two reasons. First, sentiments, emotions and demands evolved both during the occupation of the square and after its clearance. Second, this was not a cohesive movement and was instead characterized more by diversity than common purpose. So with these important caveats in mind we can suggest that Tiananmen was inspired by a combination of student self-interest, the long-term goal of national regeneration and the shorter-term goal of inner party political reform and rectification, as well as by those who (later) called for more fundamental political change.

In traditional China, intellectuals (zhishifenzi 知识分子) were expected to play the role of the moral conscience of the imperial system – they had a right and a duty to expose problems on behalf of the general population. With the collapse of the empire, students and intellectuals became the vanguards of new China, debating and introducing new ideas in the May Fourth movement to replace the outdated and defeated ideas of traditional China. But while these new ideas were largely 'western' creations – liberalism, Social Darwinism, socialism and anarchism – they were embraced as a way of saving and reinvigorating China; the ideologies were means to other ends rather than ends in themselves Thus, for many of those who brought the CCP to power in 1949, promoting Communism like the self-strengthening movement before it and Deng's transition from socialism afterwards was a means to the end of China's restoration.

In many respects, the students took on these dual historical roles in 1989, self-associating themselves with both the loyal critics of traditional China and the innovators and saviours of the nation from the first quarter of the twentieth century. Moreover, there was a feeling that this generation had been forced into action because of the sell-out of the older generation. Establishment intellectuals had been co-opted to become part of the system rather than 'loyal' critics from without, while government officials were too concerned with their own positions and privilege to provide the leadership the people needed.

Student activism in 1989 did not emerge from a void, and previous bouts of activism occurred with at least some official approval (Crane 1994) and also reflected this combination of national pride, self-interest and the need for the Party to become more pluralistic. For example, demonstrations against Japanese imports (perceived to be being dumped on China) in 1985 were not opposed by the state even if it was not an officially state-sanctioned movement. Demonstrations in 1986 calling for more democracy were inspired by the then party leader Hu Yaobang's own call for a search for new ways to democratize the Party – to make the system more transparent and fair, rather than to overthrow it. And in retrospect, perhaps we can identify the Christmas 1988 protests against African students in Nanjing as the start of what became Tiananmen 1989. While antipathy towards African students had long run deep, in Nanjing it escalated into complaints about the much better treatment and conditions that international students – and 'even' African students! – enjoyed compared to Chinese university students. This in turn escalated into a call for Chinese students to be given human rights (Sullivan 1994).

So like previous bouts of unrest, Tiananmen was partly aimed at redressing specific grievances under the banner of a national patriotic campaign – against the lack of choice and individual freedom outlined early in this chapter, but also against boring and poor classes and curricula, compulsory political education classes, student dorms housing 12 to a room, only an hour's hot water a day, terrible food, and so on. It was also aimed at making the Party less introverted – more open to new ideas, new people and new processes; to make the Party live up to its promise of a new 'socialist democracy' of transparency, predictability and legality and to deal with the corruption that seemed to be providing the sons and daughters of the elites with all the benefits of economic reform. And all of this was necessary in itself, but also to allow for China's resurgence as a great power.

Making authoritarianism work

Demanding democratization: transparency and legalism

These demands have been echoed since 1989 by not just the 'New Left' and 'say no' generations, but also by Chinese from every sort of political persuasion and group (including from within the Party itself). People want the state to actually do in practice what it already says that it does – to implement at the local level laws that are passed at the centre. Perhaps most clearly of all,

148 *Shaun Breslin*

they want the state to listen to them. There is also a demand for honesty. For Ngkok (2007), the consequences of the SARs (severe acute respiratory syndrome) outbreak brought home to the new leadership of Hu Jintao and Wen Jiabao the extent to which the party–state structure had become out of tune with the needs and demands of ordinary people and had become a self-serving organization. Officials not only lied to the people but lied to each other and gave the impression of a network of officials solely concerned with saving their own face and positions, not saving those who were most at risk and dependent on the system for health-care and reliable information.

As a brief aside here, it is interesting to compare the response to SARS with the May 2008 earthquake in Sichuan Province. At first sight, the two crises are not readily comparable. Although SARs did have victims, the longer-term problem was more to do with the (non)governance of risk. After the earthquake, while the risk of aftershocks, floods and disease were important, there were more tangible and direct challenges in terms of saving the trapped and finding food and shelter for the homeless. Nevertheless, the very open and transparent way in which the earthquake was dealt with shows a party–state that was not only helping the people, but keen to show the people that it was helping them. The army were the people's saviours, and the party–state had nothing to hide. Helping those affected (and not helping officials cover their own backs) was the agenda – and if corruption was partly responsible for the speed at which some buildings collapsed, then this would be dealt with openly once the immediate crisis was dealt with.

Notably, however, this new openness was not unconditional. Foreign reporters and those protesting against the collapse of schools were removed (at the very least) as soon as protests began to appear coordinated and out of the State's control. While the Party encourages what Shai (2004) calls 'managed participation', it reacts very differently when it feels that it cannot control or manage political action. And it is how it handles this tension that will perhaps determine whether the attempt to construct a consultative participatory authoritarianism ultimately can be successful.

Supplying democratization

Debates over the need to reform the political system have been ongoing for many years, but the Fourth Plenum of the 16th Central Committee in September 2004 marked the start of a renewed focus on the failings of the Party's leadership or 'ruling capacity' (zhizheng nengli 执政能力).The plenum's final communiqué noted that while both 'history' and the 'Chinese People' had 'chosen' the Party to rule, its continued tenure in power could not be taken for granted. The Party needed to 'heighten an awareness of suffering, and draw deep lessons from the experience of ruling parties across the world' to ensure 'good government for the people'. In short, 'constructing a clean and honest administration and fighting corruption are a matter of life and death for the Party' (Central Committee 2004).[8]

Democratizing one-party rule in China 149

A number of academics with close links to the Party have responded by proposing alternatives. Xie Tiao (2007) has perhaps been the most radical, looking to the Swedish model of social(ist) democracy for lessons that the Chinese leadership can learn in undertaking political system reform, and appearing to suggest that Leninist-Marxism had cheated the Soviet people (though refraining from commenting on whether the Chinese people had been similarly taken in). But Xie also echoes the dominant conclusion that there is a need for greater popular participation and more checks and balances on the abuse of power (Fewsmith 2007). And without pushing the analogy too far, this message is very similar to what the demonstrators were saying in 1989, which in turn has echoes of Mao's critique of the Party before the Cultural Revolution. For Mao, the Party had become both isolated and insulated from the people; isolated in terms of having different sets of interests and demands than the normal people, and insulated in restricting ways in which normal people could make their voices heard.

Mao's solution in the 1960s was to immerse the cadres in the masses – a process that went beyond probably what even he expected and wanted, as the radicalism eventually paralysed the party–state structure and led to all but civil war in some parts of China. This is not the intention today. Rather, it is to re-engage the party–state with the people in four main ways. First, the leadership has renewed its commitment to promoting equable growth, and helping those who have been left behind by providing more social welfare. Whether this constitutes a new fourth pillar of legitimacy to add to the three outlined earlier, or whether it is simply a rethinking of the existing balance between stability and growth is something that is yet to become clear. The rhetoric appears to suggest a new paradigm, but the actual policies are not quite the radical departures from the status quo ante that the current leadership might want the Chinese people to believe. Second, there is yet another widespread and high profile campaign against corruption. Third, there have been key policy changes intended to reduce the way in which officials can exert their influence over the population. Fees have been abolished and transferred to more transparent and predictable taxes, and land rights have been enshrined. In keeping with the understanding that what is said in Beijing doesn't always happen on the ground, these have been supported by high profile, cumbersome and expensive enforcement campaigns.

Finally, the Party is promoting democratization, apparently defined by Hu Jintao as 'perfecting a socialist democratic system' that guarantees 'full participation' in democratic elections, 'democratic decision making, and democratic supervision of power'.[9] This can and does entail the extension of elections to more levels of the political system – something that is likely to continue to expand in the future. But when the Chinese talk about democratization, what they are really referring to is making the existing one party–state more democratic – increasing transparency, predictability and the rule of law – and more efficient. For Pan Wei (2003), it is about constructing a 'consultative rule of law regime' – though again terminology can be

150 *Shaun Breslin*

confusing. Fazhi 法治 can be translated as rule of law, but when used in China does not have the same connections with the provision of basic political and human rights as it does in the West. Rather, like democratization, it entails ensuring that citizens know what they can and cannot do; and also that party–state officials know the limits to their authority and can be challenged through the legal system if the exceed their powers.

Democracy in this sense entails giving the individual protection from the arbitrary power of the party–state and providing new checks and balances on the power of individual leaders to pervert or ignore official policy. In this latter respect, democratization is also about enforcing the central leadership's authority over the political system – an alliance between central government and the people to combat the authority of the local state. Democratization is also about creating a more transparent and predictable policy-making process – one that can accommodate more of the diverse interests and demands that exist in the increasingly diverse and complex Chinese society, making the people feel part of the system and also ensuring that policy reflects the interests of the people. What it is certainly not about is introducing multiparty democracy through which the CCP might be challenged for overall power.

Conclusion: towards democratization with Chinese characteristics

Is this limited democratization enough to satisfy those who feel that their voices are not being heard? And is the state able to deliver on its promises? In economic terms, the much vaunted move to a new economic paradigm based on development and equity has had some concrete results, but the task of satisfying the demands of those who feel unfairly left behind is simply too huge to be accomplished any time soon. Politically, one of the key objectives of democratization with Chinese characteristics is to make the local state subject to the oversight of the people in accordance with central government aims and objectives. But unless central organizations dispatch inspection teams to stand over the shoulder of every local official, then ensuring that local authorities do what they are meant to do remains hugely problematic. This is particularly so when the task of implementing democratization is largely in the hands of those who might come under unwelcome scrutiny by the people if the new system is made to work.

Perhaps more important, there seems to be an internal tension between the perceived need to encourage debate and participation, on the one hand, and the desire to manage it, on the other. In a major report that has become known in English as *Storming the Fortress*, the Central Party School promoted a 'comprehensive political system reform plan' to be undertaken by 2020, that requires the State not just to tolerate but also to embrace and promote non-state action and a multitude of different ideas (including religious beliefs) (Zhou et al. 2007). If this is going to work, then non-governmental organizations need to emerge and develop to articulate the interests that the elites know they should take into account in developing policy. There also needs to be

Democratizing one-party rule in China   151

predictability and certainty. If those who respond to the new consultative climate and participate as required are then periodically victims of renewed bouts of policy tightening, as some seem to have been in the run-up to the Olympics, then the desire to participate is likely to decline: the belief that the system can live up to its promises could well diminish.

But when push comes to shove, the system – whatever level of the system we are talking about – is ultimately wary in the extreme of allowing (let alone facilitating) truly independent participation in the political arena. Or more correctly, it is wary of what appears to be concerted and organized political participation. The Party wants 'managed participation' and it becomes very nervous as soon as participation appears unmanageable, or managed and organized independently from the state – or even when individual action becomes unorganized collective action (Shai 2004). And in many respects, the way that the leadership responds to this contradiction – the desire to consult versus the desire to control – will go a long way to determining how the democratization process works out in the future.

Add these challenges together, and there is a distinct possibility that the drive for democratization might backfire. Yu Jianrong (2008: 75–6) argues that this has already happened, with new trends in the mass protests. Riots are no longer just responses to single issue concerns, such as corrupt excising of taxes, workplace disasters, land seizures, and so on. There is always a specific spark, but they are flamed by:

> a more profound sense of social discontent, reflecting a present crisis of governance in China. After three decades of rapid economic development, China's political system is increasingly incapable of harmonizing relations between the disparate interest groups that exist in the market economy. The government's failure to establish a just and equitable adjudication system to arbitrate between them has engendered widespread social despair.

But as argued throughout this chapter, dissatisfaction with the current system does not necessarily mean that there is a demand to replace it with liberal democracy. The most important objective – the coherent political aspiration – is national regeneration and resurgence, with some form of authoritarian government deemed the best way of achieving this. The current system might need reforming, but into a better form of authoritarian control – governance by a form of benevolent and benign consultative strong state that oversees a more equitable distribution of growth at home, and defends Chinese interests in an uncertain and perhaps even hostile environment abroad.

Moreover, the idea of China as a developmental authoritarian state holds considerable appeal as a model for others to follow. It might be a stylized model that ignores many of the challenges that the Chinese leadership itself has identified, but what model isn't an ideal type? As an alternative to the liberalizing conditionalities of the international financial institutions and the

152 *Shaun Breslin*

major western powers, China's experience of achieving rapid economic growth while not abandoning authoritarian control through democratization has considerable appeal in some areas – particularly among authoritarian elites in parts of the developing world. In developing his conception of the end of history, Fukuyama (1989) argued that 'the People's Republic of China can no longer act as a beacon for illiberal forces around the world'. In that he was talking about the Maoist alternative at the time, he was right. But in abandoning the Maoist model, then China might have developed a beacon for illiberalism that is an even greater challenge to the global spread of liberal democracy.

Notes

1 Criminal Law of the People's Republic of China, available at: www.com-law.net/findlaw/crime/criminallaw1.html.
2 The following section is adapted from the discussion on class reformation in Breslin (2007: 174–84).
3 Official Chinese reports tend to refer to stratification and use the term jieceng 阶层 or social strata, rather than class (jieji 阶级)
4 Zhao (2004) prefers to divide the discourse into three: state, intellectual and popular. Given that some intellectuals are very close to the State, and that others have promoted agendas that are similar to the popular approach identified in this chapter, a bipartite division seems to be the simplest way of establishing that Chinese nationalism has different facets.
5 For a good overview of the 'say no' literature, see Des Forges and Luo Xu (2001).
6 I am grateful to the late Zeng Huaguo for this observation.
7 Friedrich List, German political economist (1789–1846).
8 Author's translation, others may differ.
9 According to Xie Tao (2007), this was how Hu Jintao described it orally during a trip to France in 2007. Author's translation – note that 充分 chong fen is translated here as 'full', but can also be 'ample' which has a slightly different nuance.

9 Democratization by whom?
Resistance to democracy promotion in the Middle East

Bassma Kodmani

This chapter sets out to explain the failure so far of international democracy promotion in the Middle East. It offers a number of essential conditions applying to relations with the West that must be met first, if democratic objectives are to have a chance of being realized. While locating the present and future prospects within a past history of troubled foreign involvement in the region, the account is positive about the democratic possibilities. At the same time it argues that these can only be damaged by the continuation by outsiders of an unreformed approach to promoting democracy and other foreign policy objectives there.

In the Middle East, the credibility of democracy promotion, irrespective of its timing, circumstances and of the identity of its promoters, is undermined by a number of fundamental realities and constraints that are difficult to ignore. These are, first, there is no consensus on the model of democracy to promote, beyond a few stated principles. Second, no foreign power is likely to promote change that runs against its vital interests. And third, there are vital needs and concerns, such as physical security and integrity of the social body that supersede aspirations to democracy. Added to those, factors of a more circumstantial nature can also discredit the noble design of democracy promotion. As it was waged by the democracy bureaucracy created under the presidency of George W. Bush in the United States, democracy promotion in the region occurred at a time when the West was renewing its tutelage there and accompanying the message of soft power with the heaviest instruments of hard power (in Iraq), thus killing any chance of a fair and serene discussion of the idea altogether.

Yet for all its ugly resonance and nasty consequences in the region to date, the democracy promotion agenda has undeniably triggered a change of attitude in the Arab world by governments and societies alike. The less credit western governments claim for any achievements, however modest, the easier it will be to assess the impact with some objectivity. As a new Obama-led administration takes control of foreign policy in the US, the fact that it has made clear its intention of restarting a genuine peace process between Israel and the Palestinians and is not making democracy promotion a priority is likely to help. At no point did Arab public opinion accept the idea that the

154 *Bassma Kodmani*

question of Palestine should be set aside to give precedence to domestic change. More importantly, the large majority of public opinion in the Arab world continues to think that western powers do not have the interests of the Arabs at heart, largely because they have failed to promote a fair solution for the Palestinians.

There are important lessons to learn from the failures of the Bush administration. Whether this will be enough to rehabilitate democracy promotion as an acceptable let alone legitimate goal, is an open question. Whatever the fate of this agenda under the Obama administration, advice to the region on what it should and should not do needs to be coupled with sober and realistic thinking about what outside powers can and cannot do, as well as greater sensitivity to the complex realities and intrinsic fragility of the region and of the states that compose it. Questions about how to promote democracy in multi-sectarian societies, and in a fundamentally unstable security environment as well, have been left without a satisfactory answer or rather they have not been posed at all. After the traumatic experience of the war on Iraq and the quagmire of Afghanistan, Arab societies are calling on western promoters of democracy to be more humble about their ability to bring change. The message is clear: You (the West) have proved that you can wreak havoc in a country, overthrow a brutal regime, dismantle the state apparatus, but nothing indicates so far that you are equipped to rebuild a country socially or politically.

While Arab societies beg for greater understanding of these realities, they also seek ways to prevent their governments from using those same realities as excuses to delay the fulfilment of their long-standing aspiration to live a dignified life as free citizens.

The democracy promotion agenda as articulated by former President Bush in 2003 has been widely loathed and rejected by Arab societies. Five or more years after it was launched, no Arab country has moved away from authoritarianism and established stable democratic rule. The fact that the agenda has alienated public opinion in the Arab world and has not succeeded so far in bringing stable democracy to any country in the region leaves little room to discuss its merits and no justification for persisting in trying to enforce it. Any serious observer could have predicted that change could not be a matter of a few years but would take a decade or probably two. However, the more fundamental question remains one of principle: can democracy be fostered from outside? Do public opinions accept the idea itself, and if they do, by whom and through which means?

There are few precedents in history to suggest that democracy can be deployed by outsiders in a country to transform an authoritarian system. With the notable exception of the years 1945–48, transition to democracy was a slow and endogenous process. The most frequently cited examples are those of the aftermath of World War II, when Germany, Austria, Italy and Japan witnessed massive foreign military intervention, defeat and regime change. The other exception is the de-colonization era when democracy was

Resistance to democracy in the Middle East   155

introduced from the outside and even then, the only successful major example is that of India. Barring those historical cases, all other successful democratization has resulted from internal change, whether in Southern Europe, Asia or Latin America.

For a time, the collapse of the communist countries of Central and Eastern Europe in the 1990s revived the belief that democracy could be promoted from outside. Western democracies lauded the impact of Radio Free Europe and the role of the Conference on Security and Cooperation in Europe (CSCE) as decisive factors in the establishment of democratic political systems. The reality is more complex: change in Eastern Europe resulted from a combination of the domestic upheaval of social and political forces, on the one hand, and the strategic and ideological shift from the socialist order with its military architecture, on the other.

In the Middle East, the debate on the democracy promotion agenda in the past five years has slowly shifted too. The main disagreements are no longer over whether to accept or reject a foreign role. Between the minority who embraced it and were dubbed 'the marines' by their opponents, and a large section of the intellectual and political elites who denounced it vociferously, there are interesting nuances to be captured.

The foreign factor is a component of Middle Eastern realities

Beyond the knee-jerk reactions and irritation at the 'heavy US hand', it is important to consider what exactly is rejected, and how societies have been interacting with the discourse on democracy proposed from abroad.

The reality is that key developments and major ideological debates in the Arab world were strongly influenced, if not determined, by the foreign factor, whether in opposition to it or in support of it. It is actually impossible to analyze the political situation in the Arab world in isolation from external factors. The Egyptian national movement in the years 1910–20 was encouraged by the Declaration of the Fourteen Points that US President Woodrow Wilson enunciated in a speech to the US Congress at the end of World War I. All the political forces that began to appear then were influenced by external factors. The influence did not come from the colonial states only. The Muslim Brotherhood organization was formed in reaction to the collapse of the Caliphate in Turkey. When fascist ideas emerged in Italy and Germany in the 1930s, fascist forces took shape in Egypt in the form of the 'Young Egypt' (Misr al-Fatat) Party and the like. A few years after the communist revolution took place in Russia in 1917, Communist Parties were formed in most Arab countries that closely coordinated their activities with Moscow and the socialist countries of Eastern Europe (Al-Ghazali Harb 2007). Even the Nasserist revolution in Egypt might not have taken place altogether had it not been for outside influence. In 1952, Washington encouraged the Free Officers to carry out their coup against the monarchy because the US believed that Nasserism was the only way that Arab communist movements could be kept

156   *Bassma Kodmani*

in check. In the Gulf, meanwhile, the British played the role of king makers by supporting the Saud family to rise to power in Saudi Arabia, and by crafting the entities and establishing the ruling families of the small Gulf states in the 1960s and 1970s.

So, cases where debates and processes of change were purely endogenous are the exception rather than the norm, and this is not specific to the Middle East. Domestic debates in Central and Eastern Europe were always shaped by foreign influence or dominant foreign powers following a military victory. Likewise, criticism of the internal situation in Eastern and Central Europe is always made in reference to some outside model.[1]

The relevant question therefore is not whether to accept or reject outside influence. It is rather to recognize that foreign influence has always been a reality and that foreign powers continue to have a decisive role in determining the fate of political regimes, whether it is to protect them, keep them afloat or destabilize them.

Analysts recount key episodes of Arab contemporary history to show that the region was always penetrated and that foreign powers have always played a role in shaping Arab history. In many cases, they argue, events celebrated as glorious patriotic achievements were in fact triggered, supported or facilitated by foreign powers, as if collective memory had erased the foreign factor (Al-Ghazali Harb 2007).

While very few people in the region would publicly admit the potentially positive role of pressure from outside, there is arguably more support for some aspects of it than appears at first sight. Arab societies have come to believe that their governments are more sensitive to pressure from outside than from their own society. Advocates of external pressure on current governments (and there are few of them who openly call for it) argue that such external pressure is effective because the ruling elites have a sense that they derive part of their legitimacy from their good relations with the outside world. Requests and sometimes instructions, conditions or other forms of pressure from abroad produce tangible effects. Given this objective (albeit regrettable) reality, accountability vis-à-vis the outside is seen as preferable to no accountability at all, provided of course that the outside powers are sincere about pursuing the objective of democratic transformation.

When democratic transformation becomes an explicit goal

Western governments had been promoting reforms and good governance for more than ten years before the Bush administration, followed by Europe, made democracy promotion an explicit goal in the Middle East.

There is much ambiguity and misunderstanding around the word reform. Retrospectively, we can consider it was constructive ambiguity because reform was not seen as a threatening scheme. It led governments to integrate 'reform' into their discourse, to engage in some changes such as modernization of their administration, to introduce new legislation, constitutional reforms,

Resistance to democracy in the Middle East 157

the rationalization of some practices and other measures that they felt would boost economic growth, attract foreign investment and improve their image abroad. They pursued measures aimed at satisfying their outside partners while renewing their control over their societies. None of these measures required a commitment on their part to yield any of their prerogatives, nor to relate to their societies in any way that was fundamentally different from before. Governments manipulated reforms to consolidate their control. The discourse on good governance and reform allowed governments to de-politicize the measures they agreed to implement, thus removing any content that might challenge the prevailing political order.

With the motto of reform, the region went some way down the road to change but reached a definite limit. Administrative modernization led to replacing old politicians with younger professionals that had no or only shallow social roots, bringing some progress on the level of greater efficiency but not on accountability. The space has been opened for pressure from below though it remains highly constrained. Governments enjoy greater capacity for top-down control, but it became clear that the onus of developing countervailing powers to check the power of the executive would not come from the top but would have to be initiated by the societies. Reform schemes were becoming meaningless as long as the objective of democratization was not made explicit, and as long as rulers were not told more sharply that democracy is about reconciling the objective of good governance with that of political representation; that institutions delivering services are not just neutral administrations or machines but forms of governance, and that the key political question is not only what services they provide (no matter how valuable these services are, as security for example) but how much control citizens have over them.

When democracy promotion became the stated goal of the West, Arab governments hurried to integrate it in their discourse. They designed new strategies aimed at pleasing or reassuring foreign powers. Their attitudes only confirmed the fact that the Middle East is a deeply penetrated region. Monarchs in Morocco, Jordan, Bahrain, started talking about installing constitutional monarchies. Presidents in Egypt, Yemen, Algeria, Mauritania like almost every other country in the region organized elections and designed reform programmes for their institutions that gave priority to the areas most visible to outsiders. When criteria or indicators of good governance and democratic practices are put forward, the leaders are careful to give an impression of fulfilling the requirements: they tailor their reform measures so as to ensure positive evaluation and a good image vis-à-vis the outside. When a prominent columnist in a major American newspaper writes a critical piece on the regime, this will be the first thing that a president or king wants to read in the morning, lest the article influence the US Congress and its debates on the fate of vital financial aid, a trade agreement, foreign investments or military and security support to the country.

Shifting to a new paradigm that set out explicitly the objective of democratic transformation without dilution should have increased the chances of

158 *Bassma Kodmani*

achieving some successes. Only when clear-cut contours are defined can effective strategies be derived. This does not require an agreement on the exact outcome in terms of the desired model of democracy in each national context. The shift towards democratic transformation as the stated goal was meant to lay the ground for expanding the range of instruments to mobilize, processes to experiment and actors to involve. If only the objectives had been more modestly stated and a more humble assessment had been made of what the West can and cannot do, a great deal more might have been achieved.

Public space and the strategic role of the media

One actor that can claim to have played a strategic role in inducing a change of attitude is the media – first, international television networks, then local independent media. Given that most regimes are more concerned about looking good than they are about introducing genuine reforms, image-making becomes a critical tool for exerting pressure. It is pressure of a neutral kind, one that does not suggest directions or models but that merely exposes governments and discredits their bad practices, leading them to alter their behaviour at their own initiative. When the international media started to provide wide coverage of protest movements, a signal was given, the lid of fear that had kept societies from mobilizing was lifted and citizens dared take to the streets to express their demands.

Media played a critical role in re-injecting politics into the public space, from where it had been banned for decades. If we take the three-level functions of public space – expression, protest, participation – then the Arab world has clearly witnessed progress on the first two, though only limited progress on the third.[2] The public space of expression has been broadened everywhere, including in even the most authoritarian systems. Media is the first space in which this opening occurred. It began with pan-Arab satellite television as a de-territorialized public space, then, more significantly, it became grounded in countries that allowed independent media to develop. The diversification in media sources and ownership was the key to this change in the landscape from a state monopoly to the emergence of a variety of privately-owned local TV channels, newspapers and internet sites. In Egypt, over a dozen independent newspapers and half a dozen TV channels have emerged in the past decade. In Morocco, Algeria, Kuwait and Lebanon where the state monopoly was broken earlier, independent newspapers exist. In countries where the state monopoly continues to prevail (Syria, Saudi Arabia), blogs have become a major source of information for society, albeit limited to those equipped with computers.

The public space for protest is more limited, though it has clearly flourished as well. Demonstrations, sit-ins, strikes, even when they are banned by law, are happening. Countries in Northern Africa like Morocco and Algeria, Tunisia before President Ben Ali came to office in 1987 have a longer tradition of street demonstrations. Egypt started tolerating demonstrations and

Resistance to democracy in the Middle East 159

reduced the level of violent suppression by security forces once independent and international satellite television began to cover them. First, these demonstrations were organized as a reaction to regional conflicts (Palestine, Iraq). They occurred inside university campuses and around the mosques after Friday prayers. But they quickly became a common mode of mobilization that spilled into the streets and expressed discontent over domestic issues, organized by activists from the opposition. Periodic demonstrations have come to serve as a test of the government's determination, its willingness to use violence to suppress and expose itself to embarrassment as pictures circulate around the world. Civil society is now using the space opened by the international as well as the new independent local media.

The reason the media is singled out here is because it proved to be a key vehicle for the expression of social concerns and demands, as well as the introduction of some diversity into a public space that had previously become dominated by the religious discourse.

When democracy promotion meets reality

With the shift towards formulating democracy as an explicit objective, came a different type of disillusion. What Arab elites have been observing since democracy promotion began to be touted by the US and others as a priority, is a mix of ignorance and arrogance that the 'democratizers' have demonstrated. Many of those Arab voices who saw some merit in the western agenda of democracy promotion were deeply disappointed when they discovered how little western governments understood about the realities of the region and the complexities of the societies. Even when the outsiders are sincere, so the argument goes, they are ignorant of the realities of the region and therefore incapable of formulating relevant strategies and inducing positive change.

Scepticism permeates the thinking of Arab public opinion, including among the advocates of a foreign role. The latter lament that over five decades, western interests crystallized around three priorities: (1) protecting Israel; (2) securing oil supplies; and (3) preventing communist control over the region up to the end of the Cold War. None of these goals, they say, required the existence of democratic regimes, but rather of strong regimes able to resist the communist threat and other dangers that impinged on access to the region's petroleum resources. It is only after September 11, 2001, that the same external powers started pressing for democracy. But since then, relations have been tainted with various forms of suspicion: suspicion of ignorance, arrogance, lack of empathy if not outright hostility, as well as suspicions of foreign ambition and greed.

Security challenges and the democratic agenda: a minefield

Unfortunately, developments on the ground in Iraq especially have nurtured the worst fears and given credit to an ideologically based discourse that

160　*Bassma Kodmani*

rejects democracy promotion from outside as a modern version of colonial politics. The fact is that concomitant with their self-assigned mission of democracy promotion, western powers were imposing new forms of tutelage on some countries of the region and resorting to practices all too reminiscent of the colonial era. Societies watch not only with suspicion but with outright fear policies that they deem irresponsible at best, because they seem to mock the territorial integrity, disrupt national and social cohesion, and ignore the fragility of Arab states.

Arab collective memory vividly retains the idea that colonial powers throughout the twentieth century used minorities to advance their own interests. The societies now continue to glorify the leaders of revolts who resisted foreign schemes at dividing their country and who protected the national integrity, examples being the national heroes in Syria, Iraq, Algeria and elsewhere. It is very difficult to erase this memory at a time when military occupation is a reality of the present, together with strategies to remodel the political institutions of a major country like Iraq along sectarian lines. Arab societies are most suspicious of any foreign discourse on minorities (ethnic, cultural, religious), their status and rights when it is articulated against the backdrop of efforts to revive tribal and ethnic loyalties in Iraq, Afghanistan, and Pakistan, thereby undermining hopes of salvaging the central modern state.

Even in situations where the opposition is muzzled by the most authoritarian governments, such as in Syria, society sincerely believes that public denunciation of and mobilization against the government are unpatriotic. To this day, a large part of the rejection of foreign interference is out of fear of being 'treasonized' (*takhwin*), literally being considered a traitor, something that governments take advantage of because they know it is a soft spot of their public opinions. This is not a specific feature of some kind of Arab paranoia and conspiracy theory. Political scientists acknowledge that among the conditions for establishing a sound democracy, the elected rulers must enjoy a high degree of autonomy vis-à-vis foreign powers. This is because the alienation of national independence disqualifies a democratic regime (Schmitter and Karl 1991).

These fears have been constantly fuelled by the ever increasing militarization of US Middle East policy. One recent example is the revelation about a 2004 classified order from then Secretary of Defense Donald Rumsfeld, under the direction of President Bush which authorized Special Operations Forces to conduct attacks against al-Qaeda and other militants anywhere in the world including even countries not at war with the United States (in Syria, Pakistan and elsewhere). Based on an expansive definition of self-defence, the order provides a legal rationale for conducting operations inside the territory of sovereign countries without the prior approval of the governments, and allows for intelligence gathering anywhere in the region.[3] Likewise, the Bush administration also persuaded many governments in the region to join security and intelligence cooperation agreements in the name of the war on terror.

National cohesion and the integrity of the state

Much as societies are unhappy with their governments, they seek to protect state institutions as the only guarantee against chaos and threats to the survival of society as a whole and of the personal security of citizens. Scenes of conflict in Iraq, Palestine, Lebanon, Sudan and in Algeria over many years act as deterrents and are shaping the attitudes of opposition forces. Radical groups advocating violence find little support within society. Islamist movements who resorted to violence in the past have repented and conducted self-criticism. It is remarkable to note that virtually all opposition movements, from left to right, secular and Islamist, are unreservedly choosing the peaceful path to promote change. This is not out of any particular esteem or belief in the legitimacy of the governing elites but rather out of fear of endangering the foundations of the state.

The outcomes of public opinion polls conducted in the region offer a clear indication of those fears. They all seem to confirm that aspirations to freedom and democratic governance are overruled by fears of instability and support for law and order. This is hardly surprising. In all extremes cases of human misery, civil strife and poverty, priority is given to holding the country together and then planning economic, social and political development. This is true of Africa but it also holds true for the Arab world, where sectarian diversity and the risks to the stability and integrity of the national states are widely perceived as existential threats, albeit with varying degrees that depend on the origins of the state as a historical construct. With the near disintegration of the Iraqi state, countries to the south of Iraq (notably the Gulf monarchies and Jordan) began to dread the emergence of a Shia state, while countries to the north (notably Turkey and Syria) feared the emergence of an Iraqi Kurdish state: both are seen as a possible source of serious long-term instability affecting all Iraq's neighbours.

The debate on security, instability and the hegemonic policies of the US was and remains so overwhelming that it has rarely allowed the discussion of more fundamental questions around the models of democracy on offer and whether or not they are worth importing. Such discussions exist, however, and the questions posed are worthy of serious consideration.

Which democracy?

Opponents of the democracy promotion agenda among Arab elites say they would like to see greater candour on the part of the 'democratizers'. They read about debates in the West over the content of a democratic system and the diversity of historical experiences, and they are aware of the tensions within democratic societies in the West. When a British, a German or a US democracy foundation or government aid agency seeks to promote democracy, which model is it actually offering? Great Britain has no clear separation of powers while the United States Constitution regards this as indispensable.

162   Bassma Kodmani

Poland and Ireland, two Catholic states, have no separation of Church and State, whereas France views this as a prerequisite for starting a process of separating the private and public spheres. Switzerland celebrates communal rights when France stresses individual rights and curses *communautarisme* as a bad word (Barber 1996).

These elites feel that the West is seeking to promote democratic practices by bringing its own achievements from the past and proposing them as a project for the future. Yet they see that societies in the West are confronted with new challenges within their own democratic systems, that their academics and ruling elites have their own doubts about the health of their political systems and are reflecting back on the democratic theory, its premises, scope and depth, and seeking ways to legitimize democracy anew (Hirst and Khilnani 1996). Middle Eastern societies sense that the model is currently facing challenges in the West and that the ideal of democratic rule that is presented there does not match the reality and cannot simply be juxtaposed in opposition to autocracy. They would certainly appreciate more candour on the part of their western interlocutors. Arab elites and democracy activists feel that their western partners would gain in credibility if they were less certain about the path they are proposing and admitted that the growth of democracy is an evolutionary process constantly in the making.

Among political currents in the Middle East, Islamist movements are more involved in these discussions than others. This is probably because Islamists claim to have a competing model of social and political order that they seek to promote. Islamists seem to question some of the fundamental principles of the western democratic model, such as the role of religion in public life, individual rights as a founding principle of social order, and the rights of women. To these values, they oppose the moral order that Islam guarantees naturally, the welfare of the community and the role of solidarity networks as the primary guarantors of a peaceful society, and the role of women as the guardians of family values, social stability and cultural identity. Many Islamists genuinely believe that they have an alternative model of democracy to offer, one that would avoid the materialistic, selfish and ultimately decadent features of Western societies that do not, according to them, secure the paramount value to the individual, namely happiness.[4]

Another political current that challenges democratic principles as defined in the West, though in a less direct way are the nationalists, for whom the sovereignty, independence and integrity of the nation make up the paramount value. Individual rights and freedoms, minority rights, while important, should remain subject to these more vital values. Thus national security is more important than human security, or expressed rather differently, national security is the only valid framework through which human security can be effectively provided.

This nationalist claim is not limited to the Arab world. It is a global phenomenon affecting developed and developing nations alike, fuelled by the anxiety of populations facing the erosion of welfare states. The tension resulting from the combination of increasing political freedoms and decreasing acceptance of social and economic responsibility by governments is seen by critics of western democracy as another, more recent feature of the crisis of the political system in the West, where the evaluation of a government's performance is no longer tied to the provision of social services or to promises of welfare. Arab nationalists see that democracy in the West has been slowly decoupled from equality and social justice, that the value of equality has been replaced by acceptance of great inequality (not just of income and assets but also education, training and participation), causing the bonds of solidarity to erode.[5] This simply means that justice is seen to be no longer at the centre of the value system of modern democracy. The result is a clear decline in its legitimacy as a political system. As noted long ago by the Italian jurist Danilo Zolo (1992), democracy, because it does not rely on tradition or force in the same way as other political systems, requires constant re-legitimizing.

Notwithstanding the exceptional increase in oil and gas revenues of many Arab countries over the past decade (see Chapter 10 by Richard Youngs in this volume), economic deprivation continues to affect at least 80 per cent of the overall Arab population. Out of 320 million Arabs, some 15 per cent at most (30 million) have benefited from the oil boom directly or indirectly. The rest remain poor even where their poverty has not increased, which in a growing population means increasing numbers of socially and politically disenfranchised. It is remarkable in this context that political protest has remained peaceful so far, even when openings for legal protest are limited.

These Arab 'masses' – an outdated word for what remains, however, a powerful reality – now watch the unfolding crisis in the international financial and economic system that started in 2008, and the accompanying questioning of the western economic model, almost with disbelief. The sobering statements by leading authorities in the US financial system admitting that they were wrong to believe the model could regulate itself and bring nothing but ever more prosperity for the many leaves developing nations in disarray. Could it be that the model which donor countries and international institutions are perceived as pushing down their throats for the past two decades was wrong after all? This would have been a historic revenge for communism, if there were communists left to celebrate!

Arab societies, however, are entitled to feel some relief in the face of the crisis of the under-regulated free market, which was fostering excessive inequality and social injustice, rapacious government and a self-absorbed private sector. What they hope is that the end of triumphant ultra-liberalism might bring with it the end of the West's triumphalism about its model of society as infallible.

Who is likely to promote a policy that goes against its own interest?

When Europeans decided to follow the US lead on democracy promotion and the European Union (EU) included language on the need for political reforms

164 *Bassma Kodmani*

in the various documents on 'neighbourhood' and 'partnership', they were keen to convey the message that Europe was also sensitive to the indigenous aspirations of Arab societies. Yet the impression in the Arab world was that Europe was giving in to its 'Atlanticist temptation': the EU confirmed that the West sees itself as a united front facing the Arab and Muslim world as a culturally problematic region.

Meanwhile the well-intentioned human rights organizations of Europe and liberal intellectuals were scrutinizing EU practices, and denouncing the hypocrisy of Europe's own discourse on democracy while it was intensifying its cooperation with certain authoritarian governments so as to fight international terrorism and criminal networks and put a stop to illegal migration. Few voices dared express outright that the priority for Europe with its southern neighbours would always be stability before democracy, and moreover that this was a legitimate concern for Europe given the geographic proximity of the Arab world.[6]

The United States' key interests in the region are just as vital: the security of Israel, the safe flow of oil, the stability of financial markets, and the US's ability to project its power and shape the strategic order of the region through the cooperation of key allies in Arab countries.

The Bush administration forgot that domestic change is likely to lead to a questioning of the established regional order. There is nothing specific about the Middle East in this. The 'deepening' of democracies in Latin America brought to power grass-roots leaders in Venezuela, Bolivia and Brazil, and resulted in more independent economic and foreign policies. Likewise, the democratic leaders of Turkey and the ruling Justice and Development Party do not consider that they owe the US anything. They refused to allow US planes to launch attacks on Iraq from its territory in 2003, and Iraqi factions, because they now have a voice, threatened to veto a security agreement with the US in late 2008. Arab countries, if governed by leaders representing the will of the people, are very likely to take similar action. Democratization of Arab countries, whatever the outcome then, means that governments will express their societies' opinions and will. History shows that when the 'Arab street' had a voice and their government's foreign policy was in tune with public opinion, the leaders did not always choose to preserve the status quo, especially when the status quo was seen as the result of deals between illegitimate governments and foreign powers with imperial designs. This was true in the 1920s in Egypt, in the 1940s, 1950s and 1960s in Syria, Egypt, Algeria and Yemen when nationalism was the bête noire of western governments, and Arab governments who had ascended to power as a result of revolutions or coups challenged the interests of imperial powers.

The real predicament of the West with the Arab world is similar to what it faced with Russia, as one Russian representative at the Helsinki Group (a non-governmental human rights monitoring body dating from 1999) said defiantly to his western colleagues: 'You claim that Russia is not ready for

Resistance to democracy in the Middle East 165

democracy but it is you in the West who are not ready for democracy in Russia.' Similarly, there are many indications that the West is not ready for democracy in the Arab world.

Does democracy promotion have a future?

All kinds of doubts and fears seem to have taken hold of the democracy promoters, and these doubts have not escaped the attention of Arab governments, who manipulate them with a certain degree of cynicism, not least by inciting public opinion against America while they themselves often depend on American support and protection.

Yet, for all the resistance that democracy promotion and external interference have caused, loss of interest in spreading democracy on the part of western powers will only harm western strategic interests over the long run. If the wind of democracy were to start blowing in the opposite direction, the democratic forces in the region are likely to face greater difficulties and increased suffering not only due to the revenge of their governments but also from other opposition forces, who will seek to disqualify them and discredit the values they promote. If and when democracy were to finally come about, Arab societies would then not have cause to be grateful to the West and would not feel that they share its values. Western ties with the region would be damaged and the feelings of hostility vis-à-vis the West and the outside world will grow stronger. So, on that basis, any rational assessment should force the West to continue supporting the democratic movement in the Arab and Islamic world. The real question is not if, but how.

Democracy promotion has stumbled over all sorts of obstacles, some of which we have described already. But a major flaw in the approach was and remains the lack of trust in Arab societies. A glance at democracy assistance programmes shows that most measures were designed to induce controlled change from above, and that outside partners remained reluctant to genuinely foster a shift of power toward societies. The Arab world sensed arrogance, lack of empathy and ignorance in the US and to a lesser extent European approaches, as the strategy slipped from freeing societies from the chains of their authoritarian rulers to treating them as suffering from pathologies from which they need to be cured. The war on terror contributed in the most unfortunate way to creating a climate of mutual suspicion between western governments and Arab societies alike.

Addressing public anxieties

To begin with, a key change will need to occur at the level of American foreign policy. According to a recent statement in the US by Armitage and Nye (2008): 'We need to use hard power against the hard-core terrorists, but we cannot hope to win unless we build respect and credibility with the moderate center of Muslim societies.' If that kind of message is heard and translates

166 *Bassma Kodmani*

into practical policies, Arab public opinion will cease to feel that distrust and lack of empathy dominate western dealings with the region.

The brief experience we can refer to suggests clearly that pressure from below is what is fostering genuine change of mentalities, of popular attitudes and of certain outdated government practices. It is public protest and the echo given by the independent media that are exposing and embarrassing governments, creating unease in some instances. Within some key state institutions such as the security sector, for example, members of the police and of security agencies are increasingly unhappy to serve as the instruments of authoritarianism and to carry the onus of public opinion's anger. The same holds true for members of the judiciary. The subservience that the executive often requires from judges is creating resentment among them because it discredits their profession and harms their public standing.

The movements from below have so far been peaceful, and there is no question that a mute complicity exists between the message from abroad and the attitude of social and political movements inside the societies. The initial message from western governments was that peaceful moderate opposition would be rewarded. This message clearly shaped the attitudes of political and social movements, not least the Islamist parties, who are going out of their way to reassure audiences inside and outside that they do not seek to monopolize the political scene, that they will respect pluralism and diversity, and will honour international agreements signed by the existing regimes.[7]

It will take some time for the withering Arab regimes to decline and fade. Before a different type of political system takes shape, the Arab world will go through a hybrid period. The challenge for outside governments is to define ways and means of accompanying this hybrid period which will be rife with dangers if the challenges are mismanaged. Knee-jerk reactions must be avoided. The profound anxieties towards change that are to be found in the region are realities that must be recognized and coped with and, adapted to, because, ultimately, it is the Arabs who will have to live in the democracies that the US and Europe say they want to build, not the Europeans or the Americans. This means that the following important conditions must be recognized and adhered to.

Democratizing plural societies

First, there is no chance that democracy can bring harmony and stability to Arab societies without acknowledging the diversity of Arab societies and defining legal measures to protect key groups against discrimination. Democracy, if reduced in its definition to the rule of the majority, will bring considerable damage to most Arab countries: it would be a recipe for imposing the tyranny of the majority. The debate on the need to contextualize universal values so as to adapt them to the region is legitimate. There are cultural specificities, a particular debate about religion, culture, social and family patterns of relations. But standing firm on certain fundamental values is an existential matter for Arab societies. Pluralism is definitely one of them.

We have not seen any responsible approaches by governments designed to manage sectarian diversity. Political authorities are not regulating inter-communal relations to build harmonious relations between communities, and the societies are neither equipped nor empowered to address the problem adequately. Other institutions within society, mainly the religious institutions, Christian and Muslim alike, often take on the role of protecting and organizing their communities, with little concern for inter-communal coexistence. Projects and programmes for improving governance and promoting the rule of law schemes should include explicit and detailed schemes concerning the management of inter-communal and inter-sectarian relations (in terms of principles, mechanisms and the right institutions to uphold them). To be acceptable as well as coherent, the western discourse should stop promoting the protection of minorities and stress instead the principle of neutrality of the state and the idea of equal citizenship.

Islam and secularism

Second, the 'Islam versus secularism' dichotomy should cease to be formulated as a dilemma. By declaring that it is not possible to separate religion from politics in Muslim societies, democracy promoters unintentionally make theirs the argument of the most conservative Islamists, namely that a popular mandate to exercise political authority cannot (must not be allowed to) completely replace a divine mandate. This leads to fostering the influence of the religious establishment which, in turn, does everything to perpetuate this belief.

Arab societies are ready to be ruled by governments whose legitimacy is based on popular vote. It is through this process that secularism will develop and that religious legitimacy, and hence authority, will gradually wane and come to be replaced by an authority based on popular suffrage. Now, secularism is defined in Europe as a cultural value but it was not so originally. It became a cultural value as a result of a purely political process. The state, its institutions, its occupation of the social sphere and the practices it brings (ranging from tax collection to elections) broaden secular space and impose secularism by carving out a space for it that grows with time. In a religious society, this space needs to be conquered, and snatched from the influence of the religious establishment. It is a political process, not a static value.

Democracy and the social contract

Third, in any developing country, democracy needs to bring first and foremost a new social contract and a more equitable distribution of resources. The more we advance on the path of liberal economic development without explicit social contracts, the more alternative networks of solidarity become

168   *Bassma Kodmani*

vital for ever larger numbers of vulnerable groups. Such community-based support systems that provide solutions to people's basic needs and avert social explosions are almost exclusively faith-based. In the Arab world, *al mujtama' al ahli*, a more identifiable sector than *al mujtama' al madani* (both translated as civil society), is the only space that citizens can call their own. There is nothing culturally specific about this civil society. Even in largely secularized countries, civil society remains the domain of the church, the family and only third, of voluntary association. While states tried to crush this space, it survived and it still remains vibrant, through religious networks.

Speaking to all democrats

Fourth, liberal democracy activists call for political and moral support to be given to any political party, whatever its ideological orientation, provided it respects legal means and is committed to democracy. Based on this, they see no justification for boycotting the Islamists as long as the latter abide by democratic rules. Islamists are not seen as a danger by the large majority of the population. They are a product of their social fabric and carry the values of the people. Islamist movements have followed a three-decade-long trajectory of building social networks, developing a political culture based on religious messages, evolved into political actors that are knocking on the door of the state and demanding their share of power. In most cases, they are joining multi-party coalitions, taking an active role in parliament, negotiating portfolios in government and advancing their agenda through peaceful means. This is true of Egypt, Morocco, Yemen, Bahrain, Kuwait, Jordan and even Syria and Tunisia, where boundaries between opposition forces with different ideological affiliations are softened through negotiating processes and the formation of coalitions.

Even in contexts where the militarization of politics has occurred as a result of conflict (as in Palestine and Lebanon), Hezbollah and Hamas sought power-sharing, though they did not resist the temptation to turn their weapons inward in order to strengthen their bargaining position and gain a larger share of power.

The exclusion of the Islamist movements sets the outside partners on a collision course with large sections of public opinion in the Arab world. Accepting the inevitable (which means the participation of Islamists) and making the best of it (which means setting appropriate conditions and restrictions) might avoid worse scenarios. By the same token, however, activists in the Arab world see no reason for western powers to single out the Islamists in order to engage in an exclusive dialogue with them. They consider that the issue of democratic reform should be clearly understood by all as a cause based on principles. Consequently, it is for Arab political forces to negotiate among themselves the principles and rules of the democratic game. Once they reach an agreement, all the parties that subscribe to it become acceptable interlocutors for outside parties, who should have no say as to who they want or don't want to talk to.

Resistance to democracy in the Middle East 169

What scares the Arab democracy activists is the political opportunism of US policy that leads to befriending Colonel Qadhafi and ignoring the Libyan opposition, then branding Hamas a terrorist organization after its victory in a free and fair election.

The role of money

America and Europe wield considerable power through the enormous financial and political support they provide to a number of regimes. If the aid were cut off, the result would be disastrous. An active strategy of promoting democracy does not imply such bold new initiatives, but instead using more wisely the influence that Western governments already have in order to exert pressure. If the US and Europe took a clear, public and consistent stance against undemocratic practices, then the governments would understand better the price they might have to pay for failing to take heed, and the social movements that are demanding democracy would be encouraged.

That said, threatening to withhold financial aid to governments is likely to be more effective than offering money to opposition forces. Although opposition political parties are generally in desperate need of money because their supporters are poor, many of them refuse to put their reputation at risk by accepting financial support from outside. What they want is the political support that can curb the repressive acts of the state. This political support provides the feeling that there exist abroad, not only in America or Europe but throughout the world, international organizations, human rights organizations that are standing beside them – beside them morally rather than behind them financially. As Al-Ghazali Harb (2007) says, 'This not only gives people a sense of moral support, it makes the government think twice before it takes any action.'

Palestine, violence and democracy: what the United States can do

Lastly and most importantly, the new administration of President Obama in Washington should undertake to expend political capital to end the corrosive effect of the Israeli-Palestinian conflict. Thus, Armitage and Nye (2008) are right to say;

> The United States must resume its traditional role as an effective broker for peace in the Middle East. We cannot want peace more than the parties themselves, but we cannot be indifferent to the widespread suffering this conflict perpetuates and passionate feelings it arouses on all sides. Effective American mediation confers global legitimacy and is a vital source of smart power.

In contrast, seeking to promote the rule of law, freedom of expression and fair elections while continuing to lead a policy on Palestine and Iraq that runs

170 *Bassma Kodmani*

contrary to the aspirations and concerns of Arab societies is definitely a dangerous strategy. Claiming to empower people and give them a voice, and then doing what infuriates and alienates them, goes a long way in explaining the failure of the democracy promotion agenda.

Conclusion

In conclusion to this chapter, then, we should reflect that the pendulum may be swinging back from focusing on promoting domestic changes to the urgency of solving the core conflict of the region. But will this entail a loss of interest in democratic transformation? The priority of peace as a short-term goal might imply working with 'nasty regimes' who can 'deliver'. But let's be clear about what these regimes can deliver: they can easily secure oil supplies, work to preserve the regional status quo and Israel's security. But they cannot guarantee domestic stability in the long run.

Political change usually results from pressure, which needs to come from somewhere: if it cannot come from domestic constituencies and ceases to come from outside pressure, then the only remaining source of pressure is crises.

Notes

1 Observation made by Pierre Hassner, Working Group on Democracy and democratization, CERI, Paris, 9 May 2006.
2 Based on observations by Fernando Calderon in a working paper presented at the seminar of the Latin America and Middle East Petra Group, Jordan, March 2006.
3 See 'Order lets US strike Al Qaeda worldwide', *International Herald Tribune*, 11 November 2008.
4 For further discussion of the compatibility of Islamist ideas with democracy and of nationalist views too, see Chapter 3 by Marina Ottaway in this volume.
5 For further discussion of expectations and their disappointment regarding the performance of democracy in the new democracies, see Chapter 6 by Renske Doorenspleet in this volume.
6 Hubert Védrine, former French Minister of Foreign Affairs (1997–2002), was among the most outspoken on this and pleaded for realism rather than idealism.
7 This is endorsed by prominent leaders of the Muslim Brothers of Egypt, Isam el Eryan and Abdel Monem Aboul Foutouh in various public debates and articles in the Egyptian press.

10 Energy
A reinforced obstacle to democratization?

Richard Youngs

Between 2001 and the summer of 2008, oil prices increased from around $20 to nearly $150 a barrel. While prices then fell back as a result of the international financial crisis, demand for energy is still expected to grow exponentially, and many predict that oil and gas reserves are on the point of peaking. Western dependence on imported supplies is set to increase. It is estimated that the European Union's (EU) reliance on imported energy supplies will rise from 50 to 70 per cent of energy requirements and the US's dependence to 60 per cent by 2025 (Cordesman and Al-Rodhan 2006: 18). It is estimated that in 2035 global energy consumption will be double that of 2005, with fast-developing economies such as those of China and India hungry for ever-increasing supplies of oil and gas. Non-democratic producer states have enjoyed the succour of increased revenues and greater international leverage. Beyond short-term fluctuations in oil prices, these regimes are widely seen as strongly placed to consolidate their influence over the medium term.

This new energy panorama raises many questions. The focus in this chapter is on one specific issue, namely its impact on democracy. Of the diverse factors affecting democracy's fortunes, energy would appear to present one of the most open-and-shut cases. As oil and democracy appear never to have mixed well, the new context is widely seen as a major factor quite unequivocally loading the dice even more strongly against democracy. Evidence abounds that the new energy panorama has worked and is working clearly to democracy's disadvantage. But the chapter digs a little deeper and asks whether the equation is quite as simple, quite as black-and-white as this. Notwithstanding the negative trends associated with the changes to international energy markets, 'the return of oil' to international geopolitics has also served as a catalyst for more far-reaching debates over democratization and governance reform. Full-scale democratic reform may be increasingly 'blocked by oil' but pressure for some degree of governance reform has itself intensified in response to that same autocratic management of energy resources.

Autocrats empowered

No developing country whose economy is dominated by oil is a consolidated democracy. Democracies such as Norway, Canada, The Netherlands, the UK

172   *Richard Youngs*

and the US produce or have produced significant amounts of oil and gas; but in the developing world the presence of oil and gas is normally seen as having reinforced existing autocratic government. The presence of oil and gas reserves has generally been associated with weak state structures, the over-centralization of executive power, higher than average military spending, and a natural resource export dependency that militates against broader social and economic modernization (Humphreys et al. 2007: 11–13). The well-established 'rentier state' argument has both a demand and supply side: first, oil means regimes do not need to raise revenues from their citizens; second, it means those citizens can be compensated for their disenfranchisement with oil largesse. Oil hinders democracy, according to the standard view, by both facilitating repression and choking modernization (Ross 2001).

In the new energy panorama of the 2000s, many experts argue that the 'rentier state' characteristics of key producer countries have become stronger, militating even further against the prospects for democratization. With state coffers overflowing, since 2002, autocratic governments have been flush with massive quantities of new funds for patronage-based distribution. One of the more pronounced versions of such a perspective is that recent years have witnessed a flourishing of the 'first law of petropolitics', namely that tighter energy markets lead directly to a repression of democratic rights. Thus, according to Friedman (2006), 'the tide of democratization that followed the fall of the Berlin Wall seems to have met its match in the black tide of petro-authoritarianism'.

The evidence demonstrates that overall political rights in non-democratic producer states have worsened modestly since 2002 (Table 10.1). Clear back-sliding has occurred recently in states such as Russia, Iran and Venezuela. In states such as Nigeria and Algeria nominally democratic reforms have failed to fuilfil their promise or have unravelled at least in part. Reforms promised by regimes in Azerbaijan, Kazakhstan and Angola have not materialized. All these regimes have used state oil funds to distribute patronage-based largesse. Saudi Arabia has enjoyed record surpluses since 2006. By 2007, Russia held the third largest stock of foreign currency reserves in the world, had paid off most of its debts, and had set aside nearly US$150 billion in an oil investment fund, used as a political slush fund. The Azeri State Oil Fund rose to $2.2 billion in 2007 and was predicted to rise to $50 billion by 2010, over which time the state budget was on course to triple.

President Ahmadinejad has placed his cronies at the head of the Iranian oil ministry, compounding his already marked tendency to distribute oil and gas revenues for populist projects. At the same time, the pension funds managed directly by Iran's Supreme Leader Ayatollah Khamenei have over-flowed (Gheissari and Nasr 2006: 144). In late 2007, Libya's Colonel Qadafi pro-mised to dismantle a number of institutional structures in Libya so that he could distribute oil revenue more directly to the population. Flush with funds, Angola's Eduardo dos Santos government rejected a liberalization package from the International Monetary Fund and continually pushed back long-

Energy: an obstacle to democratization? 173

Table 10.1 Freedom House score of key producers, 2001–2 to 2007

	2001–2			2007		
	PR	CL	st	PR	CL	st
Algeria	6	5	NF	6	5	NF
Angola	6	6	NF	6	5	NF
Azerbaijan	6	5	PF	6	5	NF
Cameroon	6	6	NF	6	6	NF
Chad	6	5	NF	6	6	NF
Colombia	4	4	PF	3	3	PF
Congo Braz.	5	4	PF	6	5	NF
Egypt	6	6	NF	6	5	NF
Eq. Guinea	6	6	NF	7	6	NF
Gabon	5	4	PF	6	4	PF
Iran	6	6	NF	6	6	NF
Iraq	7	7	NF	6	6	NF
Kazakhstan	6	5	NF	6	5	NF
Kuwait	4	5	PF	4	4	PF
Libya	7	7	NF	7	7	NF
Nigeria	4	5	PF	4	4	PF
Oman	6	5	NF	6	5	NF
Qatar	6	6	NF	6	5	NF
Russia	5	5	PF	6	5	NF
Saudi Arabia	7	7	NF	7	6	NF
Sudan	7	7	NF	7	7	NF
Turkmenistan	7	7	NF	7	7	NF
UAE	6	5	NF	6	5	NF
Uzbekistan	7	6	NF	7	7	NF
Venezuela	3	5	PF	4	4	PF
Averages	5.6	5.2		5.9	5.2	

Source: Freedom House.
Notes: PR = political rights, CL = civil liberties, st = status (NF = not free, PF = partly free). On scale 1–7, 1 = free, 7 = not free.

promised elections; when these were eventually held in September 2008, the ruling party was guaranteed a comfortable extension of its power. In East Africa, democracy-weakening rentier dynamics have emerged in response merely to the anticipation of future oil discoveries. And Venezuela's President Hugo Chávez has provided perhaps the most explicit example of petro-populism. On the basis of such rent distribution, many of these autocrats enjoy increasing domestic support, even as they dismantle democratic checks and balances.

If increased energy prices have given autocrats greater power vis-à-vis domestic constituencies, it has – the standard argument runs – also liberated them from international pressure for democratic reform. One influential study notes a trend away from a 'markets and institutions storyline' to a logic of 'regions and empires', that places greater stress on strategic alliances; the search for 'exclusive backyards'; and undercutting between Western

174　*Richard Youngs*

governments each in search of the most favourable and secure long-term bilateral energy deals (Clingendael International Energy Programme 2004: 24, 26, 91). Firm US pressure for democracy and human rights has been termed an 'outmoded' policy, no longer viable with the demise of slack oil markets (Council on Foreign Relations 2001: 30).

The energy-rich states of the Gulf of Guinea (on the west coast of Africa) are described by one analyst as 'successful failed states' precisely because their very weaknesses in fact serve both the domestic political elite and international energy interests (Soares de Oliveira 2007). Some economists claim that for poor energy-rich countries a too open political system, without extremely strong checks and balances, invariably engenders civil violence and the kind of patronage that lowers growth rates (Collier 2008: 42–3).

Most notably, the Saudi Arabian regime has manoeuvred to retain its position as indispensable energy ally to the West. After 9/11, Saudi Arabia increased output to reduce oil prices. The Saudi government then promised to temper any upward pressure on oil prices that resulted from the 2003 Iraq invasion. The regime was seen by many as robustly defending the Kingdom and its oil facilities from Islamist terrorists. The government spent well over $1 billion to strengthen security at its production facilities after attacks on the latter in 2003. By 2005, Saudi Arabia was providing 30,000 troops to protect the oil infrastructure. One effect of this was that the ruling family became less tolerant of reformist voices as it turned to conservative Salafi clerics to rein in militants.

Elsewhere in the Middle East there also appears good reason for Western governments not to risk endangering alliances with incumbent regimes. Qatar, one of the most closed political regimes in the entire region, is also one of the most open to inwards investment in the energy sector and increasingly the key player in the development of LNG exports (Shell signed the world's biggest liquified natural gas (LNG) deal with Qatar in 2006). Similarly, the United Arab Emirates (UAE) remains highly authoritarian but has an increasingly outward-oriented economy. In contrast, where some political liberalization has occurred, as in Kuwait, foreign investment in the energy sector continues to be blocked, and Islamists in Kuwait's increasingly lively parliament have hindered the ruling al Sabah family's proposals to open the oil sector to foreign investment.

Some analysts argue that the US's pressure for democratization has already been too great: as Middle Eastern regimes have begun to liberalize their political systems, they have, it is contended, felt more obliged to bend to popular sentiment to prioritize short-term revenues and thus move away from support for low oil prices (previously justified on grounds that the health and stability of Western economies are in the long-term interest of producer countries themselves) (Barnes and Jaffe 2006: 148). Producer states' more aggressive push for higher oil prices is seen by some energy experts as the result of too much political liberalization already having occurred in leading member states of the Organization of Petroleum Exporting Countries (OPEC)

Energy: an obstacle to democratization? 175

(Jaffe 2005: 4). Some observers suggest that Islamists – likely to emerge as the main beneficiaries of democratization – argue even more forcefully that production should be kept at a lower level and be more domestically oriented, rather than any effort made to reduce international prices.

Additionally, of course, the scope for pro-democracy policies is seen as having been seriously undermined by the emergence of competitor purchasers such as China. One expert argues that producer states' move away from market-based solutions and democratic norms has been hastened – even if not directly caused – by the rising demand for energy of China and India, with whom deals can now be secured that circumvent 'Western norms' (van der Linde 2005: 6, 13–14). Thus, an emerging 'Asia-Gulf nexus' is said to be ready to 'spawn political dimensions' (Armitage et al. 2002: 211). Another energy expert laments that the West will have to reverse powerful current trends to ensure that China and India veer towards cooperative solutions, based on international markets and good governance, rather than mercantilism and zero-sum competition (Yergin 2006: 75–7). In 2006, China invested 1 billion Euros in Africa and launched a 3.6 billion Euro China-Africa Development Fund. Ferguson (2006: 644), links the new 'imperial scramble' for oil to a longer-term, underlying 'descent of the West' and its political norms.

Energy and democracy promotion

Most analyses of the 'new geopolitics of energy' indeed focus on what was widely seen as the Bush administration's far-reaching 'securitization' of energy, in US policy. On one side, there appears to be a realpolitik approach to energy security from the United States and other consumer states. On the other lies 'autocracy promotion' that has itself been fuelled by increased oil revenues. Russia has increased subsidies to Central Asian republics, Venezuela to Cuba and Libya to Zimbabwe, to name but a few examples.

In 2001, the Bush administration set up the National Energy Policy Development Group, which in May 2001 produced a National Energy Policy whose main conclusion was that access to foreign oil and gas would become the over-riding security concern of US foreign policy. On this basis, the US military was, in the words of one writer, 'converted into a global-oil protection service' (Klare 2004: 7). New military deployments and partnerships were, it was argued, oriented primarily to guarantee oil supplies. Between 2000 and 2003, the Bush administration increased military aid to the US's top 25 oil suppliers by 1800 per cent, with primary increases going to Iraq, Uzbekistan, Kyrgyzstan, Azerbaijan, Colombia, Russia and Oman (see Chapter 5 by Bermeo). While such deployments were justified by the Bush administration in terms of counter-terrorism, in practice, they were – it was charged – more reflective of energy security imperatives. The 2001 Defense Review talked explicitly of deploying US armed forces where energy supplies might be impeded (ibid.: 71, 174). In February 2007, the Bush administration approved the creation of a new Africa Command for a sizeable relocation of

176   *Richard Youngs*

naval forces to protect Nigerian oilfields; indeed, West African oil was defined as a 'strategic national interest', implying that military force could be mobilized in its protection. In Colombia, US military activities increasingly went beyond counter-narcotics to fighting the guerrilla forces that were threatening key oil pipelines. The US expanded its largest military base in the Middle East, in gas-rich Qatar, acknowledging a link to the protection of energy supplies.

All this was characterized by one critic as a new, 'brazen energy imperialism', while the US's talk of democratizing the Middle East was likened to 'a drug addict asking his pusher to change his criminal activities' (Kleveman 2004: 263). The 2006 State of the Union address seemed to signal a modest change of tone, with President Bush now suggesting that the US must wean itself off its 'addiction' to oil and declaring the goal of replacing more than 75 per cent of US oil imports from the Middle East by 2025. An Advanced Energy Initiative (AEI), which followed on from the first US National Energy Plan for more than decade, was signed into law in August 2005. President Obama looks set to continue this trend. In the opinion of most observers, however, the 'securitization' of energy policy remains a striking feature of US strategy. One writer claims to have elicited from insiders of the Bush administration the statement that 'US military and energy strategy ... [are] to be one' (Engdahl 2004: 248). One of the most comprehensive studies of US policies in recent years laments that US approaches to energy security exhibit the same military flavour as other dimensions of US foreign policy and are bereft of more holistic, socio-economic understanding (Kalicki and Goldwyn 2005: 14). Even those who might feel such criticisms to be overstated would be hard pressed to deny the realpolitik strand within emerging US energy security policies.

While most European politicians and officials claim to reject this US-style securitization of energy, their own policies show clear evidence of strategic alliance-building with key producers. Even as European diplomats strenuously reject suggestions that they seek a 'hard power' link, some European states' military cooperation and deployments have increased in important producer states – for instance, by Germany in Uzbekistan, France in Algeria and the UK in the Gulf. European diplomats acknowledge that, whatever the criticisms of US policies, even the least Atlanticist of member states have sought to retain some degree of (what is deemed) necessary 'coat-tailing' on US military guarantees in supplier states.

And many see the EU itself as showing signs of a lurch away from the normative power towards a more pronounced realpolitik. Javier Solana, the European Union's High Representative for the Common Foreign and Security Policy argues that:

> The scramble for territory of the past may be replaced by a scramble for energy ... We have to take our energy from where we find it ... Thus, our energy needs may well limit our ability to push wider foreign policy

Energy: an obstacle to democratization? 177

objectives, not least in the area of conflict resolution, human rights and good governance ... The scramble for energy risks being pretty unprincipled.
(Solana 2006)

A senior French policy-maker stresses how Paris was concerned to move beyond its image as a 'status quo power' and be more supportive of political reform, with the key exception of oil-producing states where European interests would suffer from assertive democracy promotion policies and where leverage would in any case be minimal. European officials also admit that the changing structure of international politics leaves diminishing scope for issues of democratic governance.

These trends can be seen across several cases. As EU governments have competed fiercely among themselves for bilateral gas contracts with Russia, many investors welcomed President Putin as an antidote to the chaotic and unpredictable government regulations limiting multinationals' interest during the Yeltsin years (Maynes 2006: 22). In the 1990s, foreign direct investment just to Hungary was greater than to Russia; after that Russia began receiving more than the whole of central and eastern Europe (Johnson 2005: 183). In 2006, overall trade between the EU and Russia increased by a third, and the EU consolidated its position as the largest investor in Russia. Putin regularly points out that Russia remains significantly more open to energy investments than Gulf producers. He has been ambivalent over the notion of a 'gas OPEC' precisely because this would limit Russia's political room for manoeuvre in striking bilateral deals with European states, in which Gazprom commits itself to increasing supplies in return for downstream access.

The EU has signed bilateral energy partnerships with Azerbaijan and Kazakhstan that circumvent the democracy and human rights strictures of the European Neighbourhood Policy (ENP). Kazakh president Nursultan Nazarbayev has been extolled by the US and European governments as a 'reliable partner' (Commission 2006: 2). It is recognized that the tight control exerted by the presidential family over energy contracts in Kazakhstan – Nazarbayev's son-in-law was chairman of state gas monopoly, Kazmunaigaz – has directly facilitated many new investment projects. Nazerbayev's team helped set up the Caspian Pipeline Consortium, using their centralized control over government institutions to overcome resistance (Rutledge 2006: 62). The president is also judged to be pushing forward LNG plans in opposition to significant parts of the political elite. One diplomat summarized: Nazerbayev might be corrupt, vainglorious and unpredictable, but he is surrounded by good, pro-market advisors. The US very openly ceded its talk of democratizing Central Asia to a raft of new visits to Nazarbayev and his team to strengthen cooperation (Carothers 2007c: 9). Indeed, as Vice President Cheney spoke of his 'good friend' Nazerbayev, and political aid efforts in Kazakhstan diminished, this was cited as one of the most dramatic examples of Bush's 'democracy vision' going into reverse (Baker 2007).

178 *Richard Youngs*

Western sanctions were imposed against Uzbekistan in response to the November 2005 Andijan 'massacre' of democracy protestors there. However, the EU's sanctions were extremely limited; after October 2007, only an arms embargo remained in place. German and other policy-makers argued that even if the European response to Andijan looked feeble to some, it had already proved strong enough to push the Karimov regime appreciably closer to Russia, including on energy matters. In the same month that US troops left Uzbekistan, the governments in Tashkent and Moscow signed a mutual security pact. Russia's Gazprom and Lukoil moved to increase their investments in Uzbekistan (International Crisis Group 2006: 3). Recent years have seen record levels of foreign investment from not just Russia but also from China, Malaysia and South Korea as well, marking a clear change in Uzbekistan's foreign policy orientation. Moscow pushed to get its Gazprom-linked man in Uzbekistan lined up as successor to President Karimov. With many European countries counting strongly on Uzbekistan's future potential as a gas supplier, they have advocated more positive engagement with rather than isolation of the brutal Karimov regime.

Reform pressure unleashed?

Such are the twin logics – internal and external – that make energy seem such a clear-cut case of a 'new obstacle to democratization'. But at both the domestic and international levels, at least some countervailing trends can be witnessed. These do not fundamentally change the energy–democracy equation but do reveal that it contains some potential for political reform as well.

The domestic politics of oil- and gas-producing states in fact suggests a situation far more complex than that of textbook rentier state dynamics. It is unduly deterministic to posit an axiomatic link between a given change in international energy markets and domestic political outcomes in producer states, as if the fate of democratization were not mediated through the complex agency of political, social and economic actors. It is well documented that democratization is often triggered by a a sequence of growth followed by crisis – a mix of positive and negative dynamics. Just such a mix may be building up in some oil- and gas-producing states. Regardless of market shifts, some of the vulnerabilities of energy-dependent autocracies are likely to become more apparent. Even if energy prices soon return to an upward trajectory – as oil prices did by mid-2009 – the future may not be wholly comfortable for petro-dictators.

Some oil wealth has trickled down, arguably inadvertently, providing some modernization precursor to political change. Hugo Chávez spent heavily in his social missions, before being defeated in a referendum over constitutional reform in December 2007 (reversed in a later referendum, 2009). Here, whatever the president's autocratic modus operandi, it would be difficult to argue that 'oil' has had only anti-democratic effects on both the positive (redistribution) and negative (mobilization) side of the equation.

Energy: an obstacle to democratization? 179

The Freedom House scores reproduced in Table 10.1 show that very few 'partly free' countries have descended to the status of 'not free'. Semi-authoritarian oil producers mostly did not slide into absolute autocracy. Moreover, the degree of backsliding registered in oil states was matched by similar erosions in democracy in many non-oil-producing countries, reflecting an apparently general trend besetting 'grey zone' regimes rather than something causally unique to energy dynamics. (The more obvious point might also be mentioned that higher oil prices have not made already-democratic producers such as Norway, the US, Canada, the UK or The Netherlands any less democratic.)

Regimes' distribution of the massively increased oil rent accrued since 2002 has clearly not sufficed to 'buy off' popular discontent in, for example, Middle Eastern producer states, where growing numbers of people have agitated for political liberalization. In countries such as Iran, Venezuela, Nigeria and Algeria, the new oil wealth has led to unpredictable spurts of public spending that have been the root of growing social instability. If Middle Eastern regimes embarked upon cautious processes of political liberalization during the 1990s period of low oil prices – eager to 'share' the responsibility of difficult economic readjustment with their populations – these processes engendered domestic expectations that could not simply or safely be completely quashed once the comfort of expensive oil returned (Ottaway and Dunne 2007: 13).

Questioning the standard line that the rentier states of the Gulf were well protected from democratic dynamics, some analysts suggest that in fact two different dynamics have come into play. First, in some Gulf states, resentment has grown over government failures to deliver adequate wealth distribution and effective economic policy for long-term growth, as well as over the lack of transparency in the allocation of resources. Second, over time, an incipient middle class has become more independent of the state than assumed by state rentier theory. At the same time, under conditions where reasonably comfortable lifestyles are assured, it is probable that political change could be less violent and destabilizing than in many other regions. It is argued that the combination of wealth and the legitimacy of the region's royal families means that, in the Gulf, open politics could be ushered in without complete collapse and discontinuity of the system. In these ways, political opening could be more of a stabilizing force than strategic danger. Incipient reform began as a means of re-empowering regimes, but it now grapples with the question of just how far to enfranchise citizens in the Gulf (Ehteshami and Wright 2007: 916).

In Saudi Arabia, a source of popular anger is precisely the fact that oil revenues flow directly into the royal budget, with no accountability; in some senses, the increase in oil prices after 2002 actually exposed the regime to greater public criticism, even though the budget surplus reached a record high in 2006. Limited reforms in fact commenced at precisely the moment that oil prices began rising. Oil-related calculations indeed conditioned the modest

180　*Richard Youngs*

process of political reform initiated by the Saudi royal family after 2001. This reform process allowed the holding of municipal elections, the creation of a National Organization for Human Rights, an increased deliberative role for the Shura Council and several rounds of a reform-oriented National Dialogue. While change was carefully modulated by the regime, in particular after the succession of King Abdullah in August 2005, political debate became freer, and differing positions within the ruling family itself were debated more openly (Hamzawy 2006: 6). Observers suggest that the royal family has been concerned to deflect criticism of its management of oil revenues, and also that the post-2004 oil price increases will not overcome the budget constraints that are of a more structural nature (Glosemeyer 2005: 224).

In Kuwait, higher oil prices have also been seen as helping to explain the growing intensity of political debate, with the regime coming under greater pressure to explain and justify its use of increased revenues. After the death of Shaikh Jabir in January 2006, members of the ruling family and the opposition in parliament together blocked the direct succession of the Crown Prince in favour of Sheikh Sabah, demonstrating that succession was no longer an internal family matter. Elections have become freer, and women are allowed to stand as candidates. The Sabah family retains all key posts in government, including energy and foreign affairs, but a new spirit of open debate has taken root. Increased cooperation between Islamists and liberals has put the ruling family under meaningful pressure for the first time, especially on the profligate and corrupt use of oil revenues. While Islamists continue to oppose opening energy contracts to international bidding, opposition platforms are increasingly organized around pressure for the more transparent and efficient use of oil revenues, as a means of assisting stability and moderation. It has been the Kuwaiti parliament that has pressured increasingly for the regime to release more accurate and transparent information on the state of the country's reserves (Luciani 2008: 7).

In several other cases, it is clear that increased oil revenues have not been a recipe for quiescence but have rather magnified discontent with regimes and even spurred additional opposition activity. Increased gas revenues are widely cited as one factor driving more vibrant oppositional politics in Egypt. Here higher energy prices have not assuaged critics – the traditional dynamic expected of the rentier state – so much as increased pressure on the regime and provided a fillip to opposition groups. In Spring 2008, the influential Al Azhar religious institution issued a *fatwa* (religious pronouncement) declaring that the Egyptian government should respect the principle of *zakat* (alms) by transferring 20 per cent of oil and gas revenues to the population. A similar logic can be witnessed in Iran, where some local observers opine that liberal reformers have regained strength in part through a focus on the regime's hugely wasteful and corrupt management of the gas reserves. With patronage-based subsidies now accounting for 15 per cent of the country's Gross Domestic Product and stoking inflation, increasing discontent was heard from social groups excluded from such benefits, especially those left outside a

Energy: an obstacle to democratization? 181

rapidly overheating housing market. In general, throughout the Middle East, the recent years of oil revenue bonanza have also seen growing inequalities and unravelling social safety nets, potentially putting at risk regimes' strategies of self-preservation (Heydermann 2007: 15–16).

In Central Asia, an incipient middle class has pushed for a stronger rule of law precisely in order to protect their newly acquired oil-related wealth. Azerbaijan recorded the world's fastest rate of economic growth in 2005 and the government confidently announced that the country would free itself from external aid within five years. In practice, the increased revenue flowing into the Azeri State Oil Fund has been used for political patronage, leaving large pockets of worsening poverty in Azerbaijan and a far more frustrated and brittle society. The president of the Azeri Public Finance Monitoring Centre observes a growing 'syndrome of social injustice' sowing popular discontent – the result of immense new wealth (and a rapidly rising military budget) co-existing with an actual decline in the level of public service provision.[1] In Kazakhstan, it is notable that pressure from local non-governmental organizations for greater transparency in the management of oil revenue has emerged as the foundation for stronger political opposition to President Nazarbayev. The fact that the oil fund is run by Nazarbayev cronies and used as a patronage fund is increasingly the source of public discontent. Kazakhstan provides a good example of this discontent combining with the 'trickling down' of some oil wealth to an incipient middle class: precisely the combination of negative and positive dynamics that has been associated with advances in political openness elsewhere (von Grumpennberg 2007).

Due to oil revenues, Angola was by 2006 taking its turn as the world's fastest growing economy. This growth has massively increased wealth disparities and social tension and palpably re-awakened the tensions of the civil war. The state oil firm, Sonangol, functions increasingly as the creature of a small cabal of the political elite. Revenues and deals are controlled by the apocryphal '100 families'. But behind the confident façade, domestic discontent has mushroomed. Some 60 per cent of Angola's oil production comes from the Cabinda enclave, where conflict has deepened between separatists and government forces, revolving in large measure around differences over the sharing of oil revenue. Grievances stem from the lack of local democracy in Cabinda, where all officials are appointed by central government. In 2006, the central government distributed additional oil revenues to local leaders in Cabinda in an effort at pacification, but low-level violence remains with many rebel groups rejecting the peace deal. Angola provides one of the best examples of the tension between external and internal energy policy: as increasing quantities of oil are shipped out of Angola, the majority of the country's population still lacks access to modern energy. After long postponing elections, the dos Santos government held a poll in September 2008; while the ruling party emerged victorious from these elections, the regime is seen by many as increasingly embattled and obliged to reform the murky governance of Sonangol, sooner or later.

182   *Richard Youngs*

In Nigeria, the government of President Obasanjo chose not to embed the rule of law, but rather sought to buy off militants in the oil-producing Delta with oil contracts and government positions. This merely provided the incentive for a perpetuation of violence and increasing opposition to the central government. Several companies linked to militant groups were granted security contracts. At the 2005 National Political Reform Conference, groups from the Delta demanded that 25–50 per cent of oil revenues go direct to local communities in oil-producing areas, and that this not be channelled through corrupt federal government bodies. The government offered only a 17 per cent transfer, further enraging local communities. As prices rose, oil companies channelled increased sums in bribes to local governors, which simply inflamed the population more, as the distribution of such largesse was erratic and patronage-driven. Local governors stormed out of the 2005 national forum on political reform, but they themselves were responsible for siphoning off much of the revenue that did flow back into the Delta – as the 2007 elections approached, 33 of Nigeria's 36 state governors were under investigation. Nigeria provides perhaps the clearest example of increased oil revenues engendering greater, and even destabilizing, pressure for far-reaching governance reform in a country where institutional structures proved unable to fairly manage the post-2002 bonanza. President Yar'Adua has been forced to promise far-reaching governance reforms to the oil sector in reaction to popular protest at the scale of corruption emerging from the Obasanjo era.

Governance and international energy security

Another nuance to the apparently open-and-shut argument relates to the international level. Recent trends have rendered increasingly questionable the presumption that Western interests are well served by alliances with autocratic suppliers.

Many examples demonstrate that non-democracy is very far from providing for Western energy security in a predictable and sustainable fashion, even where nominally pro-Western authoritarian regimes present themselves as a bulwark. Most producer state regimes have exhibited a combination of unpredictable policy-making, weak technical capacity, a limited prioritization of long-term investment to increase productive capacity and a tendency to target foreign investors as a means of shoring up their weak domestic legitimacy.

In Saudi Arabia, the complex politics of the royal family are seen by some critics as breeding increasingly unpredictable and changeable policy-making (Al-Rasheed 2005: 201, 208). Where Middle Eastern regimes have bent to domestic concerns, it often has not augured well for Western interests. The Saudi regime scaled back its National Gas Initiative because it feared the political consequences of any significant market opening (Rutledge 2006: 190). Similarly, Saudi Arabia won an exception for the energy sector when it joined the World Trade Organization (WTO) in December 2005, because the

Energy: an obstacle to democratization? 183

government realized that continued control over this sector was crucial to its political leverage both domestically and internationally.

In the summer of 2006, the Algerian government reversed a tentative liberalization of the energy sector as a means for President Bouteflika to shore up his support with oil clans, amid rumours that he might be pushed out of office (Estrada 2006: 5). The Algerian company Sonatrach was henceforth automatically to be given a controlling stake in investment projects involving foreign companies. In 2007, the effective renationalization of the energy sector led Sonatrach to break a flagship 5 billion Euro contract signed in 2004 with Spain's Repsol and Gas Natural to develop the Gassi Touil gas field in the east of the country. With the exception of Saudi Aramco, no national (producer-state) oil company in the Middle East has a good record in exploration or development, their resources having been dispersed across a wide range of politically-motivated activities and not focused in an efficient way on increasing efficiency and production capacity (Jaffe 2005: 6). National oil companies across the Middle East enjoy preferential fiscal regimes and are expressly used by regimes to further political power rather than invest in additional oil and gas capacity. The International Energy Agency reports that nowhere near the level of investment needed – $1 trillion over the next decade – is finding its way into augmenting productive capacity.

Iran suffers from an increasing shortfall in energy sector investment that many see as related to the nature of its political system. Iran has been unable to meet its own OPEC oil production quotas since prices rose after 2003. Despite sitting on 10 per cent of the world's oil reserves the Iranian government has had to ration domestic petrol use. Even more strikingly, Iran is still a net importer of gas. Under-investment in production capacity is directly linked to the subsidization of domestic fuel prices, which depresses revenues for re-investment. This subsidization is in turn seen as a populist measure offered by an embattled regime seeking the means to perpetuate its own survival. Buy-back terms have been toughened, thereby deterring foreign investors, quite apart from any geopolitical disincentives. Iran's energy sector operates at well below full capacity. The influence of the Revolutionary Guards has grown significantly, both over the nuclear programme and energy policy; one reason for the limited opening in the energy sector is the Revolutionary Guards' determination to direct energy contracts towards their own operators (*The Economist* 2007).[2] Experienced energy technocrats have been replaced by patronage-placed government supporters untrained – and 'completely incompetent' according to one European government official – in energy questions.

Perhaps most notably, Vladimir Putin's centralization of power within Russia is of a piece with the attempt to re-establish Russian influence abroad. Experts concur that Russia's assertive energy diplomacy cannot be delinked from the abuse of good governance and market principles internally (Milov 2006: 20). Far from breaking up Gazprom, as he originally promised, Putin has come increasingly to rely on and support the latter as a vehicle for

184 *Richard Youngs*

projecting Russian influence. The political backing for Gazprom has certainly sufficed to give the latter a striking international self-confidence.

The energy sector is increasingly managed by the Kremlin 'as a strategic asset which it can use to assert itself on the world stage' (Monaghan and Montanaro-Jankovski 2006: 21). KGB secret service veterans have moved into senior positions in Gazprom and key *siloviki* (recruits from the military and security sectors) have become generally influential in the energy sphere; one of its number, for example, assumed the chairmanship of Rosneft, the largest state oil company. Most dramatically, Shell and then BP in relation to their contracts for the SakhalinII and Kovykta gas fields respectively were forced to cede control to Gazprom and accept more minor operational roles. In December 2006, a new law was introduced requiring a minimum 50 per cent Russian ownership of gas pipelines and 75 per cent for oil pipelines, and placing additional restrictions on foreign ownership (Kausch 2007: 5). Many observers link the strengthening of the Kremlin's political control to decreases in oil and gas production. An increasing lack of transparency means that it is not clear even what levels Russian reserves and production levels actually stand at.

In Azerbaijan, the state oil company, Socar, and decisions affecting anything related to oil remain firmly under the control of Presidents Aliyev's family, with often unpredictable consequences for European investors. Diplomats complain at an increasing lack of transparency, for example when a hefty energy price rise in February 2007 was announced out of blue and without consultation, including with the EU. Fragility is compounded by the prospect of Karabakh refugees ejected by Armenia, and now in Baku, being funded by oil money to reclaim the Nagorno-Karabakh enclave.

In Kazakhstan, corruption is increasingly rampant and the president is known to have requested extravagant personal kickbacks (a personal jet, presents for his daughters) in return for concessions to foreign companies. Although foreign investment has increased, after 2003, access conditions were toughened to allow foreign investment only in Kazakh-controlled joint ventures (Kleveman 2004: 85). Some EU officials expressed concern that Nazerbayev was increasingly set on emulating Vladimir Putin, using high energy prices as the basis for assertive foreign policy, while attempting to drive wedges between EU states. EU Commission officials in Kazakhstan lament that the effective implementation of laws is increasingly rare, rendering the whole business and economic climate unpredictable. The flawed 2007 elections were followed by Kazakhstan mimicking Gazprom and taking back greater control over the Kashagan field from the foreign consortium led by Italy's Eni. In response to Kazakhstan reopening the Kashagan contract, Andris Piebalgs (EU Commissioner for Energy) criticized the lack of 'mutual respect, transparency and predictability'and strong complaints followed from the European Business Association, which urged stronger European governmental involvement.[3]

In Uzbekistan, the Karimov regime has kept the energy sector relatively closed to foreign investment as part of its strategy of self-survival. European

Energy: an obstacle to democratization? 185

investment is negligible, foreign companies often targeted by the regime's arbitrary rules and restriction of private sector activity. Only small independents, such as UK firm Trinity Energy, have been willing to risk much involvement in Uzbekistan. For all the West's willingness to please, Karimov has drifted towards preferential partnership with Russia's Gazprom.

In Africa, conflict and autocratic power have combined to work against Western energy interests. The French company Total negotiated a deal in southern Sudan that was rendered void by the rebel Sudan People's Liberation Army. When a key Total drilling licence came up for renewal in Angola it was transferred to a Chinese company. In Equatorial Guinea, President Obiang is a dictatorial bully but increasingly finds it difficult to get his orders obeyed. A crumbling institutional system means effective implementation of presidential decisions has become impossible (Shaxson 2007: 36, 143, 125). Although Britain's BP was awarded the first LNG contract with Equatorial Guinea in 2007, in general, European investment there is modest. In Nigeria, observers note the same kind of emerging resource nationalism as in other producer states. Obasanjo introduced new quotas on minimum Nigerian participation in oil licences and in his final months in office in 2007 the president handed licensing offers for 45 oil blocks to political cronies. Between 2003 and 2007, all major new oil contracts went to Asian companies, who offered development packages in return.

In short, democracy's absence presents serious and growing problems for Western energy interests. To some degree, recognition of this can increasingly be seen in the design of European policies. For a brief moment, an instrumental link between democratic governance and energy security was promoted by some US neo-conservatives – who argued that high oil prices were the result of autocrats needing to whip up popular resentment against the West, and hence international efforts to bring about a change of regime would be beneficial for Western energy interests. While rejecting such logic, the EU's declared approach to energy security is to extend the rules and principles of its own internal market, as part of what might be termed a 'market-governance' nexus (Youngs 2009). Official policy documents and statements most commonly assert that sustainable energy security requires the EU to maintain pressure for governance reforms and better human rights protection around the world. The rise of 'resource nationalism' is seen as integrally linked to the non-democratic politics of producer states like Iran, Nigeria and Venezuela. EU Energy Commissioner Piebalgs has spoken of his acute 'concern that 80 per cent of global oil reserves are in the hands of state-controlled entities' (Piebalgs 2007).

The EU orientation towards energy strategies based on rules-based governance reform is distinctive of the EU's own internal market. External Relations Commissioner Benita Ferrero-Waldner claims that the EU's 'added value' to external energy policies would be to ensure that rule of law principles prevailed through 'enhanced legal framework[s]' (Ferrero-Waldner 2006). The series of new energy partnerships – signed with Ukraine, Azerbaijan, and

186 *Richard Youngs*

Kazakhstan – represent a familiar EU-style approach of attempting to use contractual agreements to attain adherence to rules-based behaviour on market regulations, transport and safety. Officials stress that rules-based governance also offers the most promising way to approach China's rise as energy consumer: according to one diplomat, an increasingly prominent part of European energy strategy was the effort to convince China 'to trust the market'.

Several European governments have been strong supporters of the Extractive Industry Transparency Initiative (EITI). This aims to gain commitments from multinationals to publish details of their payments in producer states, as a means of reducing the scope for bribery. Some governments are currently supporting proposals for a new 'EITI plus' in response to the limited focus of the current initiative on auditing government income from oil and gas resources (and not on the manner in which that income is spent).

In sum, there could be a governance, if not an outright democracy, dividend from these developments in EU relations with energy producers. Furthermore, in so far as western governments have begun to prioritize the development of alternative technologies to fossil fuels in the interests of greater energy independence, climate change mitigation or on simple economic grounds, the increase in oil and gas prices of recent years might in the long term prove to be more boon than bane for democracy. If demand patterns change sufficiently to force a diversification of oil and gas rentier states away from these primary industries, what appears to have been a golden age for the 'petrolist' regime might ultimately prove to have been rather more benign for political liberalization.

Conclusion

The new energy era has helped empower autocratic regimes. Overall, the data show no dramatic decline in political freedoms in energy-producing states since 2001, but modest backsliding has occurred in a select number of such states. High energy prices have worked to entrench the absence of democracy in producing states. But claims of a powerful and mechanistic law – 'higher oil prices equals less democracy' – look patently overblown. Energy represents one factor among many that have engendered 'new obstacles to democracy', and in the case of most countries has not been the most potent democracy-spoiler.

Many autocratic leaders have skilfully used increased oil and gas revenues to divert some pressure for reform. Some producer states targeted by Western democracy promotion policies in the immediate aftermath of 9/11 have seen critical external pressure subside. And China's search for new energy supplies has been a significant factor tilting the balance of international relations towards alliances not conditioned on democracy-related criteria. Even within Europe, echoes resound of the beggar-thy-neighbour competitive policies of the 1970s – the return to which grates with the whole aim of 30 years of European integration.

At the same time, two countervailing trends have taken shape. First, while the oil and gas bonanza may underpin some leaders' new popularity, in some places their patronage-based distribution of revenues has also ignited significant pro-democracy opposition activity, in Africa, Central Asia, Russia, the Middle East and Latin America. Producer governments are under the spotlight from their domestic constituencies to a degree that they were not when international energy markets were far less tight. Successive oil booms have heightened domestic expectations: the repeated frustration of such expectations sows the seeds of potential instability and political rupture. Such frustration is likely to come increasingly to the fore now.

Second, consumer governments have begun to press for a set of international governance norms capable of mitigating the pathological effects of resource mismanagement in non-democratic producer states. Again, in a tighter market, good governance is seen to matter more, as profligacy becomes more costly. Western governments' and international institutions' 'governance reform' logic remains fully to be implemented, but it does demonstrate that the new energy panorama has engendered new debates and initiatives related to good governance. Good governance is not now seen as a mere appendage to development policy but rather as a geostrategically-pertinent framework needed for the better management of globally scarce energy resources. This is not tantamount to Western pressure for full-scale democratization but it does bring into sharper focus a more limited range of meaningful good governance reforms. Neither of these two factors changes the fundamentally problematic relationship between 'oil and democracy', but they do mean that below the surface of the new autocracy-boosting energy panorama, more positive fires might be kindled.

Acknowledgments

The author wishes to thank colleagues at FRIDE and Peter Burnell for their input. The chapter also benefitted from participants' comments at a seminar organized by FRIDE on 'Oil and democracy' in May 2008.

Notes

1 Observation shared with a FRIDE seminar in Madrid, November 2007.
2 See *The Economist* (2007: 6).
3 *The Times of Central Asia*, 25 September 2007, and *New Europe*, 22 October 2007, respectively.

11 Addressing democracy's challenges

Peter Burnell and Richard Youngs

This volume set out to explore the widespread contention that new challenges and obstacles have arisen to democratization. The book's chapters have analyzed this perceived phenomenon in its component parts, in order better to investigate critically if new challenges to democracy really have emerged, and, if so, in what form and to what degree. A number of very different factors tend to get thrown into the mix and sometimes conflated when the so-called 'pushback' is debated; this book has consequently been predicated on the contention that each part of the overall picture must be examined with greater precision.

This concluding synthesis draws out from the preceding chapters a number of select points that add nuance to our understanding of democracy's new challenges, and that speak more specifically to how the challenges to democracy might be addressed. Here we revisit the different components of the democracy puzzle presented in the opening chapter, namely the questions of competing ideologies, loss of morale, heightened opposition to democratization efforts, doubts about Western democracy promotion policies and the effects of democracy assistance, and the changing international context that requires established democracies to come to terms with an increasingly multipolar world. It is suggested that challenges might be distinguished and tackled at three levels: first, what peoples and politicians can do to protect, preserve and improve their democracy and the prospects for democratization; second, the lessons for international policy-makers and democracy practitioners; and third, lessons for researchers and the directions that future research might most usefully take.

Nuancing the trends

The foregoing chapters allude to a number of different factors that have coalesced to engender doubts over the prospects for further democratization around the world. The contributing authors offer many interpretations that confirm pessimistic readings of democracy's international prospects. It is clear that the incremental expansion in the number of democracies witnessed since the beginning of the 'third wave' has in recent years ceased. States such as

Addressing democracy's challenges 189

Russia, Uzbekistan, Venezuela and Thailand have suffered democratic reversals; apparent reform potential in the Middle East continues to disappoint; economic opening in countries like China and Vietnam does not appear to be spilling over to extensive political liberalization; and few chinks have appeared in the world's most illiberal or closed political systems, such as Myanmar (Burma), Cuba, Turkmenistan, Belarus, North Korea, or even Zimbabwe, where President Mugabe and his cronies mount a protracted struggle to retain their monopoly of power. It has become clearer that authoritarian breakdown does not necessarily lead to democratization. Pessimists contend that the vast majority of states with the structural prerequisites of democracy are already democratic.

Much debate has been ignited by the observation that autocrats are learning to defend themselves from democracy promotion efforts, often cooperating amongst themselves to do so. Leaders including Putin (Russia), Karimov (Uzbekistan), Mubarak (Egypt), Ahmadinejad (Iran) and Chávez (Venezuela), for example, have clamped down on the kind of low-level civil society support previously tolerated; the lesson they took in particular from Ukraine's Orange revolution was that over the longer term such support could prove threatening to their own regimes if allowed to go unchecked. In Chapter 7, Regine A. Spector and Michael McFaul observe that Russia has become more active against democracy than the West has been in its favour. The British Council has closed operations in Tehran following intimidation from Iranian authorities and Russia is accused of a cyber-attack on Kyrgyzstan aimed at convincing the latter to close its US military base. Closely related to all this, doubts have emerged over the impact of and tactical strategies available to democracy assistance programmes. With some commentators speculating that around 30 of the new democracies could be at risk over the next decade, the democracy agenda now would seem to be more about trying to preserve gains made than 'spreading freedom' further.

At the same time, the book's chapters serve to add some nuance to the now standard citing of the 'backlash'. Countries such as Indonesia and Brazil have quietly been making impressive progress in consolidating and improving democratic process. In Africa, the degree of public contestation is clearly greater than a decade ago. In Chapter 6, Renske Doorenspleet unpacks the statistical data to find that trends are actually mixed: while the obstacles to democratization of authoritarian regimes have become more prohibitive, most of the emerging democracies have gradually become less illiberal. Another point worth emphasizing is that we must take care not to think that all challenges to democracy are new. Many problems and concerns identified did exist in the supposedly halcyon decade for democratization, of the 1990s. Some challenges have undoubtedly deepened and multiplied, but we must avoid creating a straw figure of idealized conditions prior to the difficulties now arising in the twenty-first century. Kagan's (2008) suggestion that a more conventional historical pattern of international politics – one based on the struggle for power between contending national states – is now

190 Peter Burnell and Richard Youngs

recommencing, downplays the fact that rivalry between liberal democratic and autocratic values far from disappeared at the end of the Cold War. The larger claim that international competition in the market place for political ideas is largely a reflection of the relative standing of competing powerful states, while troubling for democratization, reflects a long-established realist perspective on international relations that many theorists will continue to argue is ill equipped to understand international politics in today's increasingly globalized world – the coming of a more truly global society, in particular.

The rise or reinvigoration of several regional powers and widely predicted emergence of a multipolar will fundamentally change the democracy promotion calculus, in complex ways that are hard to determine. Non-Western international development aid is an emerging and growing phenomenon; some of this offers the prospect of additional support for democracy (India has been one of the biggest contributors to the UN Democracy Fund), some risks neutralizing the West's governance programmes (China's aid to Africa). So far, India, South Africa and South Korea have vetoed a number of democracy-promoting initiatives within the so-called Community of Democracies; their more positive involvement in international democracy support will be of great importance in the future. Even so, analysts represented in this book concur that most of the initial impulse against democracy promotion came from the singular factor of Russian reactions to the colour revolutions and Moscow's subsequent success in siding with 'authoritarian resistance' in a number of non-democratic regimes.

Beyond this, two other distinct strands of issues can be identified: one relating to developments within non-democratic states; and one related to the democratic world's efforts to support the spread of democracy. Any account of democracy's new challenges, while trying to distinguish between domestic and international challenges, should also acknowledge that the two can be hard to separate; indeed, the spheres are to some extent mutually constituted. Much comment has understandably focused on the damage inflicted by the policies of the Bush administration and Russia's current assertiveness; but this book has drawn out the fact that the impact of these factors appears to be compounded by changes of a more structural kind. A key finding here is that the challenges to democracy extend well beyond the narrower interpretation of the 'backlash' that concentrates too heavily on the intensified resistance to democracy assistance on the part of autocratic regimes. Also, care should be taken not to over-state the negative effect of the dip in US credibility: for many ordinary citizens in developing states this is not necessarily the main determinant of the prospects for reform in their own societies or indeed of the strength of democracy's ethical appeal. It is perhaps too easy to attribute too much – for good or bad – to the vicissitudes of US policies.

The implications of this are mixed. Thomas Carothers (in Chapter 4) stresses that policy-makers in the Bush administration fundamentally misunderstood the nature of the 'backlash' as simply an embedding of authoritarianism. He

Addressing democracy's challenges 191

opines that while to some degree the backlash may diminish in intensity as the factors related to the invasion of Iraq and the colour revolutions fade, it could also endure and shift in focus. Notwithstanding the policy responses that he recommends here and elsewhere (see, for example, Carothers 2008), there must be a question mark against whether democracy promotion is likely to regain momentum unless a new spurt in democratic opening and democratic transition comes about first.

Additionally, in overall terms, the book suggests that care is needed not to over-state the emergence of successful ideological competitors and alternatives to democracy. Russia and China may offer a challenge in the sense of their 'output legitimacy', principally their recent economic performance, but not necessarily in terms of their representing a political aspiration widely shared by individual citizens around the world. Many now speculate that the high tide of Russian 'soft power' may already have passed. Marina Ottaway (in Chapter 3) expresses doubts over whether a strong coherent ideological challenge to democracy has emerged at all: political Islam is incapable of becoming anything like a universal model and in any case appears divided along several fault lines. Bassma Kodmani in Chapter 9 confirms that we should not exaggerate the antipathy of Islamism and democracy in the Arab world. Socialism seems unlikely to reclaim its former widespread appeal, notwithstanding global capitalism's current financial and economic woes. Populism seems a more likely outcome at the national level, but although a populist strain in politics can persist over several decades, the larger significance for democracy very much revolves around the political personalities who orchestrate or take advantage of it, and their intentions. Similarly, while nationalism can fuel anti-democratic impulses, this does not have to be the case: history proves there are varieties of nationalism that are entirely compatible with democracy. Of course, as Ottaway makes clear, these judgements about democracy's ideological competitors do not necessarily encompass all the political challenges that democracy faces, let alone the security dangers that established democracies face and anticipate having to address for some time to come, for example, those arising from international terrorism or growing dependence on unreliable foreign sources of energy.

Furthermore, the challenge differs across states at different stages of political development. It is helpful to distinguish between challenges to democratic opening; to democratic transition; to democracy maintenance; to democratic consolidation; and to democratic improvement. There consequently exists significant variation across regions and states. In Chapter 7, Regine A. Spector and Michael McFaul observe that if democracy has been discredited in Russia, this is linked to the way in which during the 1990s reform was promoted from outside. In contrast, Kodmani's account of the Middle East highlights that disappointment stems from the feeling that the West in practice has done very little to assist citizens gain a stronger voice in relation to authoritarian regimes, and is guilty of insincerity or hypocrisy. Shaun Breslin meanwhile argues convincingly (in Chapter 8) that the

192 *Peter Burnell and Richard Youngs*

situation in China is different again. While democracy promotion there would have to overcome resentment about the way Western intervention in the nineteenth century served to undercut Chinese sovereignty – an episode that fuels suspicions about Western intentions even to the present day – Chinese aspirations for political liberalization continue to mount. At present these are couched not in terms of Western-style liberal democracy but rather of the 'national project'. But increased accountability, private freedom, legal redress and political access for non-party members have together ensured that today's China is far freer than even a decade ago. While these and other cases might all be lumped together as examples of democracy being resisted, the reasons for such resistance are very different and the underlying trends relating domestic change (or lack of change) to international dimensions are very varied.

Finally, Chapter 10 argues that while high energy prices have filled the coffers of non-democratic producer states and driven leading consumer states into bilateral energy deals with them, a uniform inverse correlation between 'oil' and democracy is not a justifiable conclusion. Indeed, in many oil-producing states increased energy prices have triggered new pressure from society for political reform. Price volatility could yet expose some illiberal rentier regimes facing large social pressures, Iran, for instance, to increased political vulnerability.

In sum, it emerges clearly from the book that a comprehensive understanding must embrace a multiplicity of factors – ideological competition, major new currents in international politics, shifts in the balance of power among nations, developments in the status that ideas of sovereignty and non-interference now attract, the role played by structural factors, the disappointing performance of some new democracies in delivering societal aspirations, as well as the more routinely covered issue of authoritarian resistance to reform support. Crucially, this mix of factors combines in different ways in different contexts; equally crucial, the factors themselves are dynamic, not static.

Re-energizing democracy

Not having the luxury of managing the difficulties of democratization in isolation, societies must find ways of coping simultaneously with the other major political challenges too, such as those to the state and to national security, without compromising the conditions for democracy and its advancement. The chapters on China and Russia both show that the possibilities for maintaining a democratic momentum are at the mercy of considerations to do with other priority public goals. Indeed, the various regions and countries examined in this volume indicate how far democracy is still perceived as having consequential or instrumental rather than intrinsic value. The chapters also suggest that in practice even such consequential value can easily be judged as expendable in the context of short-term perspectives on other policy

Addressing democracy's challenges 193

goals – an observation that applies to the West's commitment to democracy promotion too.

All this presents a demanding challenge for policy-makers. Yet none of the authors concludes that democracy has reached a definitive limit. Democracy's progress may have stalled in some places, but the implication of the foregoing analyses is that democracy can be re-legitimized. Managing popular expectations of democracy and responding appropriately to disappointment will be crucial, as demonstrated in Chapter 6. There Dooreenspleet again points to significant variation in what lies behind the current dissatisfactions. In new democracies there seems to be very little appetite among the public for a return to authoritarianism. Yet while some citizens regret the limits to democratic quality, others appear to express a desire for government to assume a firmer hand. Exactly where and in what way democracy needs re-energizing is in this sense complex and to some degree context-specific.

One inference is that politicians must modify their own behaviour, for example, committing to less corruption and showing a stronger empathy with the people's needs but without becoming populist. Institutional reforms may have to be introduced in order to help make this happen, for instance, strengthening institutions of horizontal or intra-state accountability like the judiciary, as government and society comes to recognize the weaknesses in the existing democratic architecture. Additionally, in this regard, stronger international support for coping with the economic challenges posed by international shocks including sharp fluctuations in world markets and the international terms of trade might also be required. As shown by the resort to urgent financial support from the International Monetary Fund by countries as different as Iceland, Hungary and Ukraine in October 2008, the buffeting of international financial forces makes no exception for newly democratized countries or, for that matter, some well-established democracies.

At the time of writing, the full force of the 2008 meltdown in international banking has yet to be felt, but it is certainly not too early to inquire into what the consequences of a prolonged global economic recession might be for democratization. Five observations stand out here. First is the well-established conviction that prosperity, while not a necessary condition does help underpin stable democracy. Where economic tightening sharpens domestic conflict, emerging democracies are rendered that much more fragile, especially any that already experience deep social unrest. Second, as the experience of Europe in the 1930s demonstrates, the personal insecurity and fear that economic hard times usually bring can be fertile ground for the rise of values that give priority to stability and order over individual liberties and social diversity, in short, opportunities for authoritarian socialization. Third, the association of liberal democracy with prosperity – which previously burnished democracy's international reputation – now takes a knock, especially if the 'authoritarian capitalism' or 'illiberal capitalism' displayed by China is seen to escape the economic downturn or at least cope with it better (outcomes that are not guaranteed). Fourth, and somewhat at odds with the previous

194 *Peter Burnell and Richard Youngs*

proposition, is the often-voiced concern that economic difficulties could cause a retreat from economic policies embodying market thinking almost anywhere. In turn, this would be bad for democratization to the extent that a market economy and political pluralism are believed to go together. Fifth, the spread of democracy around the world is pushed further down the agenda of political leaders in the West, as domestic constituencies compel governments to focus on reworking the regulatory framework for a return to orderly national and international financial markets while defending the world's trading system against pressures for economic protectionism at the same time.

The above presents a formidable list. However, we should not forget that financial turmoil and/or poor economic prospects contributed to the downfall of undemocratic regimes and brought in today's more democratic arrangements in countries ranging from the socialist states in Central and Eastern Europe to Indonesia. As further illustration that challenges might create opportunities, there is the reasoning of the US National Intelligence Council report on *Global Trends 2025* released in November 2008, which mused that slowing growth in China and diversification of Russia's economy in the event of sustained falls in the price of fossil fuels could make democratization there more likely, albeit not immediately.

Looking further ahead, even these issues on the international agenda may come to be seen as relatively secondary as world leaders are forced to come to terms with the need to agree, implement, monitor and enforce adequate mitigation measures for greenhouse gases, in the face of climate change. Just addressing the adverse political as well as economic and human consequences of global warming and weather-related disasters will pose heavy demands. While democratization's place on the international agenda could be one casualty, political reform may offer the only viable strategy for authoritarian and semi-authoritarian rulers to maintain political order in the face of climate change's harmful effects. This would turn to democratization's advantage the commonly accepted view that democracies are better stewards of the environment, notwithstanding the questionable application of that generalization to the particular environmental issue of carbon emissions and climate change.

Lessons for democracy promotion

Consensus exists among the book's contributors that attempts to promote democracy have been weakened by fragmentation within the policy community at both the international and national levels. The negative impact of US policies related to Iraq and the wider Middle East is also strongly noted, not least by Kodmani. Although US government advocacy of and financial commitment to democracy promotion increased after the terrorist attacks of 9/11, the durability of such commitment has since been widely doubted. Of particular concern are findings from annual opinion surveys that suggest a sharp fall in public support: in 2007, only 37 per cent of people questioned in the US and 31 per cent of Democratic Party supporters agreed that their

Addressing democracy's challenges 195

government should help establish democracy in other countries, compared with 71 per cent in 12 European countries (German Marshall Fund of the United States 2007). Moreover, the US government's own respect for liberal democratic credentials and basic human rights (of suspected terrorists, for instance) is increasingly under the spotlight. The Bush administration alienated democrats around the world. In its closing phases the Bush administration retreated into a more realist foreign policy stance. Looking to the new administration of President Obama, the question arises of whether this loss of credibility will prove ephemeral or of longer-lasting significance.

Ambivalence has taken root in Europe, with support for democracy promotion among leading figures suffering from its (sometimes confused) association with doubts over the ethics of military intervention and conflation with American unilateralism (Mathieson and Youngs 2006). All this requires significant rethinking in the way that democracy promotion aims are formulated and presented – and an understanding of the way in which mistaken policy choices in one area are now, in a more hostile environment for democracy policy, much more likely to have negative spill-over to other areas. A perception clearly confirmed in this book is that 'dissemination' dynamics must now be fully conceived as capable of working in both a pro- and anti-democratic direction, not as a one-way transmission belt of liberal political values. And yet, partly in recognition of this possibility, none of the chapters argues that concessionary, largely consensual international support for democratic reform should now be abandoned, notwithstanding the many criticisms of its performance in the past.

Instead, Thomas Carothers draws attention to the case for formalizing international norms to guide democracy promotion as a means of creating a more permissive environment for pro-reform efforts. He laments that so far practitioners within democracy institutes and foundations, other non-governmental organizations and Western governments have generally declined fundamentally to reassess their basic approaches to democracy assistance in response to the backlash. Several of the book's authors agree that a prerequisite for democracy support to regain the initiative is at the very least some reconsideration of the way such policies are justified to the public and explained – both at home and abroad. Greater transparency may be in order, especially as authoritarian regimes tend to overstate the impact of donors' democracy work because they assume (or profess to believe) that such organizations are engaged in the kind of behind-the-scenes manipulation that they themselves rely upon. This serves to make successful democracy assistance more difficult.

Laurence Whitehead, in Chapter 2, and Bassma Kodmani, in Chapter 9, concur that wider external influences outside the sphere of democracy support militate against the recovery of commitment to political reform. The foreign policies pursued by democracies are clearly – and probably increasingly – influenced by policy goals that at times have over-ridden democracy support, and enjoy political backing from powerful bureaucracies possessed of greater resources and more strategic location within the machinery of government than the democracy units. If this situation continues, as seems quite likely, the challenges facing democratization and the challenges facing democracy promotion will continue to intertwine in ways that may not be favourable for either. Indeed, for Whitehead, a fundamental challenge remains to reconcile internationalist principles with democracy's necessary grounding in state sovereignty.

Nancy Bermeo, in Chapter 5, provides a dramatic illustration of this in respect of US military aid and sales. Assistance to security sector reform offers a specific example (together with development aid for governance capacity-building) where everyone should now pay closer attention to the implications of such involvements for democracy and democratization. Bermeo argues for a better understanding of exactly how military aid impacts on democracy aid and its objectives in different political contexts. The concern is that military aid will continue to empower hard-liners in non-democracies to quash the very reformists who are receiving support in varying (often modest) degrees by the same or other Western donors. The lesson is stark: increasing military aid in this way represents a far more significant obstacle to democratization than was previously realized – by democracy practitioners and independent analysts alike.

A more positive link also needs to be crafted between democracy policies and energy security strategies. What has so far been a largely problematic trade-off in Western policies between democracy and energy imperatives could be turned into a positive use of governance reforms as a means of bridging the security and democracy support agendas. This in turn may require greater interaction between the democracy and energy policy-making communities. However, even if greater overall policy coherence is essential, this should not provide a coda for democracy being submerged by competing foreign policy objectives. Calls for mainstreaming democracy promotion within overall foreign policy are often made. For example, the enshrining of democracy promotion as one of the key pillars of US foreign policy in the National Security doctrine formed one of the joint recommendations of the National Democratic Institute and International Republican Institute to the incoming Obama administration. However, they should be greeted with considerable caution: as has been displayed in a European context (see, for instance, Jünemann and Knodt 2007), security considerations tend to be overbearing, and rather than democracy support gaining more weight from a closer relationship, the opposite could be the real outcome.

Both Russia's reaction to the colour revolutions elsewhere and Russian attempts to influence the course of the Orange Revolution in Ukraine, which some commentators believe was counter-productive, tell everyone to be prepared for the possibility of unintended consequences. How far such possibilities should be allowed to influence decisions on democracy support tactics and strategy is a matter for case-by-case interpretation. Even if a more absolutist reading of national state sovereignty is 'back' in international

Addressing democracy's challenges   197

politics – as argued by Laurence Whitehead in Chapter 2 – this need not function as an impermeable barrier to all external pro-democratic influences, especially where significant domestic support for political reform already exists within the political elite or society generally At the very least some such influences can proceed by way of what the literature calls 'linkage' (as distinct from 'leverage') and from the exercise of 'soft' (not 'hard') power. Although China's representatives miss few opportunities to claim that the country's reliance on cultivating soft power distinguishes China from more assertive countries in the West, it would be a serious mistake to lend credence to the notion that everything China stands for exerts a stronger international appeal than western-based ideals. Moreover, as Breslin shows, politics in China is changing, and in certain ways that can only be welcomed. Elsewhere in the world, it is as well to recall that even the most stringent adherence to ideas of state-based national sovereignty offers no guarantee of protection to an unpopular or failing regime against internal implosion or revolution from below.

In this sense, the preceding chapters imply that practitioners should not be discouraged but do need to take the long view. Democratic despondency about recent developments in Russia and Chinese resistance to international pressure over human rights should be placed in perspective: both countries are freer now than they were more than two decades ago and at least some of the gains are probably irreversible. In this sense, the tendency, especially in the United States, to paint the demise of unipolarity and 'liberal hegemony' in unremittingly negative light for democracy should be tempered at least to a degree. Concerns over the backlash should not blind practitioners to new opportunities, especially those that become available if flexibility is shown in reassessing approaches to supporting democratic opening, defence or advance. There is indeed much talk of the necessity to establish a 'new democracy promotion paradigm'. But the details of what this will mean in practice await decisive resolution by the relevant policy communities, national and multilateral. For instance, it could mean concentrating on strengthening the emerging democracies and neglecting the semi-authoritarian or hardened authoritarian regimes; abjuring the more coercive approaches seems likely; higher levels of cooperation among European, American and other democracy practitioners is another possibility but by no means assured.

Analytical lacunae

An observation that can be drawn from the various chapters is that in politics, actors do matter. Much is contingent. For example, things might have turned out differently in Russia (although not necessarily more favourably to liberal democracy) if Yeltsin had not been succeeded by Putin and Putin had not interpreted events in Russia's near abroad as a threat to Russia. Similarly, the skill of China's leadership in managing dramatic economic and social changes appears to be crucial to determining that country's political future: the

198 *Peter Burnell and Richard Youngs*

possibilities, which are diverse and some of them unpredictable, range from political instability or increasingly xenophobic nationalism to more freedom and something like democracy 'with Chinese characteristics'. Breslin confirms that there is still a weak grasp of whether the 'China model' is sustainable over the long term, or conversely whether 'consultative authoritarianism' (and authoritarian capitalism more generally) is simply akin to opening a Pandora's box of unsustainable contradictions and unintended consequences. More research is needed on such path-dependency and variation in outcomes. This suggests a theoretical as well as empirical challenge for analysts.

Also, while structural economic factors must be incorporated so that particular requirement should not be exaggerated: the effects on democratization of secular trends in energy prices, for instance, might not be uniform; the further ahead the time frame is, the more uncertain are both the trends and their political consequences. In other words, analytical approaches to making sense of the international dimensions of democratization still struggle to incorporate satisfactorily a due deference to both structure and agency and their interactions, especially given that both of these can change quickly and quite drastically. The steep rise in the international oil price to a peak close to $US150 a barrel in July 2008 followed by an even sharper fall (to around $US40) only five months later, is illustrative of the former; and for the latter, Robert Mugabe's political exit in Zimbabwe could prove key to transforming that country's political and economic fortunes. This book suggests that many misunderstandings of the 'backlash' stem from wider shortcomings in our knowledge of how to bridge the structural conditions and human choice-making. This prompts also a renewal of the familiar plea for a better conjoining of international relations and political theory in future research on democratization – both to take account of shifts in the moving and broken line where the domestic and the foreign, the national and the international dimensions interact, and to remind ourselves that if authoritarian values really are now staging a comeback, then political theorizing has always ranged well beyond western liberal democratic theories. Perhaps now is the time to revisit opposing traditions in both normative and descriptive or explanatory theory, if we want a better grasp of where the future might lead.

Furthermore, research still has to work with data shortcomings. Some of these stem from choices over methodology: by themselves, different choices can be responsible for variations in our assessments of the true state of democracy and democratization, that is, the real trends. To illustrate, the scores the Bertelsmann Transformation Index 2008 provided for all of its 52 'defective democracies' in 2007 improved across the five criteria for political transformation (Bertelsmann Stiftung 2008); the Economist Intelligence Unit's Index of Democracy 2008 (based on 2006 data) found no recent global trend of outright democratic regression but merely stagnation instead; while the new Ibrahim Index of African Governance actually came up with a positive picture. Two-thirds of countries in Sub-Saharan Africa – a region often considered one of the toughest for democratization – improved their

Addressing democracy's challenges 199

governance performance during 2006, with political participation and human rights featuring particularly strongly (Mo Ibrahim Foundation 2008) The point is not that inconsistencies among figures like these and those reported by Freedom House (see Chapter 1), Polity IV, and so on are enormous (for they are not), or that the 'babel' surrounding alternative regime classifications and nomenclature is insurmountable. Rather, the moral is that considerable care should continue to be taken in the way data are presented, interpreted, and used. The parallel life of terms like democratic regression, recession, decline, decay, rollback, reverse wave and, even, pushback has much potential to confuse, unless attention is paid to the definitions and the value of comparing different data sets is recognized. While patterns that emerge over several years certainly should carry weight with analysts, instant reactions to a selective and very short-run set of figures and the way they are reported in the headlines can be misleading and are best avoided.

Even so, there are instances where more and better data clearly are needed. Shortcomings in the data for military aid, covert military intervention and arms exports by Russia and China are perhaps to be expected. But Doorenspleet shows that even the results of attitude surveys in democracies have to be interpreted very carefully (in particular, over using the same questionnaire in very different socio-cultural environments coloured by different historical experiences with various types of political regime). The choice of questions asked and the way the questions are understood by respondents may distort the findings in unforeseen ways; reliable data on attitudes towards democracy in the most illiberal states remain out of bounds. Moreover, if the responses send mixed messages or appear to be inconsistent with the respondent's observed behaviour, then we are hard pushed to divine the real meaning for democracy. As to what matters most, dissatisfaction with the local experience of democracy or the gap between dissatisfaction and support for democracy, is a question that hangs in the balance: answers may depend on precisely how the dependent variable is defined (democracy's quality versus its resilience and sustainability, for instance) as well as on who is making the judgement (the analysts or the citizens themselves). Further investigation must be made in order to better assess the crucial matter of what triggers dissatisfaction and whether it must be good or, conversely, bad for democratization.

Finally, the imprecise art of evaluating the performance of democracy assistance, where recent efforts at quantifying the effects of US democracy and governance assistance (see Finkel et al. 2008) have yet to be matched by counterpart studies of European democracy aid, may soon be joined by the new challenge of how to assess the performance of international endeavours to maintain (export, even) authoritarian or illiberal rule. Comparing the effectiveness of the various international strategies in upholding different types of democratic and non-democratic political regimes suggests much scope for innovative and detailed analytical and empirical research, as does the very idea that authoritarian values can be diffused across societies through channels or by mechanisms that compare with democratic diffusion, social

200 *Peter Burnell and Richard Youngs*

learning and acculturation. More modest there will be growing case studies to find out more about the raft of new recruits to the democracy support industry. That includes both nation-level foundations and institutes of the sort that now exist in some of Europe's post-communist democracies and intergovernmental or multilateral bodies such as the United Nations Democracy Fund.

Implications for the future

As a recent comprehensive history of democracy points out, there have been periods of democratic fatalism in the past: Keane (2009: 571) notes that the early twentieth century was one such time, when the German sociologist Max Weber expressed views that were far from sanguine about democracy's failure. However, although democratic progress around the world in very general terms now appears to have reached a plateau, this does not mean it is not still moving forward in some countries, or that a reverse wave of democratization is definitely under way. Although the progress of democratization appears to have stalled for now, that does not mean it has reached its final limit. However, part of the challenge currently facing democratization is to overcome the disappointment of discovering afresh (if not for the first time) that democratization is not as easy or straightforward as was presumed in some quarters in the early 1990s. A more specific challenge faces international democracy support, namely to regain the legitimacy and credibility that have been eroded over recent years, and to find new strategies adapted for a changed international environment, one where the established democracies do not have a free hand in determining the agendas of international politics. Although there is general agreement that the role of international factors must be taken fully into consideration, a broad consensus still exists that democracy support's capacity to exert a positive influence is modest at best, and on occasions may even be counterproductive, notwithstanding the very positive contribution it has made in special circumstances and at exceptional moments. However, none of the chapters in this book conclude that international democracy support has no role at all to play. Rather the implication is that devising appropriate responses to the new challenges that both democracy support and democratization now face poses its own major new challenge. But above all, continuing to persuade ordinary people that, all things considered, democratization has more to offer than do the available alternatives, while not a brand new challenge, may remain crucial for the foreseeable future. It would be wrong to conclude that the world now stands on the threshold of a new 'reverse wave' of democracy. However, the present juncture could be decisive in terms of whether the years ahead see broad consolidation of democracy's recent gains in overall terms or a resumption of forwards movement instead.

Bibliography

Ackerman, P. and Duvall, J. (2005) 'People power primed: civilian resistance and democratization', *Harvard International Review*, 27(2): 42–7.

Agence France Presse (2003) 'Russia grumbles at US role in Shevardnadze's overthrow', 25 November.

Al-Ghazal Harb (2007) 'The role of the West in internal political developments of the Arab region', Arab Reform Initiative Thematic Studies, April. Online. Available at: www.arab-reform.net (accessed 15 December 2008).

Almond, G. and Verba, S. (1963) *The Civic Culture: Political Attitudes and Democracy in Five Nations*, Newbury Park, CA: Sage.

Al-Rasheed, M. (2005), 'Circles of power: royals and society in Saudi Arabia', in P. Aarts and G. Nonneman (eds) *Saudi Arabia in the Balance: Political Economy, Society, Foreign Affairs*, London: Hurst and Company.

Ambrosio, T. (2009) *Authoritarian Backlash: Russian Resistance to Democratization in the Former Soviet Union*, Farnham: Ashgate.

Armitage, R., Bloomfield, L. and Kelly, J. (2002) 'Preserving US and allied interests in a new era', in L. Bloomfield (ed.) *Global Market and National Interests: The New Geopolitics of Energy, Capital, and Information*, Washington, DC: Center for Strategic and International Studies.

Armitage, R. and Nye, J. (2008) 'Implementing smart power: setting an agenda for national security reform. Statement before the US Senate Foreign relations Committee, 24 April'. Online. Available at: www.csis.org (accessed 15 December 2008).

Armony, A. and Schamis, H. (2005) 'Babel in democratization studies', *Journal of Democracy*, 16(4): 113–28.

Arnold, C. (2007) 'Russia: Nashi celebrates victory: public steers clear', *RFE/RL*, 3 December 3, 2007.

Baker, P. (2007) 'As democracy falters, Bush feels like a "dissident"', *Washington Post*, 20 August.

Barber, B. (1996) 'Three challenges to re-inventing democracy', in P. Hirst and S. Khilnani (eds) *Reinventing Democracy*, Cambridge, MA: Blackwell, pp. 144–56.

——(2003) *Fear's Empire: War, Terrorism and Democracy*, New York: Norton and Co.

Barma, N. and Ratner, E. (2006) 'China's illiberal challenge', *Democracy: A Journal of Ideas*, 2(Fall): 56–68.

Barnes, J. and Jaffe, A. M. (2006) 'The Persian Gulf and the geopolitics of oil', *Survival*, 48(1): 143–62.

Beissinger, M. (2007) 'Structure and example in modular political phenomena: the diffusion of bulldozer/Rose/Orange/Tulip revolutions', *Perspectives on Politics*, 5(2): 259–76.

202 Bibliography

Bell, D. (1960) *The End of Ideology: On the Exhaustion of Political Ideas in the Fifties*, New York: Free Press of Glencoe.

Belton, C. (2008) 'Copy China and invest abroad, says Medvedev', *Financial Times*, 31 January.

Bennendijk, A.L. and Marovic, I. (2006) 'Power and persuasion: nonviolent strategies to influence state security forces in Serbia (2000) and Ukraine (2004)', *Communist and Post-Communist Studies*, 39(3): 411–29.

Bermeo, N. (2003) *Ordinary People in Extraordinary Times: The Citizenry and the Breakdown of Democracy*, Princeton, NJ: Princeton University Press.

Berrigan, F. and Hartun, W. (2005) 'U.S. weapons at war 2005: promoting freedom or fueling conflict?', World Policy Institute Special Report. Online. Available at: www. worldpolicy.org/projects/arms/reports/wawjune2005.html (accessed 28 December 2008).

Bertelsmann Stiftung (2008) *Bertelsmann Transformation Index 2008*. Online. Available at: www-bertelsmann-transformation-index.de (accessed 28 October 2008).

Blagov, S. (2008) 'Moscow wants to strengthen CIS and other post-Soviet groups', *Eurasia Daily Monitor*, 5: 114, 16 June.

Boonstra, J. (2007) *OSCE Democracy Promotion: Grinding to a Halt?*, Working Paper 44, Madrid: Fundación para las Relaciones Internacionales y El Diálogo Exterior.

Boubekeur, A. (2008) *Salafism and Radical Politics in Postconflict Algeria*, Carnegie Paper No.11, Beirut: Carnegie Middle East Center.

Bratton, M. (2002) *Wide but Shallow: Popular Support for Democracy in Africa*, Afrobarometer Working Paper 19 (MSU, IDASA, CDD). Online. Available at: www.afrobarometer.org (accessed 28 October 2008).

Bratton, M. and Mattes, R. (2001) 'Support for democracy in Africa: intrinsic or instrumental?', *British Journal of Political Science*, 31(3): 447–74.

Bratton, M., Mattes, R. and Gyimah-Boadi, E. (2005) *Public Opinion, Democracy, and Market Reform in Africa*, New York: Cambridge University Press

Breslin, S. (2007) *China and the Global Political Economy*, Basingstoke: Palgrave.

Brown, N. J., Hamzawy, A. and Ottaway, M. (2006) *Islamist Movements and the Democratic Process in the Arab World: Exploring the Gray Zones*, Carnegie Paper No. 67, Washington, DC: Carnegie Endowment for International Peace.

Brubaker, R. (1999) 'The Manichean myth: rethinking the distinction between "civic" and "ethnic" nationalism', in H. Kriesi, K. Armingeon and H. Siegrist (eds) *Nation and National Identity: The European Experience in Perspective*, Zurich: Ruegger, pp. 55–71.

Bruneau, T. and Trinkunas, H. (2006) 'Democratization as a global phenomenon and its impact on civil relations', *Democratization*, 13(5): 776–90.

Budge, I., Newton, K. *et al.* (1997) *The Politics of the New Europe: From the Atlantic to the Urals*, London: Longmans.

Bunce, V. and Wolchik, S. (2006a) 'Favorable conditions and electoral revolutions', *Journal of Democracy*, 17(4): 5–18.

——(2006b) 'Youth and electoral revolutions in Slovakia, Serbia, and Georgia', *SAIS Review* 26(2); 55–65.

——(2006c) 'International diffusion and postcommunist electoral revolutions', *Communist and Post-Communist Studies*, 39(3): 283–304.

Burnell, P. (ed.) (2003) *Democratization through the Looking-glass*, Manchester: Manchester University Press.

——(2006) *Promoting Democracy Backwards*, Working Paper 28, Madrid: Fundación para las Relaciones Internacionales y el Diálogo Exterior.

Bibliography 203

——(2007) *Evaluating Democracy Support: Methods and Experiences*, Stockholm: IDEA and SIDA.

——(2008a) 'From evaluating democracy assistance to appraising democracy promotion', *Political Studies*, 56(2): 414–34.

——(2008b) 'International democracy promotion: a role for public goods theory?', *Contemporary Politics*, 14(1): 37–52.

Bush, G.W. (2007) 'Remarks to the Democracy and Security Conference in Prague', 5 June. Online. Available at: www.whitehouse.gov/news/releases/2007/06/20070605-8.html (accessed 28 December 2008).

Carothers, T. (1999) *Aiding Democracy Abroad: The Learning Curve*, Washington, DC: Carnegie Endowment for International Peace.

——(2002) 'The end of the transition paradigm', *Journal of Democracy*, 13(1): 5–21.

——(2006) 'The backlash against democracy promotion', *Foreign Affairs*, 85(2): 55–68.

——(2007a) 'Ousting foreign strongmen: lessons from Serbia', in T. Carothers (ed.) *Critical Mission: Essays on Democracy Promotion*, Washington, DC: Carnegie Endowment for International Peace, pp. 53–61.

——(2007b) 'The democracy crusade myth', *The National Interest*, 90(July/August): 8–12.

——(2007c) *U.S. Democracy Promotion During and After Bush*, Washington, DC: Carnegie Endowment for International Peace.

——(2008) 'Does democracy promotion have a future?' in B. Berendsen (ed.) *Democracy and Development*, Amsterdam: Koninklijk Instituut Voor de Tropen, pp. 121–38.

Central Committee (2004) 中共中央关于加强党的执政能力建设的决定 *Zhonggong Zhongyang Guanyu Jiaqiang Dangde Zhizheng Nengli Jianshe de Jueding* [The Party Central Committee Decision on Strengthening Governing Capacity Construction]. Online. Available at: www.china.com.cn/chinese/2004/Sep/668376.htm (in Chinese) (accessed 23 September 2008).

Chavusaw, Y. (2005) 'Revolution and anti-revolution in the post-Soviet Space', *Eurozine*, 25 November 2005. Online. Available at: www.eurozine.com/articles/2005-11-25-chavusaw-en.html.

Chua Chin Hon (2004) 'Chinese middle class? It's just a myth, study finds', *The Straits Times*, 27 January.

Clingendael International Energy Programme (2004) *Study on Energy Supply Security and Geopolitics.* Online. Available at: www.clingendael.nl/publications (accessed 12 January 2009).

Clinton, B. (1994) 'Address before a Joint Session of the Congress on the State of the Union', 25 January. Online. Available at: www.c-span.org/executive/transcript.asp?year=1994 (accessed 28 December 2008).

Coleman, J.S. (1965) *Education and Political Development*, Princeton, NJ: Princeton University Press.

Collier, P. (2008) *The Bottom Billion*, Oxford: Oxford University Press.

Collier, P., Elliott, L., Hegre, H., Hoeffler, A., Reynal-Querol, M. and Sambanis, N. (2003) *Breaking the Conflict Trap* Washington, DC: The World Bank.

Commission of the European Communities (2006) *The EU's Relations with Kazakhstan.* Online. Available at: www.ec.europa.eu/external_relations/Kazakhstan.

Congressional Research Service Report for Congress (2007) *Democracy Promotion: Cornerstone of U.S. Foreign Policy?* 26 December. Online. Available at: www.fas.org/sgp/crs (accessed 17 March 2008).

Cooley, A. (2008) *Base Politics: Democratic Change and the U.S. Military.* Ithaca, NY: Cornell University Press.

204 Bibliography

Cordesman, A. and Al-Rodhan, K. (2006) *The Geopolitics of Energy: Geostrategic Risks and Economic Uncertainties*, Washington, DC: Center for Strategic and International Studies.

Cornell, S., Popjanevski, J. and Nillson, N. (2008) 'Russia's war in Georgia: causes and implications for Georgia and the world', *Central Asia-Caucasus Institute Silk Road Studies Program Policy Paper*, August.

Corwin, J. (2005) 'New youth movement to foil US plot to take over Russia', *RFE/RL* 9: 40, 2 March.

Council on Foreign Relations (2001) *Strategic Energy Policy Challenges for the 21st Century*, Report of an Independent Task Force, by the James A. Baker III Institute for Public Policy of Rice University and the Council on Foreign Relations.

Crane, G. (1994) 'Collective identity, symbolic mobilization, and student protest in Nanjing, China, 1988–89', *Comparative Politics*, 26(4): 395–413.

Crozier, M., Huntington, S. P. and Watanuki, J. (1975) *The Crisis in Democracy*, New York: New York University Press.

Dahl, R.A. (1971) *Polyarchy: Participation and Opposition*, New Haven, CT: Yale University Press.

Dalton, R. J. (1999) 'Political support in advanced industrial democracies', in P. Norris, *Critical Citizens: Global Support for Democratic Governance*, Oxford: Oxford University Press, pp. 57–78.

——(2004) *Democratic Challenges, Democratic Choices. The Erosion of Political Support in Advanced Industrial Democracies*, Oxford: Oxford University Press.

Darden, K. and Grzymala-Busse, A. (2006) 'The great divide: literacy, nationalism and the communist collapse', *World Politics*, 59(1): 83–115.

Demes, P. and Forbrig, J. (2006) 'Pora – "It's Time" for democracy in Ukraine', in A. Åslund and M. McFaul (eds) *Revolution in Orange: The Origins of Ukraine's Democratic Breakthrough*, Washington, DC: Carnegie Endowment for International Peace, pp. 85–102.

Democracy Digest. The Bulletin of the Transatlantic Democracy Network (2008) February. Online. Available at: www.demdigest.net (accessed 17 March 2008).

Des Forges, R. and Luo Xu (2001) 'China as a non-hegemonic superpower? The use of history among the China can say no writers and their critics', *Critical Asian Studies*, 33(4): 483–507.

Diamond, L. (1999) *Developing Democracy: Toward Consolidation*, Baltimore, MD: The Johns Hopkins University Press.

——(2002) 'Thinking about hybrid regimes', *Journal of Democracy*, 13(2): 21–35.

——(2003) *Squandered Victory*, New York: Times Books.

——(2008a) *The Spirit of Democracy*, New York: Henry Holt.

——(2008b) *Stemming the Recession of Democracy*, Stanford, CA: Stanford Story Bank, 29 September. Online. Available at: www.storybank.stanford.edu/stories/stemming-recession-democracy (accessed 10 January 2009).

Diamond, L. and Plattner, M. (1996) *Civil Military Relations in Democracy*, Baltimore, MD: The Johns Hopkins University Press.

Dickson, B. (2003) *Red Capitalists in China: The Party, Private Entrepreneurs, and Prospects for Political Change*, Cambridge: Cambridge University Press.

Ding, X. L. (2000) 'Informal privatization through internationalization: the rise of nomenklatura capitalism in China's offshore business', *British Journal of Political Science*, 30(1): 121–46.

Doorenspleet, R. (2000) 'Reassessing the three waves of democratization', *World Politics*, 52(3): 384–406.

Bibliography 205

——(2005) *Democratic Transitions: Exploring the Structural Sources during the Fourth Wave*, Boulder, CO: Lynne Rienner Publishers.

Dunning, T. (2008) *Crude Democracy: Natural Resource Wealth and Political Regimes*, Cambridge: Cambridge University Press.

Easton, D. (1965) *A Systems Analysis of Political Life*, New York: Wiley.

——(1975) 'A reassessment of the concept of political support', *The British Journal of Political Science*, 5(4): 435–57.

Economist Intelligence Unit (2008) *Index of Democracy (2008)*. Online. Available at: www.eiu.com (accessed 28 October 2008).

Ehteshami, A. and Wright, S. (2007), 'Political change in the Arab oil monarchies: from liberalisation to enfranchisment', *International Affairs*, 83(5): 913–32.

Engdahl, W. (2004) *A Century of War: Anglo-American Oil Politics and the New World Order*, London: Pluto.

Estrada, A. M. (2006) *Argelia: ¿retorno al nacionalismo energético?* Real Instituto Elcano, September.

Fairbanks, C. (2004) 'Georgia's Rose Revolution', *Journal of Democracy*, 15(2); 110–24.

Fang N., Wang X. D. and Song Q. (1999) 全球化阴影下的中国之路 *Quanqiuhua Yinying xia de Zhongguo Zhilu* [China's Path Under the Shadow of Globalisation], Beijing: China Social Science Press.

FBIS Report (2004) 'Russia: media accuse West of engineering Ukraine election crisis', 1 December.

Ferguson, N. (2006) *The War of the World*, London: Penguin.

Ferrero-Waldner, B. (2006) 'Opening address', External Energy Policy conference, 20 November, Brussels.

Fewsmith, J. (2007) 'Democracy is a good thing', *China Leadership Monitor*, 22.

Finkel, S., Pérez-Liñán, A. and Seligson, M. (2007) 'The effects of U.S. foreign assistance on democracy building, 1990–2003', *World Politics*, 59(3): 404–39.

Finkel, S., Pérez-Liñán, A., Seligson, M. and Tate, N. (2008) *Deepening Our Understanding of the Effects of US Foreign Assistance on Democracy Building: Final Report*, Democracy Assistance Project. Online. Available at: www.pitt.edu/~politics/democracy/FINAL_REPORT%20v18b.pdf (accessed 28 December 2008).

Finn, P. (2008) 'Russia pumps tens of millions into burnishing image abroad', *Washington Post*, 6 March, A1.

Fish, S. (2001) 'The dynamics of democratic erosion', in R. Anderson, M. Steven Fish, S. Hanson and P. Roeder (eds) *Postcommunism and the Theory of Democracy*, Princeton, NJ: Princeton University Press.

——(2005) *Democracy Derailed in Russia: The Failure of Open Politics*, Cambridge: Cambridge University Press.

Fishman, R. (1990) 'Rethinking state and regime: Southern Europe's transition to democracy', *World Politics*, 42(3): 422–40.

Fox, G. and Roth, B. (eds) (2000) *Democratic Governance and International Law*, Cambridge: Cambridge University Press.

Franck, T. (1992) 'The emerging right to democratic governance', *American Journal of International Law*, 81(1): 46–91.

Friedman, T. (2006), 'The First Law of petropolitics', *Foreign Policy*, 85(2): 28–36.

Fuchs, D., Guidorossi, G. and Svensson, P. (1998) 'Support for the democratic system', in H.-D. Klingemann and D. Fuchs (eds) *Citizens and the State*, Oxford: Oxford University Press, pp. 323–54.

206 Bibliography

Fuchs, D. and Klingemann, H.-D. (1998) 'Citizens and the state: a relationship transformed', in H.-D. Klingemann and D. Fuchs (eds) *Citizens and the State*, Oxford: Oxford University Press, pp. 419–44.

Fukayama, F. (1989) 'The end of history', *The National Interest*, Summer, 3–18.

——(1992) *The End of History and the Last Man*, New York: Free Press.

Fukuyama, F. and McFaul, M. (2007), 'Should democracy promotion be promoted or demoted?', *The Washington Quarterly*, 31(1): 23–45.

Fuller, L. (2008) 'Analysis: Armenian coalition partner lambasts former president', *RFE/RL*, 23 May.

Gaddy, C. G. and Kuchins, A. C. (2008) 'Putin's plan', *The Washington Quarterly*, 31(2): 117–29.

Gallagher, M. (2002) 'Reform and openness: why China's economic reforms have delayed democracy', *World Politics*, 54(3): 338–72.

——(2007) *Contagious Capitalism: Globalization and the Politics of Labor in China*, Princeton, NJ: Princeton University Press.

George, J. (2008) 'Minority political inclusion in post-Soviet Georgia', *Europe Asia Studies*, 60: 7, 1151–75.

German Marshall Fund of the United States (2007) *Transatlantic Trends Key Findings 2007*. Online. Available at: www.transatlantictrends.org (accessed 28 October 2008).

Gheissari, A. and Nasr, V. (2006) *Democracy in Iran: History and the Quest for Liberty*, Oxford: Oxford University Press.

Gisselquist, R. (2008) 'Democratic transition and democratic survival in Benin', *Democratization*, 15(4): 789–814.

Glosemeyer, I. (2005) 'Checks, balances and transformation in the Saudi Political system', in P. Aarts and G. Nonneman (eds) *Saudi Arabia in the Balance: Political Economy, Society, Foreign Affairs*, London: Hurst and Company.

Goldier, J. and McFaul, M. (2003) *Power and Purpose: US Policy toward Russia after the Cold War*, Washington, DC: Brookings Institution Press.

Goodman, D. (1998) 'In search of China's new middle classes: the creation of wealth and diversity in Shanxi during the 1990s', *Asian Studies Review*, 22(1): 39–62.

——(2008) 'Why China has no new middle class: cadres, managers and entrepreneurs', in D. Goodman (ed.) *The New Rich in China: Future Rulers, Present Lives*, London: Routledge, pp. 23–37.

Goodman, D. and Zang, X. W. (2008) 'The new rich in China: dimensions of social change', in D. Goodman (ed.) *The New Rich in China: Future Rulers, Present Lives*, London: Routledge, pp. 1–20.

Gorbachev, M. S. (1987) *Perestroika: New Thinking for Our Country and the World*, New York: Harper & Row.

Granovetter, M. (1983) 'The strength of weak ties: a network theory revisited', *Sociological Theory*, 1: 201–33.

Greenfeld, L. (1992) *Nationalism: Five Roads to Modernity*, Cambridge, MA: Harvard University Press.

Haber, S. and Menaldo, V. (2007) 'Does oil fuel authoritarianism?', unpublished draft paper, 11 June.

Habermas, J. (1973) *Legitimationsprobleme im Spätkapitalismus*, Frankfurt am Main: Suhrkamp Verlag. Published as *Legitimation Crisis*, Boston: Beacon Press (1975).

Hadenius, A. and Teorell, J. (2007) 'Pathways from authoritarianism', *Journal of Democracy*, 18(1); 143–56.

Bibliography 207

Hale, H. (2005) 'Regime cycles: democracy, autocracy, and revolution in post-Soviet Eurasia', *World Politics*, 58(1): 133–65.

——(2006) 'Democracy or autocracy on the march? The colored revolutions as normal dynamics of patronal presidentialism', *Communist and Post-Communist Studies*, 39(3): 305–29.

Hale, H., McFaul, M. and Colton, T. J. (2004) 'Putin and the "delegative democracy" trap: evidence from Russia's 2003–4 elections', *Post-Soviet Affairs*, 20(4): 285–319.

Halperin, M. and Piccone, T. (2008) 'A league of democracies: doomed to fail?' *International Herald Tribune*, 6 June, p. 6.

Hamzawy, A. (2006) *The Saudi Labyrinth: Evaluating the Current Political Opening*, Working Paper 68, Washington, DC: Carnegie Endowment for International Peace.

Han, D. Q. (2000) *Pengzhuang: Quanqiuhua Xianjing yu Zhongguo Xianshi Xuanze* [Collision: The Globalisation Trap and China's Real Choice], Beijing: Economic Management Press.

Harris, L. and Vinci, A. (2000) 'Yugoslav revolt: Putin recognizes Kostunica as newly elected President', *CNN Breaking News Transcript*, 6 October.

He L. (2003) 'Middle class: friends or foes to Beijing's new leadership?', *Journal of Chinese Political Science*, 8(1 and 2): 88–100.

Heintz, J. (2000) 'Russia warns the West to stay out of Yugoslavia', *The Associated Press*, 28 September.

Helmke, G. and Levitsky, S. (eds) (2006) *Informal Institutions and Democracy: Lessons From Latin America*, Baltimore, MD: The Johns Hopkins University Press.

Herd, G.P. (2005) 'Colorful revolutions and the CIS: "manufactured" versus "managed" democracy?' *Problems of Post-Communism*, 52(2): 3–18.

Heydermann, S. (2007) *Upgrading Authoritarianism in the Arab World*, Brookings Saban/Center for Middle East Policy, Analysis Paper 13.

Hill, F. and Jones, K. (2006) 'Fear of democracy or revolution: the reaction to Andijon', *The Washington Quarterly*, 29(3): 111–25.

Hirst, P. and Khilnani, S. (eds) *Reinventing Democracy*, Cambridge, MA: Blackwell.

Hofferbert, R. and Klingemann H.-D. (1999) 'Remembering the bad old days: human rights, economic conditions and democratic performance in transitional regimes', *European Journal of Political Research*, 36(1): 155–74. Online. Available at: www.ec. europa.eu/comm/external_relations/kazakhstan/intro/index.htm (accessed 28 August 2006).

Hughes, C. (2006) *Chinese Nationalism in the Global Era*, London: Routledge.

Human Rights Watch (2003) *In the Name of Counter-Terrorism: Human Rights Abuses Worldwide*. A Human Rights Watch Briefing Paper for the 59th Session of the United Nations Commission on Human Rights, 25 March 2003. Online. Available at: www.hrw.org/un/chr59/counter-terrorism-bck.htm (accessed 1 October 2008).

——(2008) 'Choking on bureaucracy: state curbs on independent civil society activism', 20: 1(D), February. Online. Available at: www.hrw.org/reports/2008 (accessed 1 October 2008).

Humphreys, M., Sachs, J. and Stiglitz, J. (eds) (2007) *Escaping the Resource Curse*, New York: Columbia University Press.

Huntington, S. P. (1981) *American Politics: The Promise of Disharmony*, Cambridge, MA: Harvard University Press.

——(1984) 'Will more countries become democratic?', *Political Science Quarterly*, 99(2): 193–218.

208 Bibliography

——(1991) *The Third Wave: Democratization in the Late Twentieth Century*, Norman, OK: University of Oklahoma Press.

Hurrell, A. (2007) *On Global Order: Power, Values, and the Constitution of International Society*, Oxford: Oxford University Press.

Ignatieff, M. (1993) *Blood and Belonging: Journeys into the New Nationalism*, London: BBC Books.

Inglehart, R. (1997) *Modernization and Postmodernization: Cultural, Economic, and Political Change in 43 Societies*, Princeton, NJ: Princeton University Press.

——(1999) 'Postmodernization erodes respect for authority, but increases support for democracy', in P. Norris (ed.) *Critical Citizens: Global Support for Democratic Governance*, Oxford: Oxford University Press, pp. 236–57.

Interfax (2003) 'Russia advises Georgia to seek political and not "street" solution to current crisis', 14 November, as reported by BBC Monitoring Service.

International Crisis Group (2006) 'Uzbekistan: Europe's sanctions matter', Policy Briefing (November).

International Journal for Non-for-Profit Law (2006) 'Recent laws and legislative proposals to restrict civil society and civil society organizations', 8(4). Online. Available at: www.icnl.org.

Jackson, R. H. (1993) *Quasi-states: Sovereignty, International Relations, and the Third World*, Cambridge: Cambridge University Press.

Jaffe, A. M. (2005) 'The outlook for future oil supply from the Middle East and price implications', speech, Tokyo, 20 July, available from the James Baker III Institute for Public Policy of Rice University.

Johnson, D. (2005) 'EU-Russia energy links', in D. Johnson and P. Robinson (eds) *Perspectives on EU-Russia Relations*, London: Routledge.

Johnson-Sirleaf, E. (2007) 'Africom can help governments willing to help themselves', *allafrica.com*, 25 June. Online. Available at: www.allafrica.com/stories/200706251196.html (accessed 1 January 2009)

Journal of Democracy (2007a) 'The debate on "sequencing"', 18(3): 5–22.

——(2007b) 'The Democracy Barometers (Part I)', 18(3): 65–125.

Jünemann, A. and Knodt, M. (eds) (2007) *European External Democracy Promotion*, Baden Baden: Nomos Verlagsgesellschaft.

Kagan, R. (2008) *The Return of History and the End of Dreams*, New York: Knopf.

Kalicki, J. and Goldwyn, D. (eds) (2005) *Energy and Security: Toward a New Foreign Policy Strategy*, Washington, DC: Woodrow Wilson Center.

Karatnycky, A. (1999) 'The decline of illiberal democracy', *Journal of Democracy*, 10 (1): 112–25.

Karumidze, Z. and Wertsch, J. V. (2005) *'Enough! The Rose Revolution in the Republic of Georgia 2003*, New York: Nova.

Kausch, K. (2007) *Europe and Russia, beyond Energy*, Madrid: FRIDE, Working Paper 33.

Keane, J. (2009) *The Life and Death of Democracy*, New York: Simon and Schuster.

Kelley, J. (2008) 'Assessing the complex evolution of norms: the rise of international election monitoring', *International Organization*, 62(Spring): 221–55.

Khanna, P. (2008) 'Waving goodbye to hegemony', *New York Times Magazine*, 27 January.

Kimmage, D. (2005) 'Uzbekistan: Karimov battens down the hatches', *RFE/RL*, 1 August.

Klare, M. (2004) *Blood and Oil*, London: Penguin.

Kleveman, L. (2004) *The New Great Game: Blood and Oil in Central Asia*, London: Atlantic Books.

Klingemann, H.-D. (1999) 'Mapping political support in the 1990s: a global analysis', in P. Norris (ed.) *Critical Citizens: Global Support for Democratic Governance*, New York: Oxford University Press, pp. 31–56.

Kommersant (2006a) 'Voters left beyond the threshold', 9 November.

——(2006b) 'No more non-profit funding sources for parties', 15 November.

Kostenko, N. and Romanov, I. (2007) 'Terrarium of like-minded people', *Nezavisimaya Gazeta*, 30 July.

Krastev, I. (2006) 'Sovereign democracy, Russian-style', *Opendemocracy.net*, 16 November.

Krickovic, A. (2001) 'International intervention and recent regime changes in Croatia and Serbia', *UC Berkeley CEEES Newsletter*, Fall.

Lagnado, A. and Evans, M. (2000) 'Moscow calls time on "beaten" Milosevic', *The Times* (London), 26 September.

Legler, T., Lean, S. and Boniface, D. (eds) (2007) *Promoting Democracy in the Americas*, Baltimore, MD: The Johns Hopkins University Press.

Lennard, J. (2000a) 'Russia and the West draw swords over Yugoslav election outcome', *Agence France-Press*, 25 September.

——(2000b) 'Russian ultranationalist calls for Russia to back Milosevic', *Associated Press*, 29 September.

——(2000c) 'Russian Parliament head blasts "drunken coup' in Serbia"', *BBC Monitoring Newsfile*, 6 October.

Levitsky, S. and Way, L. (2002) 'The rise of competitive authoritarianism', *Journal of Democracy*, 13(2): 51–65.

Li C. L.(2004) '中产 阶层 ： 中国社会值得关注的人群 Zhongchan Jieceng: Zhongguo shehui zhide guanzhu de renqun' [The middle stratum: a group in Chinese society worth paying attention to], in Ru Xin, Lu Xueyi, and Li Peilin (eds) (2004) 年 ： 中国社会形势分析与预 *2004 Nian: Zhongguo Shehui Xingshi Fenxi yu Yuce* [Analysis and Forecast of the Features of Chinese Society: 2004], Beijing: Social Science Literature Press.

Li H. B. and Rozelle, S. (2003) 'Privatizing rural China: insider privatization, innovative contracts and the performance of township enterprises', *The China Quarterly*, 176: 981–1005.

Li L. J. and O'Brien, K. (1996) 'Villagers and popular resistance in contemporary China', *Modern China*, 22: 28–61.

Lijphart, A. (1999) *Patterns of Democracy: Government Forms and Performance in Thirty-Six Countries*, New Haven, CT: Yale University Press.

Lindberg, S. (2006) *Democracy and Elections in Africa*, Baltimore, MD: The Johns Hopkins University Press.

Linz, J. J. and Stepan, A. (1996) *Problems of Democratic Transition and Consolidation*, Baltimore, MD: The Johns Hopkins University Press.

Lipset, S. M. (1959) 'Some social requisites of democracy: economic development and political legitimacy', *American Political Science Review*, 56(1): 69–103.

——(1981) *Political Man*, Baltimore, MD: The Johns Hopkins University Press.

Lu, D. (2002) '鸦片战争胶片战争和国际化 Yapian Zhanzheng Jiaopian Zhanzheng he Guojihua' [The Opium War, film war and internationalisation], in Yin Hong (ed.) 全球化和媒体 *Quanqiuhua he Meiti Globalisation and Media*, Beijing: Qinghua University Press, pp. 217–28.

Lu X. Y. (ed.) (2004) 当代中国社会流动 *Dangdai Zhongguo Shehui Liudong [Mobility in Contemporary Chinese Society]* Beijing: Social Sciences Academic Press.

Luciani G. (2008) 'Arab states: oil reserves and transparency', *Arab Reform Bulletin*, 8(2) (March), Washington, DC: Carnegie Endowment for International Peace.

210 Bibliography

Magen, A. and Morlino, L. (eds) (2008) *International Actors, Democratization and the Rule of Law*, London: Routledge.

Mann, M. (1988) *States, War and Capitalism*, Oxford: Basil Blackwell.

Markov, S. (2005) 'Oranzhevaya revolutsiya – primer revolutsii global'nogo soobshchestva XXI veka', in M. Pogrebinskii, *Oranzhevaya Revolutsiya: Versii, Khronika, Dokumenty*, Kiev: Optima, pp. 52–75.

Mathieson, D. and Youngs, R. (2006) *Democracy Promotion and the European Left: Ambivalence Confused?* Working Paper 29, Madrid: Fundación para las Relaciones Internacionales y el Diálogo Exterior.

Maxwell, K. (1995) *The Making of Portuguese Democracy*, Cambridge: Cambridge University Press.

Maynes, C. (2006) 'A soft power tool-kit for dealing with Russia', *Europe's World*, Summer. Online. Available at: www.europesworld.org (accessed 12 January 2009).

McFaul, M. (1998) 'Russia's "privatized" state as an impediment to democratic consolidation. Part I', *Security Dialogue*, 29(2): 25–33.

——(2002) 'The fourth wave of democracy and dictatorship: noncooperative transitions in the postcommunist world', *World Politics*, 54(2): 212–44.

——(2004–5) 'Democracy promotion as a world value', *The Washington Quarterly*, 28(1): 147–63.

——(2005) 'Transitions from postcommunism', *Journal of Democracy*, 16(3): 5–19.

——(2006) 'Conclusion: the Orange Revolution in comparative perspective', in A. Åslund and M. McFaul (eds) *Revolution in Orange*, Washington, DC: Carnegie Endowment for International Peace, pp. 165–96.

McFaul, M. (2007) 'Ukraine imports democracy: external influences on the Orange Revolution', *International Security*, 32(2): 45–83.

McFaul, M., Petrov, N. and Ryabov, A. (2004) *Between Dictatorship and Democracy: Russian Post-Communist Political Reform*, Washington, DC: Carnegie Endowment for International Peace.

Medvedev, D. (2008) 'Responses to questions from German political, parliamentary and civic leaders', 5 June 2008. Online. Available at: www.kremlin.ru/eng/speeches/2008/06/05/2239_type82914type84779_202294.shtml.

Mendelson, S. (1993) 'Internal battles and external wars: politics, learning, and the Soviet withdrawal from Afghanistan', *World Politics*, 45(2): 327–60.

Mill, J. S. (1867) 'A few words on non-intervention', in J. S. Mill, *Dissertations and Discussions*, vol. III, 2nd edn, London: Longmans, Green, Reader and Dyer.

Milov, V. (2006) 'The use of energy as a political tool', *The EU-Russia Review*, Issue 1, Brussels: EU-Russia Centre.

Mishler, W. and Rose, R. (1999) 'Five years after the fall: trajectories of support for democracy in post-Communist Europe', in P. Norris (ed.), *Critical Citizens: Global Support for Democratic Governance*, Oxford: Oxford University Press, pp. 78–103.

Moffett, G. D. III. (1991) 'Democratic ideals replace fading isms', *The Christian Science Monitor*, 23 May.

Mo Ibrahim Foundation (2008) *The Ibrahim Index of African Governance*. Online. Available at: www.moibrahimfoundation.org/index (accessed 28 October 2008).

Møller, J. (2007) 'The gap between liberal and electoral democracy revisited: some conceptual and empirical clarifications', *Acta Politica* 42(4): 380–400.

Monaghan, A. and Montanaro-Jankovski, L. (2006) *EU-Russia Energy Relations: The Need for Active Engagement*, Brussels: European Policy Centre, Issue Paper No. 45.

Bibliography 211

Mott, W. (2002) *United States Military Assistance: An Empirical Perspective*, Westport, CT: Greenwood Press.

Najibullah, F. (2008) 'Moscow seeking alliances in energy-rich Central Asia', *RFE/RL*, 4 September.

Nardulli, P. (ed.) (2008) *International Perspectives on Contemporary Democracy*, Urbana, IL: University of Illinois Press.

Nasar, A. (2008) 'All eyes on Medvedev for policy clues', *St. Petersburg Times*, 6 June.

National Endowment for Democracy (2006) *The Backlash Against Democracy Assistance*, Report for US Senate Foreign Relations Committee, 8 June 2006. Online. Available at: www.ned.org/publications/reports/backlash (accessed 1 October 2008).

Ngok, K. L. (2007) 'State capacity, policy learning and policy paradigm shift: the case of the implementation of the "theory of scientific development" in China', paper presented at International Conference on the State Capacity of China in the 21st Century, Hong Kong, April.

Norris, P. (ed.) (1999a) 'Introduction: the growth of critical citizens?' in P. Norris (ed.) *Critical Citizens: Global Support for Democratic Governances*, Oxford: Oxford University Press, pp. 1–31.

——(ed.) (1999b) 'Conclusions: the growth of critical citizens and its consequences', in P. Norris (ed.) *Critical Citizens: Global Support for Democratic Governances*, Oxford: Oxford University Press, pp. 257–73.

North, D. and Weingast, B. (1989) 'Constitutions and commitment: the evolution of institutions governing public choice in seventeenth-century England', *Journal of Economic History*, 49(4): 813–32.

Nowak, D. (2007) 'Nashi spinoff operating exit polls', *The Moscow Times*, 29 November.

Nye, J. S. (1997) 'Introduction: the decline of confidence in government', in J. Nye, P. Zelikow and D. King (eds) *Why People Don't Trust Government*, Cambridge, MA: Harvard University Press, pp. 1–18.

O'Brien, K. and Li L. J. (2004) 'Suing the local state: administrative litigation in rural China', *The China Journal*, 51: 76–96.

O'Donnell, G., Schmitter, P.and Whitehead, L. (eds) (1986) *Transitions from Authoritarian Rule: Prospects for Democracy*, Baltimore, MD: The Johns Hopkins University Press.

Ottaway, M. (2003) *Democracy Challenged: The Rise of Semiauthoritarianism*, Washington, DC: Carnegie Endowment for International Peace.

——(2008) *Democracy Promotion in the Middle East: Restoring Credibility*, Policy Brief No. 60, Washington, DC: Carnegie Endowment for International Peace. Online. Available at: www.carnegieendowment.org/files/pb_60_ottaway_final.pdf (accessed 10 January 2009).

Ottaway, M. and Carothers, T. (2005) *Uncharted Journey: Promoting Democracy in the Middle East*, Washington, DC: Carnegie Endowment for International Peace.

Ottaway, M. and Dunne, M. (2007) *Incumbent Regimes and the King's Dilemma in the Arab World*, Working Paper No. 88, Washington, DC: Carnegie Endowment for International Peace.

Ottaway, M. and Hamzawy, A. (2008) *Islamists in Politics: The Dynamics of Participation*, Carnegie Paper No. 98, Washington, DC: Carnegie Endowment for International Peace.

Pan W. (2003) 'Toward a consultative rule of law regime in China', *Journal of Contemporary China*, 12(34): 3–43.

212   *Bibliography*

Panitch, L. (2001) *Renewing Socialism: Democracy, Strategy and Imagination*, Boulder, CO: Westview Press.

Peerenboom, R. (2007) *China Modernizes*, Oxford: Oxford University Press.

Pei M. X. (2003) 'Rights and resistance: the changing contexts of the dissident movement', in E. Perry and M. Selden (eds) *Chinese Society: Change, Conflict and Resistance*, London: Routledge, pp. 23–46.

Petrov, N. (2006) 'Organizing a civil society', *Moscow Times*, 4 April. Online, Available at: www.moscowtimes.ru/stories/2006/04/04/008.html (accessed 20 December 2008).

——(2007) 'All smoke and mirrors', *Moscow Times*, 20 July.

Petrov, N. and Ryabov, A. (2006) 'Russia's role in the Orange Revolution', in A. Åslund and M. McFaul (eds) *Revolution in Orange: The Origins of Ukraine's Democratic Breakthrough*, Washington, DC: Carnegie Endowment for International Peace, pp. 145–64.

Piebalgs, A. (2007) 'Speech, Oil and gas geopolitics', Lisbon Energy Forum, 2 October. Online. Available at: www.europa.eu/rapid/pressReleases (accessed 12 January 2009).

Posner, D. and Young, D. (2007) 'The institutionalisation of political power in Africa', *Journal of Democracy*, 18(3): 126–40.

Prytula, O. (2006) 'The Ukrainian media rebellion', in A. Åslund and M. McFaul (eds) *Revolution in Orange: The Origins of Ukraine's Democratic Breakthrough*, Washington, DC: Carnegie Endowment for International Peace, pp. 103–24.

Puddington, A. (2007) 'The 2006 Freedom House survey: the pushback against democracy', *Journal of Democracy*, 18(2): 125–37.

——(2008) 'Findings of freedom in the world 2008: freedom in retreat: Is the tide turning?' Online. Available at: www.freedomhouse.org (accessed 28 October 2008).

Putnam, R. (2000) *Bowling Alone: The Collapse and Revival of American Community*, New York: Simon & Schuster.

Radyuhin, V. (2005) 'Shifting balance in Central Asia', 20 July. Online. Available at: www.yaleglobal.yale.edu/display.article?id=6035.

Ramo, J. (2004) *The Beijing Consensus: Notes on the New Physics of Chinese Power*, London: Foreign Policy Centre.

RFE/RL Newsline (2007) 'Belarusian President slams partisans of democracy on victory day', 10 May.

Rice, C. (2005) 'The promise of democratic peace: why promoting freedom is the only realistic path to security', *Washington Post*, 11 December, B07.

Rose, R., Mishler, W. and Haerpfer, C. (1998) *Democracy and its Alternatives*, Baltimore, MD: The Johns Hopkins University Press.

Rose, R., Shin, D. C. and Munro, N. (1999) 'Tensions between the democratic ideal and reality: South Korea', in P. Norris (ed.) *Critical Citizens: Global Support for Democratic Governance*, Oxford: Oxford University Press, pp. 146–69.

Rosenau, J. N. (1974) *Citizenship Between Elections. An Inquiry into the Mobilizable American*, New York: The Free Press.

Ross, M. (2001) 'Does oil hinder democracy?', *World Politics*, 53(3): 325–61.

Roy, O. (2004) *Globalised Islam: The Search for a New Ummah*, New York: Columbia University Press.

Rutledge, I. (2006) *Addicted to Oil: America's Relentless Drive for Energy Security*, London: I.B. Tauris.

Saakashvili, M. (2008) 'Russia has aggressive intent', interview organized by The Henry Jackson Society, 27 May.

Bibliography 213

Saradzhyan, S. (2006) 'United Russia backs sovereign democracy', *Moscow Times*, 3 October.

Sarles, M. (2007) 'Evaluating the impact and effectiveness of USAID's democracy and governance programmes', in P. Burnell (ed.) *Evaluating Democracy Support: Methods and Experiences*, Stockholm: IDEA and SIDA, pp. 47–68.

Schedler, A. (1998a) 'What is democratic consolidation?', *Journal of Democracy*, 9(2): 91–107.

——(1998b) 'How should we study democratic consolidation?', *Democratization*, 5(4): 1–19.

——(ed.) (2006) *Electoral Authoritarianism: The Dynamics of Unfree Competition*, Boulder, CO: Lynne Rienner.

Schmitter, P. and Karl, T. L. (1991) 'What democracy is ... and is not', *Journal of Democracy*, 2(3): 75–8.

Schmitter, P. and Treschel, A. (2004) *The Future of Democracy: Trends, Analyses and Reforms*, Strasbourg: Council of Europe.

Sen, A. (1999) 'Democracy as a universal value', *Journal of Democracy*, 10(3): 3–17.

Shai Y. C.(2004) 'Managed participation in China', *Political Science Quarterly*, 119(3): 425–51.

Shaxson, N. (2007) *Poisoned Wells: The Dirty Politics of African Oil*, Basingstoke: Palgrave Macmillan.

Shen, S. (2007) *Redefining Nationalism in Modern China: Sino-American Relations and the Emergence of Chinese Public Opinion in the 21st Century*, Basingstoke: Palgrave.

Shin, Doh C. (1999) *Mass Politics and Culture in Democratizing Korea*, New York: Cambridge University Press.

——(2006) *Democratization: Perspectives from Global Citizenries*, Paper Series for Center for the Study of Democracy, University of California Irvine, 25 January.

——(2007) 'Democratization: perspectives from global citizenries', in R. Dalton and H.-D. Klingemann (eds) *The Oxford Handbook of Political Behavior*, Oxford: Oxford University Press, pp. 259–82.

Soares de Oliveira, R. (2007) *Oil and Politics in the Gulf of Guinea*, London: Hurst.

Solana, J. (2006) 'Towards an EU external energy policy', address to the EU External Energy Policy conference, 20 November, Brussels. Online. Available at: www.ue.ed.int (accessed 12 January 2009).

Song Q., Zhang Z. Z., Qiao B., Gu Q. Z., and Tang Z. Y. (1996) 中国可以说不 *Zhongguo Keyi Shuo Bu* [China Can Say No], Beijing: Zhonghua Gongshang Lianhe Press.

Spector, R. (2006) 'The anti-revolutionary toolkit', *Central Asia-Caucasus Analyst*, 13 December.

Spector, R. and Krickovic, A. (2007) 'The anti-revolutionary toolkit', unpublished paper given at the 2007 annual American Political Science Association meeting.

State Council (2005) *White Paper: Building of Political Democracy in China*, Beijing: Information Office of the State Council.

Stohl, R. (2008) 'Questionable reward: arms sales and the war on terrorism', *Arms Control Today*, Online. Available at: www.armscontrol.org/act/2008_01–02/stohl (accessed 28 December 2008).

Stoker, G. (2006) *Why Politics Matters*. Basingstoke: Palgrave.

Sullivan, M. (1994) 'The 1988–89 Nanjing anti-African protests: racial nationalism or national racism?', *The China Quarterly*, 138: 438–57.

Surkov, V. (2006) 'Nationalizing the future: excerpts from speech', *Ekspert*, 43, 20–26 November.

214 *Bibliography*

Sushko, O. and Prystayko, O. (2006) 'Western influence', in A. Åslund and M. McFaul (eds) *Revolution in Orange: The Origins of Ukraine's Democratic Breakthrough*, Washington, DC: Carnegie Endowment for International Peace.

Tessman, B. and Sullivan, P. (2008) 'United States military aid and recipient state cooperation', presented at the annual meeting of the ISA's 49th Annual Convention: Bridging Multiple Divides, San Francisco, 26 March.

The Economist (2007) 'Special Report on Iran', 21 July, p. 6.

Tilly, C. (1985) 'War making and state making as organized crime', in P. Evans, D. Rusechemeyer and T. Skocpol (eds) *Bringing the State Back In*, Cambridge: Cambridge University Press.

——(2004) *Contention and Democracy in Europe, 1650–2000*, Cambridge: Cambridge University Press.

Triesman, D. (2007) 'Putin's Silovarchs', *Orbis*, 51(1): 141–53.

Tsai, K. (2007) *Capitalism Without Democracy:The Private Sector in Contemporary China*, Ithaca, NY: Cornell University Press.

Ulfelder, J. (2008) 'International integration and democratization: an event history analysis', *Democratization*, 15(2): 272–96.

United Nations Development Programme (2005) *Democracy in Latin America: Towards a Citizens' Democracy*, New York: UNDP.

United States National Intelligence Council (2008) *Global Trends 2025: A Transformed World*. Online. Available at: www.dni.gov/nic/NIC_2025_project.html (accessed 24 November 2008).

USAID (2002) 'Promoting democratic governance', in *Foreign Aid and the National Interest: Promoting Freedom, Security, and Opportunity*, Washington, DC: U.S. Agency for International Development. Online. Available at: www.usaid.gov/fani/ch01 (accessed 28 December 2008).

——(2006) 'U.S. Overseas Loans and Grants: Obligations and Loan Authorizations, July 1, 1945–September 30, 2006' ('The Greenbook'). Online. Available at: www. qesdb.cdie.org/gbk/index.html (accessed 28 December 2008).

US National Research Council (2008) *Improving Democracy Assistance: Building Knowledge Through Evaluations and Research*, Washington, DC: The National Academies Press.

US Open Source Center (2006) 'Nashi youth camp used to push anti-US philosophy', 28 November.

van der Linde C. (2005) 'Energy in a changing world', inaugural lecture, Clingendael Energy Papers No. 11.

Volkova, Y. (2003a) 'Russia calls for settling Georgian crisis constitutionally', *ItarTass*, 21 November.

——(2003b) 'Russian lawmaker says US "obviously" behind Georgia turmoil', *Xinhua News Agency*, 22 November.

von Grumpennberg, M-C. (2007) *Kazakhstan – Challenges to the Booming Petro-Economy*, Working Paper 2, Swiss Peace Foundation.

Walder, A. (2002) 'Privatization and elite mobility: rural China, 1979–96', Stanford Institute for International Studies A/PARC Working Paper.

Waldermann, A. (2007) 'The Nashi movement', *Der Spiegel Online*, 2 November.

Walt, S. (2005) *Taming American Power: The Global Response to U.S. Primacy*, New York: W.W. Norton & Company.

Wang J. C. (2004) '从洋葱到橄榄中国社会结构 将如何优 Cong "Yangcong" Dao "Ganlan" Zhongguo Shehui Jiegou Jiang Ruhe Youhua [How to modernise China's social structure from 'onion' to 'olive' shaped], Beijing Television News Report Transcript. Online. Available at: www.cpirc.org.cn/yjwx/yjwx_detail.asp?id=2793 (accessed 23 September 2008).

Watts, J. (2008) 'Chinese dissident jailed for five years after human rights petition', *The Guardian* (London) 25 March.

Waxman, C. (1968) *The End of Ideology Debate*, New York: Funk & Wagnalls.

Way, L. and Levitsky, S. (2006) 'The dynamics of autocratic coercion after the Cold War', *Communist and Post-Communist Studies*, 39(3): 387–410.

Wen, J. B. (2007) 'Guanyu Shehuizhuyi Chuji Jieduan de Lishi Renwu he Woguo Duiwai Zhence de Jige Wenti' [On the historical mission of the primary stage of socialism and several issues of our foreign policy], *People's Daily*, 26 February.

Wheatley, J. (2005) *Georgia from National Awakening to Rose Revolution: Delayed Transition in the Former Soviet Union*, Farnham: Ashgate Publishing.

Whitehead, L. (2009) 'Losing "the force"? The "dark side" of democratization after Iraq', *Democratization*, 16(2): 215–42.

Williams, D. (2004) 'Putin opposes rerun in Ukraine', *Washington Post*, 3 December, A16.

Wilson, A. (2005) *Virtual Politics*, New Haven, CT: Yale University Press.

Wright, L. (2002) 'The man behind Bin Laden', *The New Yorker*, 18 September.

Wright, T. (2002) 'The China Democracy Party and the politics of protest in the 1980s–1990s', *The China Quarterly*, 172: 906–26.

Xie T. (2007) '民主社会主义模式与中国前途 Minzhu Shehui Zhuyi Moshi yu Zhongguo Qiantu' [The Democratic Socialist model and China's future], 炎黄春秋 *Yanhuang Chunqiu Annals*, 2.

Yergin, D. (2006) 'Ensuring energy security', *Foreign Affairs*, 85(2): 69–82.

Yermukanov, M. (2006) 'Pro-presidential forces in Kazakhstan unleash covered war on "colored revolution"', *CACI-Analyst*, 15 June.

York, G. (2000) 'Kremlin deserts Milosevic', *The Globe and Mail*, 7 October.

Youngs, R. (ed.) (2006) *Survey of European Democracy Promotion Policies 2000–2006*, Madrid: Fundación Para Las Relaciones Internacionales y el Diálogo Exterior.

——(ed.) (2008) *Is the European Union Supporting Democracy in its Neighbourhood?* Madrid: Fundación Para Las Relaciones Internacionales y el Diálogo Exterior.

——(2009) *Energy Security: Europe's New Foreign Policy Challenge*, London: Routledge.

Yu J. R.(2008) 'Emerging trends in violent riots', *Chinese Security*, 4(3): 75–81.

Yu K. P. (2003) 增量民主与善治 *Zengliang Minzhu yu Shanzhi* [Incremental Democracy and Good Government], Beijing: Social Science Literature Press.

Zakaria, F. (1997) 'The rise of illiberal democracy', *Foreign Affairs*, 76(6): 22–43.

Zhao S. S. (2004) *A Nation State by Construction: Dynamics of Modern Chinese Nationalism*, Stanford, CA: Stanford University Press.

Zheng S. P. (2003) 'Leadership change, legitimacy, and party transition in China', *Journal of Chinese Political Science*, 8(1 and 2): 47–63.

Zheng Y. N. (2008) 'China: an originator of ideas', *China Review*, 43: 4–5.

Zhou T. Y., Wang C. J., and Wang A. L. (eds) (2007) 攻坚：十七大后中国政治体制改革研究报告 *Gongjian: Shiqi Da Hou Zhongguo Zhengzhi Tizhi Gaige Yanjiu Baogao* [Storming the Fortress: A Research Report on China's Political System Reform, after the 17th Party Congress], Beijing: Central Party School Press.

Zolo, D. (1992) *Democracy and Complexity*, Philadelphia, PA: Penn State University Press.

Index

Afghanistan 7, 10, 90
Africa, 4, 14, 21n.5, 104, 189, 198–99;
  governance index 198; *see also*
  individual countries
Africa-Caribbean-Pacific (ACP) 31
Ahmadinejad, M. 12, 172
Algeria 15, 46, 47, 50, 61, 157, 158, 172,
  183; Front Islamique du Salut (FIS)
  15, 50, 84
Al-Ghazali Harb 156, 169
al-Qaeda 45, 46
Amalrik, A. 73
Ambrosio, T. 21n.10
Angola 185; oil and politics 172, 181
ANOVA test 105
Arab countries *see* Middle East;
  individual countries
Armitage, R. 165, 169
Authoritarianism: regeneration 1, 3, 9,
  11, 29, 42, 59, 61, 179;
  petroauthoritarianism 172–74, 186;
  see also oil, democratization obstacle
Azerbaijan 172, 181, 184

Bahrain 47, 61, 157
Bakiev, K. 130
Baltic Republics 36
Bangladesh 18
Barber, B. 22n.19
Benin, democracy 102, 106–8, 109, 113
Bermeo, N. 12, 21n.9, 196
Bertelsmann Transformation Index
  21n.2, 198
Bhutan 1
Bolivia 61, *see also* Morales, E.
Boonstra, J. 10
Bosnia 52
Bouteflika, A. 183
Brazil 189

Bratton, M. 101
Brezhnev doctrine 9
Breslin, S. 13, 191, 197, 198
Budge, I. 100
Burma *see* Myanmar
Burundi 51
Bush, George H. 85
Bush, George W. 1, 11, 16, 38, 65, 66,
  67, 73, 85, 90, 92n.11, 117, 153, 154,
  156, 160, 164, 175, 176, 195

Carothers, T. 11, 15, 17, 190, 195
Central Asia 60, *see also* individual
  countries
Central-Eastern Europe 155, 156, 194;
  see also individual countries
Chávez, H. 9, 36, 54, 173, 178
China 1, 9, 13–14, 16, 26, 29, 39, 54, 61,
  62, 134–52, 175, 178, 186, 189, 190,
  197–98; in Africa 13, 175; Beijing
  consensus 142; Beijing Olympics
  (2008) 1, 135, 138, 151; China
  Democracy Party 135; Communist
  Party (CCP) 135, 138, 140, 141, 142,
  144, 147–49 (reform) 148–50, 151;
  2002 constitutional reform 141;
  corruption 134, 146, 148, 149, 151;
  democracy suspicion 142, 143, 144
  (democracy promotion) 135, 192;
  economic growth 1, 138–39, 142, 152;
  fourth plenum communiqué (2004)
  148–49; liberalization 134, 136–38,
  142, 145, 192; 'managed participation'
  148, 151; middle class 139–41
  (relationship with state) 134, 140–41;
  model 44, 131, 151, 152, 191, 197,
  198; nationalism/patriotism 134, 135,
  141, 142–47 (popular) 143, 144–45
  (state sponsored) 143–44 (criticisms of

US) 144, 145 (and sovereignty) 144, 145; 'national project' 135, 143, 144, 145, 151, 192; 'New Left' 145–46; pillars of legitimacy 138–47, 149; political stability 141, 142; response to disasters 148; social contract 138, 143; socialism 139, 146 ('socialist democratic system') 149; state reform 146–51; Tiananmen Square (1989) 135, 146–47; White Paper on building political democracy 142
civil society 14, 56, 59–60, 62, 64, 118, 168, 189; support 56
civil-military relations 74
climate change 186, 184
Clinton, W. 79, 85, 92n.11
coercive democratization *see* democracy promotion
colour revolutions 8, 61, 117–18; and democracy promotion backlash 61–63, 71; Western involvement 62–63; *see also* Georgia; Ukraine
Commonwealth of Independent States (CIS) 128, 129
Community of Democracies 12, 32, 190
Conference on Security and Cooperation in Europe (CSCE) 155
Cooley, A. 37, 38
Croatia 52
Cuba 31, 69

Dahl, R. 95, 113n.1
democracy assistance *see* democracy promotion
democracy barometers 9, 102, 105, 106, 108, 111; *see also* democracy trends
democracy: developmental conditions 12–14; dissatisfaction 94, 95, 99, 101–2, 104–13, 199 ('critical citizens') 94, 100–102, 109, 112, 113, 114n.9, 115n.12 (managing dissatisfaction) 111–12 (threat to democracy) 109–11, 112; ideas 2, 91n.4, 94; ideology 43, 56, 57–58; ideological challenges 7, 9–10, 35, 42–58, 191; internal support 9, 10, 57, 97, 98, 99–113, 199 (and democratic consolidation) 99, 100, 101, 113, 114n.10; and national sovereignty 23, 41; and peace 10, 11, 24, 32–33, 34, 83; and postmodernisation 101; satisfaction 7–8, 99, 100, 102, 104,105–13, 193 (declining) 99, 101, 103–4; threats in established democracies 19–20, 33, 162

democracy backlash 15, 43, 59–72, 189, 190, 191, 198; causes 2, 61–65; European democracy promoters' response 66, 195 (diplomatic response) 66, 67; US democracy promoters' response 15, 65, 66, 67, 70–71 (diplomatic response) 66 (report to Congress) 2; *see also* democracy promotion
democracy promotion 3, 8, 15–17, 42, 194–97; in Arab world 43, 153–70; assistance evaluation 15, 17, 74, 75, 199 (*see also* Finkel); assistance norms 67–71, 195; civil society support 56; coercive democratization 24–25, 33, 40, 154; 'democracy militant' 33–3; election observation 69; prospects 5, 194, 195, 197, 200; public support 194–95; and regional organisations 16, 22n.15, 31; *see also* democracy backlash; European Union; United States, democracy promotion
democracy trends 2, 3, 4, 8, 18, 21n.3, 42, 57, 71, 91n.4, 93, 94–97, 112, 117, 173, 188, 189, 198–99, 200; before democracy aid 84–85
democradura 29
Democratic Republic of the Congo 3
democratic consolidation 114n.10
democratization as counter-hegemony 34, 36–38, 41
democratization research, 4–6, 111–12, 115n.12, 197–200
Deng Xiaoping 142
developmental state 151
Diamond, L. 1, 42, 77, 100, 114n.10
Doorenspleet, R. 8, 189, 193, 199

Easton, D. 97
East Timor 30
economic trends 12–13; economic crisis *see* financial instability
Economist Intelligence Unit's Index of Democracy 198
Egypt 11, 37, 45, 48, 54, 60, 83, 155, 157, 158–59, 164, 180; Muslim Brotherhood 47, 49, 155, 170n.6; Nasserist revolution 155
electoral process 4, 11, 15
energy *see* oil
environmentalism 44, 55
European Union (EU) 4, 17, 19, 27, 171; Copenhagen Criteria 31, 33, 68; enlargement and democratization 2,

218 Index

17, 33; Europe's energy needs 176–77
178, 185–86; and neighbourhood 164;
relations with Russia 17, 177
Extractive Industries Transparency
Initiative (EITI) 186

feminism 55
Ferrero-Waldner, B. 185
financial instability, international 18, 28,
54, 163; democracy effects 193–94
Finkel, S. 74, 76, 82, 83, 86.199
foreign aid 12, 14, 190; US 'aid
interactions' 73; *see also* military aid
Fox, G. 68
France 176
Franck, T. 21n.14, 68
Freedom House 2, 96, 173
Fukuyama, F. 53, 74, 83, 152

Gallagher, M. 141, 143
gas, and politics: *see* oil
Georgia 8, 51; 'rose revolution' 61, 63,
117, 119; Russia tensions 119, 129
Germany 176
global warming *see* climate change
globalization 20, 29, 34, 38; anti-
globalization 44, 55; Chinese attitudes
145
Goodman, D. 140
Gorbachev, M. 116
Granovetter, M. 40
Grenada 30

Habermas, J. 99
Hadenius, A. 3
Haiti 24, 25, 86, 92n.14
Halperin, M. 32
Helsinki Group 164
HIV/AIDS 14
Hu Jintao 138, 148, 149, 152n.9
Hu Yaobang 147
human rights 68, 197; aid 82–83;
promotion norms 68
humanitarian intervention 16, 30
Hungary, democracy 108–9, 113, 193
Huntington, S. 6, 100
Hurrell, A. 39

Ibrahim Index of African Governance 198
Iceland 193
ideologies: 'boutique'/fragmentation
55–56, 57; democracy's ideological
competitors 7, 42–58; weak 44; *see
also* Islamism; nationalism; socialism

India 32, 155, 175, 190
Indonesia 189, 194
informal institutions 6, 21n.7
Inglehart, R. 101
Institute for Democracy and
Cooperation 130
international intervention *see*
sovereignty, state
International Monetary Fund 193
International Republican Institute 196
Iran 12, 37, 39, 60, 62, 180, 192; oil and
politics 172, 183
Iraq 7, 10, 26, 47, 51, 90, 164, 189
Islamism 42, 43, 44–50, 57, 162, 175;
and democratic beliefs 45, 46, 48, 50,
167, 168, 191; Islamic law (sharia) 48,
49; 'participating movements' 45, 46,
47–49, 168; radical 45–47; Salafi
organizations 49–50; *see also* Middle
East
Israel 13

Jackson, R. 51
Jiang Zemin 139, 141
Johnson-Sirleaf, E. 77, 91n.8
Jordan 11, 47, 48, 157
Jünemann, A. 12

Kagan, R. 72, 189
Karatnycky, A. 95, 96
Kazakhstan 60, 129, 130,133; energy
and politics 177, 181, 184
Keane, J. 200
Kenya 8, 51, 52, 102
Kérékou, M. 106
Klingemann, H.-D. 101
Knodt, 12
Kodmani, B. 12, 15, 191, 194, 195
Kosovo 26, 128
Kostunica, V.
Kuchma, L. 119
Kuwait 47, 48, 50, 158, 174, 180
Kyrgyzstan 8, 60, 130

Labour unions 54
Latin America 2, 14, 36, 164; *see also*
individual countries
League of Democracies 32
Lebanon 72, 158; Hizbollah 47, 84,
168
Li, L. J. 136, 137
liberal internationalism, *see* sovereignty,
state
Libya 169, 172, 175

Index 219

Lindberg, S. 4
Linz, J. 100
Lipset, S. M. 14, 99
List, F. 145, 146

McFaul, M. 74, 83, 189, 191
Maldives 1
'managed democracy', *see* Russia
Mao Tse-tung 136, 138, 149
Marcos, F. 89
Medvedev, D. 125, 126, 131
Melville, A. 128
Middle East 2, 15, 43, 44–50, 95, 189;
   failed democracy promotion 153–70
   (perceptions) 159–60, 161–65, 169;
   foreign influences 155–56, 157, 159,
   160, 165, 169; government reform
   strategies 156–57; media 158–59, 166;
   and minorities 160, 166; national
   cohesion 160, 161; nationalism 162–
   63; new social contract 167–68; peace
   process 154, 169–70; political parties
   168, 169; popular pressure 157, 166;
   public opinion 154, 161; *see also*
   individual countries; Islamism; oil
Miliband, D. 3, 67
military aid 199; 'aid interactions' 73–
   92, 196; European arms sales 79; and
   divided state scenario 78; and
   rationalized security scenario 78, 87;
   recipient effects 89; resource curse 89;
   and rule of law scenario 77–78, 87,
   89; and war on terror 78–79, 84, 86,
   88; US 73–92
Mill. J. S. 19
Milošević, S. 43
Minxin Pei 136
Møller, J. 95, 96
Morales, E. 36, 61
Morocco 46, 48, 157, 158; Party of
   Justice and Development (PJD) 46, 49
Mossadegh, M. 63
Mugabe, R. 198
multipolar world 72, 131, 190; *see also*
   unipolarity
Musharraf, P. 89
Myanmar 11, 69, 89

National Democratic Institute 196
nationalism 39, 43, 50–53, 57, 162–63;
   anti-colonial 50–51, 52, 160, 164;
   civic 52, 53, 191; ethnic 51, 52, 57;
   see also China, nationalism, 'national
   project'

Nazarbaeva, D. 133n.25
Nazarbayev, N. 177
Nepal 1
Nigeria: oil and politics 172, 182, 185
Non-aligned Movement 13
Norris, P. 94, 97, 100, 114n.9
North Atlantic Treaty Organization
   (NATO) 30, 31
North Korea 7
Nye, J. 107, 165, 169

Obama, B. 3, 71, 154, 169
Obasanjo, O. 182, 185
O'Brien, K. 136, 137
O'Donnell, G. 29, 99
oil 13, 163; democratization obstacle 13,
   65, 171–75, 192, 196, 198; 'energy
   imperialism' 175–76; force for reform
   178–82, 187; and governance 182–86,
   187, 196; price fluctuations 1, 65, 71,
   192; producer states 173; rentier state
   13, 172, 186
Organisation of Petroleum Exporting
   Countries (OPEC) 13
Organisation for Security and
   Cooperation in Europe (OSCE) 9, 60;
   election monitoring 10, 60, 69, 119;
   Office for Democratic Institutions and
   Human Rights 128
Organization of American States (OAS)
   16, 31; Inter-American Democratic
   Charter 68
Ottaway, M. 9, 20, 22n.17, 191

Pakistan 8, 46, 83
Palestine 15; Hamas 37, 47, 84, 168
Pan Wei 149
Panama, democracy 105–6, 109, 113
Peerenboom, R. 137
Pérez-Liñán, A. 74; *see also* Finkel, S.
Piccone, T. 32
Piebalgs, A. 184, 185
Poland 36
Polity IV 91n.4
populism 9, 54, 191; petropopulism 173
Portugal 85
poverty reduction strategies 14
Primakov, E. 132n.12
Puddington, A.
Putin, V. 1, 11, 59, 60, 64, 69, 116, 117,
   118, 119, 120, 121

Qadafi, M. 172
Qatar 174

220 *Index*

regime change 16
rentier states *see* oil
resource curse 89, 132n.13
Rumsfeld, D. 160
Russia 1, 9, 10–11, 32, 39, 62, 172, 191,
197; and Central Asia 129–30, 175,
178, 189; and colour revolutions 61–63,
64, 117–20, 125, 127, 128, 190, 191;
and democracy promotion 59–60, 64;
democratic erosion 1, 117, 120–27,
130, 183, 189; elections 69, 120, 121,
122–24, 125 (monitoring) 10, 60, 69,
128; energy 64, 117, 121, 131, 183–84;
Georgia conflict 10, 129; major events
(2001–7) 122–24; 'managed
democracy' 11, 116, 117, 120; media
122–24, 125, 130; non-governmental
organisations (NGOs) 59, 60, 65, 67,
69, 122–24, 126, 128, 132n.17;
oligarchs 121, 125; Putin's foreign
policy 117, 120, 127–31, 184;
'sovereign democracy' 11, 29, 116,
117, 125, 127, 128, 131; Yeltsin's
foreign policy 116; youth movements
126–27; *see also* Putin; Yeltsin
Russkiy Mir National Foundation 128
Rustow, D. 93
Rice, C. 83

Saakashvili, M. 119, 129
Saudi Arabia 9, 13, 182–83; after 9/11
174; oil and politics 13, 172, 174,
179–80
Schedler, A. 11
Shevardnadze, E. 119
security challenges 11–12, 28, 45, 83–84,
185, 191
Seligson, M. 74; *see also* Finkel, S.
Sen, A. 9
Senegal 102
Serbia 43, 61, 117, 118, 128
Shanghai Cooperation Organization 9,
128
Shin, D. C. 97, 98
social network theory 40
socialism: conditions 43, 53, 54, 57, 191;
decline 9, 43, 44, 53, 54, 57; Leninist-
Marxism 149; and market regulation
53–54;Marxism-Leninism 53; welfare
capitalism 54
Soros, G. 63
South Africa 18, 32, 190; Truth and
Reconciliation Commission 19
South Korea 178, 190

Southern African Development
Community (SADC) 31
'sovereign democracy', *see* Russia
sovereignty, state 197; and democracy
23–41; and democracy promotion
30–33, 40, 68, 70, 196; and liberal
internationalism 16, 23, 25, 28, 34–36,
37, 38, 39; perspectives 16, 23–41;
'sovereignty militant' 30–32; and
transnationalism 38; Westphalian
system 31; *see also* coercive
democratization; 'democracy
militant'; democracy promotion
Soviet Union 116
Spector, R. 11, 189, 191
state, failing 3, 18, 28, 51, 174; quasi-
state 51
Stepan, A. 100
Stoker, G. 94, 101, 102
Surkov, V. 125
Sweden 67
Syria 160

Taiwan 37
Tajikistan 60
Teorell, J. 3
Thailand 15, 102, 189
Tilly, C. 89
Tukey tests 107, 109
Turkey 37, 95, 164; and EU 17

Ukraine 8, 129, 193; and EU 17; Orange
revolution 61, 64, 117, 119–20
Ulfelder, J. 22n.15
unipolarity 72; see also *multipolar world*
United Arab Emirates (UAE) 174
United Nations 12, 16, 26
United Nations Conference on Trade
and Development 13
United States 34, 35, 38, 42, 52, 56, 63,
73–92, 117, 128, 131, 155, 171, 197;
energy securitisation 175–76, 177
(Advanced Energy Initiative) 176;
foreign military sales 12, 80, 87, 88,
92n.17; Helms-Burton law 31; human
rights aid 82–83; military aid 73, 74,
76, 77, 78–82, 86, 87, 175 (and security
priorities) 78–79; overseas bases 37–38,
176; presidencies compared 85;
'preventive intervention' 16, 160;
promoting democracy 2, 63–64, 65,
66–67, 70–71, 74–75, 79, 81, 83,
91n.6, 174, 190, 194 (evaluated) 74,
75, 76 (in Middle East) 153, 154, 164,

165, 169, 174, 194 (partisan) 69–71; realist foreign policy 76 (security concerns) 84, 86–87, 88, 92n.11,196; world power 72; *see also* Bush, George W; military aid; Obama; USAID; USNIC; war on terror(ism)
United States Agency for International Development (USAID) 74, 75, 76
United States National Intelligence Council (USNIC) Report on global trends 21n.4, 194
Uzbekistan 66, 129, 178, 184–85, 189; relations with US 130

Venezuela 9, 175, 189; *see also* Chávez, H.
Vietnam 189
violent conflict 8, 10, 181, 182; *see also* war on terror(ism)

war on terror(ism), effects 11–12, 20, 64, 71, 78, 84, 86, 88, 159, 160, 165
Washington consensus 14
Weber, M. 200

Wei Jingsheng 135
Wen Jiabao 138, 139, 148
Whitehead, L. 16, 21n.8, 195, 196, 197
Wilson, W. 155
World Bank 12, 14

Xie Tiao 149

Ya Keping 143
Yar'Adua, U. 182
Yeltsin, B.116, 121
Yemen 47, 61, 157
Youngs, R. 12, 13
Yugoslavia 51

Zakaria, F. 95, 114n.5
Zhao Ziyang 138
Zheng Shiping 142
Zheng Yongnian 142
Zhu Rongji 137
Zimbabwe 11, 189, 198
Zolo, D. 163

CPSIA information can be obtained
at www.ICGtesting.com
Printed in the USA
BVOW06s1800080118
504725BV00004B/149/P